the aga bible

the aga bible

amy willcock

TED SMART

First published in Great Britain by Ebury Publishing in 2006

This edition produced for The Book People Ltd, Hall Wood Avenue, Haydock, St Helens, WA11 9UL

1 3 5 7 9 10 8 6 4 2

Text © Amy Willcock 2006
Photographs © William Lingwood 2002, 2006, except p.241 © Jonathan Gregson 2005

Amy Willcock has asserted her right to be identified as the author of this work under the Copyright, Designs and Patents Act 1988.

Ebury Publishing
Random House, 20 Vauxhall Bridge Road, London SW1V 2SA

Random House Australia (Pty) Limited
20 Alfred Street, Milsons Point, Sydney, New South Wales 2061, Australia

Random House New Zealand Limited
18 Poland Road, Glenfield, Auckland 10, New Zealand

Random House South Africa (Pty) Limited
Isle of Houghton, Corner Boundary Road & Carse O'Gowrie, Houghton, 2198, South Africa

Random House Publishers India Private Limited
301 World Trade Tower, Hotel Intercontinental Grand Complex, Barakhamba Lane, New Delhi 110 001, India

The Random House Group Limited Reg. No. 954009
www.randomhouse.co.uk

A CIP catalogue record for this book is available from the British Library.

Photography: William Lingwood (except p.241 Jonathan Gregson)
Illustrator: Melvyn Evans
Editor: Gillian Haslam
Designer: Christine Wood
Food stylists: Fork Ltd, Lucy McKelvie and Jenny White
Props stylists: Liz Belton, Tessa Evelegh and Helen Trent

Diagrams on pages 7, 10 and 14 courtesy of Aga-Rayburn

ISBN: 0091910722
ISBN-13 [from January 2007]: 9780091910723

Papers used by Ebury Press are natural, recyclable products made from wood grown in sustainable forests.

Printed and bound in Singapore by Tien Wah Press

contents

introduction

It has been five years since my first Aga book, *Aga Cooking*, was published. This first book was a huge learning curve and its publication was one of the nicest things that has ever happened to me. It was the first book of its kind to reflect the cooking mood of the nation and translate it into 'Aga-speak'. I like to think of this new book as being a 'best of Amy Willcock Aga Cooking' – a compilation of all my favourite recipes, the dishes that are always requested at my workshops and demonstrations, and a good smattering of brand-new recipes, plus all the techniques and tips you will ever need.

It doesn't matter how many cookery books you buy and read, I believe the best way of learning and expanding your cooking skills is to cook, cook, cook!

Happy Aga Cooking!

Amy Willcock

aga basics

The following pages explain how each cooking area of your Aga works. No two Agas are the same, but all have a burner that heats them in the same way. The heat from the burner unit is transferred to the ovens and hot plates where it is stored. When the insulated lids are down, they hold in the heat. When the lids are up, heat is lost.

Each Aga is thermostatically controlled, so you can forget about exact temperatures. All the Aga ovens are externally vented. I recommend that new Aga users buy an oven thermometer and hang it in the middle of the ovens first thing in the morning to get an idea of the temperatures. Do this only once, just to give you an indication of what the oven temperatures are.

The heat indicator should be checked first thing in the morning, just to confirm that the Aga is up to heat. The mercury should sit on the black line, which means that the Aga has its full amount of stored heat. It is quite usual for the mercury to drop during cooking – don't worry as the heat will automatically be restored.

I only turn off my Aga for servicing, and once the temperature has been reset and I am happy with the mercury position I don't touch it until the next service (see page 13). After installation or servicing, make a note of the mercury position for the first few days, and adjust the control until the mercury consistently reaches the black central line.

There may be times when you are doing a lot of cooking and need more heat. Before you move the control knob, examine your cooking method. **There is one golden rule in Aga cooking: keep the lids down and cook in the ovens.** Around 80 per cent of cooking should be done in the ovens and just 20 per cent on the plates. The Aga's combustion system, heat path and insulation schemes are designed on this premise. Once you have taken this on board, you will never suffer heat loss again.

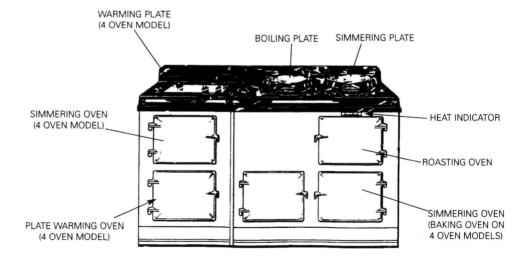

WARMING PLATE
(4 OVEN MODEL)

BOILING PLATE   SIMMERING PLATE

SIMMERING OVEN
(4 OVEN MODEL)

HEAT INDICATOR

ROASTING OVEN

PLATE WARMING OVEN
(4 OVEN MODEL)

SIMMERING OVEN
(BAKING OVEN ON
4 OVEN MODELS)

the aga plates

The 2-oven Aga has a Boiling Plate and a Simmering Plate. The 4-oven Aga also has a Warming Plate.

the boiling plate

The Boiling Plate is situated directly over the burner, making it the hottest plate. It is used when you want a fierce or high heat to bring foods to the boil or for stir-frying. Bread is toasted on it using the Aga Toaster. It is also where the Aga Kettle is brought up to the boil.

the simmering plate

The Simmering Plate gives off a gentle heat ideal for simmering, but the biggest advantage is that you can cook directly on it, like a griddle. I always use Bake-O-Glide (see page 12) on the Simmering Plate, which requires little, if any, oil, giving me a low-fat cooking option. Or you can season the plate just as you would a new frying pan by putting vegetable oil on a piece of kitchen paper and wiping the plate's surface. Do this two or three times, leaving the lid up so that some of the oil burns off and does not leave an oily build-up. If you don't use the plate as a griddle for a while, re-season before use.

Before cooking, raise the lid for a few minutes to reduce the heat a little, wipe the surface with a small amount of oil and proceed. I cook pancakes, fried eggs, toasted sandwiches and tortillas like this.

Always close the lids promptly on both plates when you have finished using them, otherwise precious heat escapes.

the warming plate
(*4-oven aga only*)

The Warming Plate is to the left of the Boiling Plate and is a very useful area to warm things such as awkwardly shaped serving dishes and teapots. It is also great for resting large joints of roasted meat.

the aga ovens

The 2-oven Aga has a Roasting Oven and a Simmering Oven. The 4-oven Aga has a Roasting Oven, a Baking Oven, a Simmering Oven and a Warming Oven. The runners in the ovens are always counted from the top downwards.

The reason foods taste so much better when cooked in an Aga is because they retain valuable moisture, which is usually lost during conventional cooking. This is because in some cases the surface of the food is sealed in by the Aga's unique radiant heat. By and large, the air in a conventional oven is hotter than in an Aga; the hotter the air, the more moisture it will absorb, which can dry food out.

As there are no dials to control the temperatures, food is cooked by **position** and **timing**. If you think in those terms, adapting conventional recipes will become second nature.

Looking at food while it is cooking is not a problem because the cast iron ovens retain the heat around the inside of the oven and opening the door will not result in a sudden heat loss.

All the ovens on the right-hand side of the Aga are externally vented, keeping cooking smells out of the kitchen and keeping succulence in the food. The stored heat is released as radiant heat, which is what locks in the flavour and moisture, giving such superb results.

The cooking times for older Aga cookers may have to be adjusted because insulation used then was not as good as it is now. New insulating materials are being developed all the time, so newer Aga models benefit from modern technology.

the roasting oven　　The Roasting Oven is the Aga's hottest oven. Think of it as having four different areas of cooking space:

　　High: top of the oven　　　*Middle:* centre of the oven
　　Low: near the bottom　　　*Floor:* the oven floor

The oven is slightly hotter on the left side, which is near the burner.

what cooks where　　*High:* the top of the oven is perfect for cooking food requiring a very high heat, such as grilled bacon and Yorkshire puddings, or for crisping the tops of cottage pies or browning meat.

Middle: the middle of the Roasting Oven is where joints of meat are cooked. Timings for roasts cooked here are the same as for conventional cookers. However, some roasts can be started here and then finished off in the Simmering Oven, but timings will be longer. For 2-oven Aga owners, this is the area to use for baking but you will need an item of cookware called an Aga Cake Baker. It is essential for cakes that need more than 40 minutes' baking time. The cake baker is an 'oven within an oven', creating a moderate temperature for a longer amount of time. For cakes requiring less than 40 minutes, using the cold Plain Shelf in the Roasting Oven creates a moderate oven temperature, but only for about 20–30 minutes. Once the plain shelf absorbs the oven's heat, it is useless until it is taken out and cooled. The Plain Shelf must not be stored in the Aga. It must go into the Aga cold. Four-oven Agas do not require a cake baker as they have a Baking Oven.

To use the cake baker, select the correct-sized tin and remove the trivet and cake tins from inside the cake baker. Put the outer container and lid on to the Roasting Oven floor to heat up. Pour the cake mix into the tin and remove the cake baker from the oven. Set the trivet and cake tin inside the cake baker. Replace the lid and put it on the floor of the Roasting Oven. Set the timer. Using the cake baker means there is no need to turn cakes round or fear of over-browning. (Also, read the baking tips on pages 212–13.)

Low: this is the part of the oven where roast potatoes, bread and sponge cakes are cooked. When making sponge cakes, do not use the cake baker; instead use heavy-based tins and place the grid shelf on the floor of the Roasting Oven and the plain shelf on the second set of runners just above, to create a moderate oven temperature.

Floor: anything you can cook on the hot plates you can do on the Roasting Oven floor. Use it to fry foods such as onions or eggs or for browning meats. Heat a frying pan with a little oil in it on the floor of the Roasting Oven; add your ingredients and fry. Do not put wooden or Bakelite-handled pans into the Roasting Oven. I find I use this part of the oven the most.

the simmering oven

This is the slow oven. On the 2-oven Aga it is on the bottom right; on the 4-oven Aga it is on the top left. On the 2-oven Aga it has three sets of runners; on the 4-oven model there is only one set in the middle. The gentle heat of the Simmering Oven is ideal for slow cooking and cooking overnight. Everything to be cooked in this oven, apart from meringues and a few other recipes, must be started either on the hot plates or in the Roasting Oven and brought up to the boil before going into the Simmering Oven. Saucepans must have tight-fitting flat lids that can be stacked one on top of the other. It is fine to put wooden and Bakelite-handled pans in the Simmering Oven.

what cooks where

Centre: this is where casseroles, soups and stocks are made. Bring to the boil on the Boiling Plate, then transfer to the Simmering Oven. Roasts such as lamb and pork can be started in the Roasting Oven, then transferred to the Simmering Oven, leaving valuable space in the Roasting Oven for other dishes. Rice puddings and baked custards are also started in the Roasting Oven, then transferred to the Simmering Oven for slow, gentle cooking. The temperature is also just right for steamed puddings.

Bottom: if you don't have a Baking Oven, this is where fruit cakes and meringues are cooked. Pin-head oatmeal can be brought to the boil on the Boiling Plate then placed on a grid shelf on the floor of the oven and left overnight for creamy porridge the next morning. This is the best place for drying fruits and vegetables

Floor: the floor of the Simmering Oven is perfect for cooking rice and root vegetables. The Aga method of cooking for rice results in delicious fluffy rice, while the Aga method for root vegetables (see page 154) is extremely easy and nutritious. The Aga is perfect for the busy person as it waits for you and there is no fear of ruining or burning foods. If you are delayed, food can wait patiently in the Simmering Oven and still taste great.

the baking oven   This oven is only available with the 4-oven Aga. It is perfect for all baking as it is a moderate oven. It can also be used like the Roasting Oven but with longer cooking times. The top of the oven is slightly hotter.

what cooks where   *Top of the oven:* small cakes are cooked to perfection.
Centre: for brownies, muffins, biscuits, breads and crumbles. Also, the right temperature for baking fish.
Bottom: when cooking soufflés or cheesecakes here, they must be off the floor. Slide a grid shelf on to the oven floor and stand the tin or dish on the grid shelf.

the warming oven   Available in the 4-oven Aga only, this is primarily a place to keep things warm. It is where plates are warmed, and it can dry out fruits and vegetables like the Simmering Oven (although they will take much longer) or infusing oils.

my biggest tip   Look at your dishes cooking and baking in the Aga frequently and don't be afraid to move the food to another location in or on your Aga. If a hot plate is too hot, then move it. The recipe timings in this book are a guide, and remember that every Aga is different. Agas create intuitive cooks because of this. You will learn to cook by instinct.

the 80/20 rule   There is just one golden rule in Aga cooking – keep the lids down and cook in the ovens. Around 80 per cent of the cooking should be done in the ovens and only 20 per cent on the plates. The Aga cooker's combustion system, heat path and insulation schemes are designed on this premise. Once you have taken this on board, you will never suffer heat loss again. If you are doing a lot of cooking and need more heat, examine your cooking methods before you move the control knob.

essential equipment

Each new Aga comes with the basic Aga kit: 2 grid shelves, 1 large roasting tin and grill rack, half-size roasting tin and grill rack, 1 plain shelf, 1 toaster, 1 wire brush. I would suggest 2-oven Aga owners invest in another plain shelf if you like to do a lot of baking, and I recommend that 2- and 4-oven Aga owners invest in a few more half-size roasting tins.

saucepans and casseroles

New Aga owners don't have to go out and buy new saucepans. However, the Aga range of saucepans has machined-flat, heavy ground bases and can reach boiling point very quickly, thereby conserving heat. Cast iron, earthenware, ceramic and copper are all suitable for the Aga. Glass Pyrex can also be used in the ovens on the grid shelves.

To test whether your existing saucepans are suitable for the Aga, fill each one with cold water and put it on the Boiling Plate. Hold either side of the pan down and see if it rocks. If the pan is flat, tiny bubbles appear uniformly over the bottom of the surface. It is not flat if the bubbles appear only in certain areas of the pan.

Buy pans that are fully ovenproof and can be used anywhere on the Aga. Saucepans and casseroles should be as wide as possible so that they cover most of the hot plate surface. The flat lids on Aga pans enable stacking in the ovens, giving you masses of room for cooking.

baking and cooking tins

When buying tins for the Aga, make sure that they slide onto the runners. This will mean the full capacity of the ovens will be realised. The one tin that I use constantly is the half-size shallow hard anodised baking tray. The full-size one can also be used as a plain shelf. They are sufficiently heavy duty to use on the hot plates and ideal for things like roasting potatoes. Make sure muffin and other specialised tins are also as heavy duty as possible. Cake tins must be heavy duty. As dark colours absorb heat more quickly than lighter ones, you may find in some cases a darker cake tin will require a slightly shorter cooking time than, say, a lighter aluminium cake tin.

kettles

To get the best from your kettle, buy a size that suits your needs. A common complaint about kettles is that they become pitted at the bottom and can take a long time to come to the boil. The first problem occurs when boiled water is not fully used and the water level is just topped up. This is bad practice as the boiled water leaves mineral deposits sitting on the bottom of the kettle which cause pitting. When this happens, it takes longer to bring water up to the boil and the kettle is less efficient. Using a smaller kettle ensures you empty the water when making pots of tea and that the kettle is always filled with fresh water. If you are using a large kettle, only fill it with the amount of water needed for the job. If you live in a hard-water area, clean the kettle once a week. A 1.5-litre kettle is the standard size for everyday use and ensures you boil fresh water every time.

Bake-O-Glide

This is a lifesaver. Use it to line baking or roasting tins (making cleaning a cinch) or on the Simmering Plate. It is dishwasher-safe and only small amounts of fat are needed, if at all, to make surfaces non-stick. Roast potatoes crisp up beautifully and the crunchy bits left in the tin lift off easily. I use the pre-cut circle on the Simmering Plate to fry eggs, cook pancakes and make toasted sandwiches.

cleaning and caring for your aga

The best way to have a clean Aga is to avoid getting it dirty. If you use the ovens for cooking foods that splatter (especially during frying and grilling), the hot plates will stay clean. Pushing pans to the rear of the oven will keep the aluminium door clean as well. Keep a damp cloth ready to wipe up spills as they happen. Be aware that acidic liquids and milk can cause pitting to the enamel top. Don't drag pans across the top as the surface will scratch.

cleaning the ovens

Oven cleaning doesn't really exist with an Aga. The ovens self-clean because the constant high heat means that food spills carbonise and only need to be brushed out with the wire brush or using a metal nozzle attachment on your vacuum cleaner. The Aga doors must NEVER be immersed in water as this would destroy the insulation.

To clean the doors, lay out a double thickness of tea towels on a flat surface and then carefully lift off the doors from the hinges. Use gauntlets to move the doors, as they will be very hot. Lay the doors on the tea towels enamel side down and leave to cool for a few minutes. Using a damp wire wool scouring pad and a little washing-up liquid, firmly go over the inside of the door – it will scratch the aluminium but not damage it. Wipe it clean and replace the doors on the hinges.

To clean the outside of the oven doors and the enamelled front and top, use a proprietary mild cream cleaner. Lightly apply it with a damp cloth, then wipe with a dry cloth to polish off any residue. A silicone polish can also be used on the front and top of the cooker to help control dust. This is a good idea for darker-coloured cookers, where the dust is more visible.

cleaning the hot plates

Clean the hot plate surfaces with the wire brush. Food will burn off and all that is needed is to clear away any carbonised bits that will interfere with the contact between saucepan bottoms and the hot surface. It is a good idea to keep the wire brush handy when making toast so that you can clear away any breadcrumbs immediately.

To clean the inside of the Simmering Plate lid (the Boiling Plate lid rarely needs cleaning as the intense heat keeps it clean), lift the lid and leave open for a few minutes to cool slightly, then place a grid shelf over the hot plate and the plain shelf on top of the grid shelf. This will reduce the heat, allowing easier cleaning in the middle of the lid, and is also a safety precaution in case your hand slips. Use a soapy wire wool pad and a damp cloth. The inside of the lid will scratch but it will not affect the cooker's performance.

Clean the chromium lids with a soapy damp cloth and buff with a clean dry tea towel. Do not use wire wool or any harsh abrasives on the chrome. To avoid the tops of the lids being scratched, either use the round Aga oven pads or a folded tea towel to protect them if you place dishes on top. Don't put heavy pans or tins on them as this may dent them.

servicing your aga

Always use an authorised Aga distributor to service your Aga. If you have moved into a house with an Aga, try to find out its service history and the telephone number and contact name of the company that services it. Gas and electric Aga cookers should be serviced once a year and oil-fuelled Aga cookers every six months. The standard check and service will take about an hour. The night before a service, remember to turn off your Aga so that it cools down. Turn the burner off and leave the pilot on (refer to the inside of the burner compartment door). After servicing, the Aga technician will re-light the Aga for you.

Converting conventional recipes is easy. As all Aga cooking is done by timing and position, just remember how the heat is distributed in each oven and once you decide where the food is to be cooked, adjust the timings accordingly. I tend to underestimate the time by roughly 10 minutes, as I can always put the dish back in for a little longer if necessary. Use the recipes in this book as a point of reference when converting conventional recipes.

Example:

Take a muffin recipe. The ingredients and method are exactly the same. The recipe calls for a pre-heated oven, a temperature of 180°C/350°F/gas 4 and a cooking time of 40–45 minutes.

For a 2-oven Aga:

There is no need to pre-heat the oven as the Aga is always ready to cook. Make the batter according to the recipe, and pour the mix into the muffin tin.

I would use the lower/bottom half of the Roasting Oven, but not the Roasting Oven floor. Place the grid shelf on the floor of the Roasting Oven and the cold plain shelf (to create a moderate oven temperature of 180°C/350°F/gas 4) on the second set of runners. Estimate the cooking time at 30 minutes, but the muffins may take up to 45 minutes if the oven is not right up to temperature. Have a look at them throughout the cooking time and check after about 25 minutes. They are done when pale golden in colour and shrinking away from the sides of the tin.

For a 4-oven Aga:

As above but cook in the Baking Oven omitting the cold plain shelf until it is needed (probably 20–25 minutes into the cooking time).

aga temperatures

Roasting Oven	Hot	Approx. 240–260°C (475–500°F) gas 8–9
Baking Oven	Moderate	Approx. 180–200°C (350–400°F) gas 4–6
Simmering Oven	Slow	Approx. 135–150°C (260–300°F) gas 1
Warming Oven	Warm	Approx. 70–100°C (150–200°F) gas ¼

These represent typical centre-oven temperatures

mercury position

Here's how to read the heat indicator:

Line in black area: less heat is stored so cooking will take longer, temperature too low.

Line in red area: more than required amount of heat stored, temperature too high.

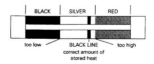

the heat indicator

the aga way of cooking

The one question that crops up at every workshop I do is: 'Halfway through cooking Sunday lunch I find the heat runs out when it comes to cooking the roast potatoes and/or Yorkshire pudding. The mercury zooms down on the thermometer. How can I prevent heat loss?'.

The answer is to examine your method of cooking. Heat loss often occurs if you use the hot plates too much beforehand. Perhaps you cooked breakfast on top rather than in the ovens that morning? Or par-boiled potatoes on the Boiling Plate instead of in the Simmering Oven? Check how much the lids are up.

If you are still experiencing problems after satisfying yourself that you are doing everything correctly, you are probably not planning your cooking timetable for the menu you have chosen. Yorkshire pudding can be cooked first thing in the morning when the ovens are at their hottest and then successfully re-heated just before serving. Roast potatoes can be cooked up to their final 20 minutes the day before. And even green vegetables can be blanched the day before, ready to be re-heated just before serving. Good cooking, whether it is in an Aga or a conventional cooker, is all about planning and preparation.

planning and preparation

Try to plan your menu around your Aga. Consider logistics. Invariably food moves around the Aga, usually ending in the Warming or Simmering Ovens, on the Warming Plate or on protected hot plate lids. Plan to use the space they leave in the ovens well. You may find that you cook food in a different order than usual as the safety net of the Simmering or Warming Ovens allows for greater flexibility. Plan in which order to cook the recipes. Decide which recipes can be cooked ahead and take into account thawing times and re-heating times if applicable. Serve some foods that can be completely done ahead and just need re-heating.

There are more tips on Aga cooking in my book *Aga Know-How* (Ebury Press, 2003).

aga at a glance

Here are some helpful general cooking positions. In my experience, 20 minutes seems to be the magic amount of time for many dishes.

techniques

Grilling: use the Aga grill pan on the Roasting Oven floor or on the Boiling Plate.

Frying: use the Roasting Oven floor and first set of runners in the Roasting Oven.

Roasting: Roasting, Baking and Simmering Ovens – use Roasting Oven for conventional timings; Baking and/or Simmering Ovens for slow roasting.

Browning meat: use the first set of runners in the Roasting Oven, then move to the floor.

Steaming: start on the Boiling Plate or in the Roasting Oven, cover, then move to the Simmering Oven.

Boiling: Boiling Plate. Once boil is established, move to the Roasting Oven floor.

Simmering: start on the Boiling Plate, cover with a lid, then move to the Simmering Oven. To reduce liquids, remove lid and continue in the Simmering Oven.

Poaching: bring to the boil on the Boiling Plate, then move to the Roasting or Simmering Oven depending on food being poached (poach eggs on the Simmering Plate).

Braising: bring to the boil on the Boiling Plate for 5–10 minutes, then move to the Simmering or Baking Oven.

foods

Jacket potatoes: third set of runners or floor of the Roasting Oven.

Roasted vegetables: first set of runners or floor of the Roasting Oven.

Frozen pizza: directly on the Roasting Oven floor.

Rice: bring up to the boil on the Boiling Plate, cover, then transfer to the Simmering Oven. In general, most quantities of rice (unless very large) take about 20 minutes.

Pasta: boil on the Boiling Plate.

Cookies and biscuits: fourth set of runners with the Cold Plain Shelf on the second set of runners in the Roasting Oven. Third set of runners in the Baking Oven.

Muffins: grid shelf on floor of Roasting Oven with Cold Plain Shelf above, or on fourth set of runners with Cold Plain Shelf on second set of runners. In Baking Oven on third set of runners.

Bread: directly on the Roasting Oven floor.

Frozen breads: third set of runners in the Roasting Oven for 10–15 minutes, covered with foil if browning too much.

Toasted sandwiches: use the round Bake-O-Glide and cook directly on the Simmering Plate.

Cheesecake: grid shelf on the floor of Roasting Oven with Cold Plain Shelf on just above for 5–10 minutes or until just set, then move to the Simmering Oven for 35–45 minutes.

Frozen fish fingers/chicken nuggets/chips: start on the Roasting Oven floor, then move to third set of runners (total cooking time about 10–12 minutes).

Crispy bacon: use Bake-O-Glide in a shallow baking tray on the Roasting Oven floor.

Melting chocolate/butter: at the back of the black enamel top, on the Warming Plate or in the Simmering Oven.

convenience food

Agas can do convenience food too. The everyday reality for many of us is that during the week dinner is just as likely to come out of a packet as it is from the latest cookbook. This is where the Aga comes in – forget the microwave, just pop the foil container on a baking tray and slide it onto the third or fourth set of runners in the Roasting Oven and dinner is ready in no time at all. Because the Aga is on 24 hours a day, there is no waiting for ovens to heat up. So even before you take your coat off, take a store-bought lasagne and garlic bread out of the freezer and they will cook in the same amount of time it takes you to hang up your coat, kick off your shoes, pour a glass of wine and kiss the children goodnight!

hidden extras

The Aga is not just a wonderful cooker, it also has hidden talents and can sometimes act like an extra pair of hands. The Aga will become the focal point of the kitchen and bottoms will have to be prised off the chrome rail!

aga ironing

One of the best things about the cooker is its ability to do the ironing! To 'iron' items such as sheets, hankies, tea towels, vests, pillow cases and so on, fold the newly washed and spun laundry. Smooth and press in creases firmly by hand and place them on the Simmering Plate lid. Turn them over when one side is dry. Take care not to drape washing over the handles of the lids and do not obstruct the air vents on the burner door when hanging sheets on the chrome rail. Press sheets by hanging them over the chrome rail, then fold and press firmly when almost dry and transfer to the lid of the Simmering Plate to press. Never place laundry on the Boiling Plate lid as it may become scorched.

hints and tips

● Buy two really reliable and accurate timers, preferably digital. Timers are crucial to the Aga cook. Or buy a timer on a long cord so that you can wear it around your neck.

● Tie a red ribbon around the rail or above so that it catches your eye and reminds you something is in the oven. A magnet with a note attached works well too.

● Dry awkwardly shaped gadgets such as graters and garlic crushers at the back of the Aga.

● Dry glassware and decanters on a tea towel at the back of the Aga.

● Keep your wooden spoons near the Aga as it will keep them dry.

● Heat unusual-shaped dishes at the back of the Aga. To warm large platters, place a tea towel underneath them to stop slipping and stand them upright, propped against the back or side of the Aga.

● Always pre-heat the Aga toaster to prevent bread sticking to it.

● To save time and energy, pre-heat pans in the Roasting Oven (do not put in saucepans with wooden or plastic handles).

● Protect open lids from splatters with a tea towel draped over the back (remove before closing the lid).

● Opening new jar lids could not be simpler. Invert the jar top onto the Simmering Plate for a few seconds and you will hear it release. Protect your hands before touching the metal lid.

● Cook poppadums directly on the Boiling Plate with the lid down – ready in seconds.

● Cook pancakes, drop scones, fried eggs and toasted cheese sandwiches directly on the Simmering Plate.

● Clean crusty pans in a biological washing powder solution by whisking the powder into some hot water to dissolve, then soak pan overnight.

● Keep salt in a salt box next to the Aga and it will remain dry.

● Use all of the black surface area on the top of the Aga – it is great for melting butter or chocolate. Break up chocolate into pieces, put it into a bowl and stand it to the left of the Boiling Plate and it will melt in no time at all. Warm flour and sugar for baking here as well.

● For 2-oven Aga owners, plan to do your baking when the ovens will be cooler, such as after a heavy cooking session.

● To bring cold red wine up to temperature, stand the bottle on a tea towel at the back of the Aga on the black enamel or wrap it in a tea towel and lay it on the Simmering Plate.

1 breakfasts

the full aga breakfast

I find that a proper breakfast can be one of the hardest meals to get absolutely right – everything must be cooked to order, usually for large numbers of people. You'll be familiar with the scene – Sunday morning and the household drifts down in dribs and drabs, all looking forward to a cooked breakfast! Co-ordinating toast, eggs, bacon and so on can become a nightmare, but not for the Aga owner!

per person:

1 or 2 free-range eggs
2 rashers bacon
1 sausage
1 large field mushroom
half a tomato
toast

1 Depending on how many you are cooking for, use either the half-size Aga roasting tin or the full-size one. Line it with Bake-O-Glide, and put the mushrooms and tomato halves, cut side up, on the bottom of the tin. Drizzle over a little oil and season with salt and pepper. Place the grill rack on top of them and put the sausages on the rack over the mushrooms and tomatoes (do not prick the sausages).

2 Slide the tin onto the first set of runners in the Roasting Oven, and cook for 10 minutes. When the timer goes off, take the tin out of the oven, turn the sausages and lay the bacon rashers on the grill rack. Pop it back into the Roasting Oven for a further 10 minutes. You may need to adjust the timings slightly depending on the thickness of the bacon and the size of the sausages.

3 When everything is cooked, take the tin out of the oven and put the bacon, sausages, tomatoes and mushrooms onto a warmed platter, cover with foil and transfer to the Simmering Oven to keep warm while you cook the eggs. If you want well-done bacon, after you remove the sausages, tomatoes and mushrooms to the platter, take off the grill rack and put the bacon on the bottom of the tin. Place the tin on the floor of the Roasting Oven and let the bacon cook to your liking.

4 If you want to make fried bread as well, cook it in exactly the same way as for well-done bacon, adding a little more oil to the tin if necessary. It will take about 5 minutes for each side.

5 There are two methods for cooking fried eggs – either in the Aga or on the Aga.

In the Aga:
When you remove the sausages, bacon and so on from the tin, add a little more oil to the tin and put it on the Roasting Oven floor to get really hot. When the oil is hot, crack the eggs into the tin one at a time. The large tin will take about 6 large eggs and the half-size tin about 3 large eggs. Baste the eggs with the fat and put the tin back into the oven for 3 minutes or until they are done to your liking.

On the Aga:

Open the Simmering Plate lid and either grease it with a little oil, or use a round, pre-cut circle of Bake-O-Glide and put it directly on to the Simmering Plate surface. Drizzle a little oil on to a piece of kitchen paper and rub it over the plate. Crack the egg on to the hot surface and close the lid. The egg will cook in about 2 minutes. The Simmering Plate surface can take about 3 large eggs at a time. (If you have an older Aga with a dented lid, check to see whether it touches the top of the egg when you close it. If it does, leave the lid open. The egg will take a little longer to cook.)

6 To make the toast, put a slice of bread in the Aga toasting rack and place it on the Boiling Plate. Close the lid but keep an eye on it as it will toast very quickly; turn over to do the other side. To stop very fresh bread from sticking to the toaster, heat the rack first on the Boiling Plate before inserting the bread. If you like crispy toast, leave the Boiling Plate lid open.

aga kippers

Put the kippers in an Aga roasting tin. Add about a tablespoon of water to the bottom of the tin and place a knob of butter on each kipper. Cover with foil and cook on the first or second set of runners in the Roasting Oven for 10–15 minutes.

conventional cooking:
Pre-heat the oven to 220°C/425°F/gas 7 and cook as above, in the centre of the oven.

aga porridge

serves 1

75g pinhead oatmeal
600ml water
brown sugar and cream, to serve

1 Put the oatmeal and water in an Aga pan and bring to the boil on the Boiling Plate. Transfer to the Simmering Plate and simmer for 2 minutes.

2 Meanwhile, put the grid shelf on the floor of the Simmering Oven. Cover the pan with the lid and put the grid shelf on the floor of the Simmering Oven. Leave overnight. Stir before serving and add brown sugar and cream.

Variation:
If using normal rolled oats, put them in a pan with the measured amount of water and leave covered on the black enamelled top at the back of the Aga overnight. Serve with brown sugar and cream.

conventional cooking:
Follow the instructions on the packet.

toasted bagel with smoked salmon, poached egg and hollandaise sauce

per person:

1 free-range egg
½ bagel
a little butter
2 slices of smoked salmon
1 tbsp hollandaise sauce (see below)
black pepper
a few snipped fresh chives

FOR THE HOLLANDAISE SAUCE:
2 large free-range egg yolks
juice of ½ a lemon
1 tbsp water
pinch of caster sugar
250g unsalted butter, cut into cubes
salt and white pepper

1 First make the hollandaise sauce. Place the egg yolks, lemon juice, water, sugar, salt and pepper in a bowl over a pan of simmering water on the Simmering Plate (do not let the bowl come into contact with the water) and whisk until the mix leaves a ribbon trail. Whisking constantly, drop in the cubes of butter one at a time – don't drop the next cube in until the previous one has been absorbed; this will take some time. When you have a thick, velvety sauce, taste for seasoning, then set aside until ready to serve.

2 Put a saucepan full of water on the Simmering Plate. When it has reached a gentle simmer, crack the egg into the water and poach for about 2 minutes.

3 While the egg is cooking, use the Aga toaster to toast the bagel. Spread the toasted bagel with a little butter and top with the smoked salmon. When the egg is ready, lift out the egg with a slotted spoon and rest the spoon on a piece of kitchen paper to drain. Place the egg on top of the smoked salmon and spoon over some hollandaise sauce. Season with black pepper and a few chives.

conventional cooking:

To make the hollandaise, bring the bowl of water to a simmer over a medium heat and proceed as in step 1. To poach the egg, bring the water to a simmer over a medium heat and proceed as in step 2.

aga yoghurt

makes approximately 950 ml

2 litres full-fat milk
300ml double cream
150ml live organic yoghurt

1 Bring the milk to the boil in a saucepan on the Boiling Plate, then simmer on the Simmering Plate until it is reduced by a third.

2 Transfer the warm milk to a clean ceramic or stainless steel bowl and add the cream. Stir well. Cool to blood temperature, then add the yoghurt. Cover the bowl with cling film, then put it on the Simmering Plate lid (protect the lid with a tea towel) and leave the yoghurt overnight to set. It will keep in the refrigerator for about 5 days.

baked eggs and bacon

serves 1

butter, at room temperature

1 rasher of streaky bacon, fried and chopped into pieces

1 free-range egg

1 tbsp double cream

salt and pepper

1 Butter the inside of a ramekin. Place the bacon pieces on the bottom of the ramekin.

2 Break the egg on top of the bacon and season with salt and pepper. Pour over the double cream and set the ramekin in a roasting tray.

3 Slide the roasting tray onto the third set of runners in the Roasting Oven and pour enough boiling water into the tray to come halfway up the side of the ramekin. Cook for 5–8 minutes.

4 Remove carefully from the oven and place the ramekin on a serving dish. Serve accompanied by hot buttered toast cut into soldiers.

conventional cooking:

Pre-heat the oven to 200°C/400°F/gas 6 and bake for 8–10 minutes.

aga french toast

There are two methods for French toast. The first method is to cook it on the Simmering Plate as for pancakes (see page 172); the second is to cook it in the Roasting Oven. For smaller numbers I would choose the Simmering Plate, but for large numbers the large Aga roasting tin holds about 6 slices of bread.

for 2 slices of bread:

1 tbsp clarified butter (see below)

1 large free-range egg

vanilla extract

2 slices cinnamon and raisin bread

1 Pour the clarified butter into an Aga roasting tin and put it on the Simmering Plate to heat up.

2 Beat the egg with a dash of vanilla extract in a flat dish and dip in the bread slices. Put the eggy bread into the tin and place the tin on the Roasting Oven floor for 3–4 minutes, then turn over and cook for a further 4 minutes. Serve immediately with sieved icing sugar, strawberry jam and clotted cream.

conventional cooking:

Melt a little clarified butter in a frying pan on the hob and cook as above.

Clarified Butter

Place a pack of unsalted butter in a saucepan and cover with a lid. Put it in the Simmering Oven or Warming Oven (which will take longer) and leave until it has melted. When melted, pour the butter into a jar or ramekin, leaving the milky residue at the bottom of the pan behind. The clarified butter may be stored for up to 6 months in the refrigerator. Clarified butter has a higher burning point than ordinary butter.

panettone french toast

serves 6

4 free-range eggs

50ml milk

1 tbsp Amaretto

generous grating of nutmeg

6 slices panettone, each about 2cm thick

TO SERVE:

unsalted butter

icing sugar

honey

1 Combine the eggs, milk, Amaretto and nutmeg In a large flattish dish, and beat well.

2 Place a large round piece of Bake-O-Glide on the Simmering Plate.

3 Dip both sides of the panettone into the eggy mix. Spread a little butter over the Bake-O-Glide, place the eggy panettone on it and cook for a few minutes, then flip and continue cooking until both sides are golden.

4 Remove the panettone to a warm plate. Spread more butter on the bread, dust with icing sugar and drizzle over some honey. Serve either for breakfast or for pudding, or to accompany the Kashmir Plums (see page 211).

conventional cooking:

Use a frying pan over a moderate heat.

breakfast muffins

makes 12

250g plain flour

150g unrefined golden caster sugar

2 tsp baking powder

pinch of salt

1 large free-range egg, slightly beaten

160ml milk

1 vanilla pod, scraped of its seeds

118ml vegetable oil or melted butter

180g fresh fruit such as blueberries, raspberries, chopped peaches, apricots, etc.

FOR THE TOPPING:

200g muesli

1 Line a muffin tin with muffin papers and set aside.

2 Mix together the flour, sugar, baking powder and salt in a large bowl. Mix the egg, milk, vanilla seeds and oil or butter in another bowl. Make a well in the dry ingredients, add the fruit and pour in the wet ingredients. Using a large rubber spatula, fold the mix together using as few strokes as possible.

3 Spoon the mix into the muffin papers until they are half-full. Sprinkle over the muesli.

4 Put the grid shelf on to the floor of the Roasting Oven and slide in the muffin tin. Slide the Cold Plain Shelf onto the third set of runners and bake for 20–25 minutes or until golden. Remove from the tin and cool on a wire rack.

conventional cooking:

Pre-heat the oven to 200°C/400°F/gas 6 and bake for 20–25 minutes as above.

panettone french toast

bacon fritters with maple syrup

serves 4

1 tbsp groundnut oil

150g maple-cured bacon, cut into small cubes

2 large free-range eggs, separated

30g plain flour

1 tbsp maple syrup

a twist of black pepper

15g unsalted butter

1 Heat the oil in a frying pan on the Boiling Plate and fry the bacon cubes until crispy. Drain them on kitchen paper and set aside.

2 Put the egg yolks, flour, syrup and a twist of pepper into a bowl and mix together thoroughly. Stir in the bacon. Beat the egg whites until stiff and fold them into the bacon mix.

3 Put a round piece of Bake-O-Glide on the Simmering Plate and grease with a little butter. Drop one heaped tablespoon of the batter at a time onto the Simmering Plate and cook until it bubbles around the edges, then turn over with a spatula and cook for a further minute. Serve immediately.

conventional cooking:

Use a frying pan over a medium heat to cook the bacon. Do not drain all the fat from the frying pan and use the same frying pan to cook the fritters as above.

popovers with fruit compote

makes 6

vegetable oil, for coating the tin

175g plain flour

½ tsp salt

freshly grated nutmeg

3 free-range eggs, beaten

300ml milk

1 tbsp vegetable oil

2 tbsp fruit compote of your choice

icing sugar, to dust

crème fraîche or cream, to serve

1 Lightly grease a 6-cup muffin tin and pre-heat it in the Roasting Oven for 5 minutes.

2 Sift the flour into a bowl. Add the salt, nutmeg, eggs, milk and vegetable oil and mix well so there are no lumps.

3 Ladle the mixture into the tin and place a teaspoon of fruit compote into each cup. Cook in the Roasting Oven for 10–15 minutes or until golden and risen.

4 Remove from the tin, dust with icing sugar and serve straight away with crème fraîche or cream.

conventional cooking:

Pre-heat the oven to 220°C/425°F/gas 7 and prepare as above. Cook the popovers in the centre of the oven for 12 minutes or until golden and risen.

bacon fritters with maple syrup

oatmeal and cinnamon oven pancakes

serves 4–6

3 free-range eggs

grating of fresh nutmeg

1 tsp ground cinnamon

175g plain flour

175ml milk

110ml water

100g oatmeal

40g clarified butter (see page 21)

icing sugar, for dusting

maple syrup, to serve

1 Whisk the eggs, spices and flour together in a bowl and, still whisking, slowly add the milk and water. Stir in the oatmeal and set aside.

2 Put 1 tablespoon of the clarified butter into a small cast-iron frying pan (I use a 21cm frying pan or my small tarte tatin dish) and heat it up in the Roasting Oven until it is smoking hot. Move the pan to the Simmering Plate and pour in a ladleful of the batter.

3 Put the grid shelf on the third set of runners in the Roasting Oven and place the pan on it. Bake each pancake for 10–15 minutes or until it is risen and golden brown. Move the pancakes to a plate in the Simmering Oven to keep warm and repeat until all the batter is used up.

4 Serve either straight away dusted with icing sugar and drizzled with maple syrup or, if cooked earlier in the day, re-heat for 8 minutes in the Roasting Oven before serving.

conventional cooking:

Pre-heat the oven to 220°C/425°F/gas 7 and bake the pancakes as above.

pumpkin muffins

makes 12

425g can puréed pumpkin

3 large free-range eggs, slightly beaten

350g plain flour

118ml vegetable oil

270g unrefined golden caster sugar

2 tsp baking powder

1 tsp baking soda

pinch of salt

1 tsp pumpkin pie spice
(this is a spice mixture I make with equal quantities of ground ginger, ground cinnamon, allspice and cloves)

1 Line a muffin tin with muffin papers and set aside.

2 Mix together all the ingredients thoroughly. Spoon the mix into the muffin tin, filling the papers to the top.

3 Put the grid shelf on the floor of the Roasting Oven and slide in the muffin tin. Slide the Cold Plain Shelf onto the third set of runners and bake for 20–25 minutes or until golden. To test if they are cooked in the middle, insert the point of a knife or a skewer and if it comes out clean they are ready. If the mix is still loose, put them back in for a few more minutes.

conventional cooking:

Pre-heat the oven to 190°C/375°F/gas 5 and bake for 20–25 minutes.

2 soups

aga stock

This is the basic Aga method for making stock which can be used as the basis for many soups.

1 Roast off the meat bones in the Roasting Oven for about 45 minutes or until brown. Then put them into a stockpot or large pot and cover with cold water. Add herbs, seasoning, a halved onion, a chopped-up carrot, celery, garlic and anything else you feel like adding (but avoid starch-based vegetables such as potatoes).

2 Bring to the boil on the Boiling Plate and boil rapidly for 5–10 minutes. Cover with a lid and transfer to the Simmering Oven for at least 6 hours or overnight.

3 Skim off the fat and strain through a sieve. Store in the fridge for up to a week, bringing it to the boil before using, or freeze for up to 3 months.

For Chicken and Game Stock:
Use a whole carcass, but do not brown. Start it in cold water.

For Fish Stock:
Do not brown the fish bones, and only cook for about an hour. Keep for 3 days in the fridge.

pancetta and chestnut soup

serves 4

2 tbsp light olive oil

2 tbsp butter

100g pancetta, chopped

2 large onions, peeled and finely chopped

435g tin chestnut purée

300ml chicken stock

300ml double cream

salt and pepper

1 Heat the oil and butter in a large casserole on the Simmering Plate and fry the pancetta pieces until the fat begins to run. Remove the pancetta and set aside. Add the onion to the fat in the pan and cook until very soft but not coloured. You can do this either on the Simmering Plate or in the Roasting Oven.

2 When the onions are soft, add the rest of the ingredients and bring the soup just up to the boil on the Boiling Plate. Add most of the pancetta and simmer for a few minutes. Taste for seasoning. (The soup can be liquidised at this stage if you wish.) Add the reserved pancetta as a garnish when you are ready to serve.

conventional cooking:
Cook the soup on the hob over a medium heat as above.

roasted vine tomato soup

This soup can be frozen and will sit in the Simmering Oven quite happily for a few hours.

serves 6

1kg vine-ripened tomatoes

3 large fat garlic cloves, unpeeled

1 tbsp olive oil

1 tbsp aged balsamic vinegar

1 handful fresh basil leaves, torn

1 heaped tbsp fresh oregano leaves, chopped

950ml vegetable stock

salt and pepper

1 Put the tomatoes and garlic cloves into the Aga roasting tin and drizzle with the oil. Season with salt, pepper and balsamic vinegar, half of the basil and the oregano.

2 Slide the tin onto the second set of runners in the Roasting Oven and cook for about 30 minutes or until the tomatoes and garlic are soft.

3 Squeeze the skin of the garlic cloves to extract the pulpy flesh into a saucepan. Pour the tomatoes into a sieve and catch the juice in the saucepan. (If you don't mind the tomato skins, don't bother to do this.)

4 Pour the stock into the saucepan and bring to the boil on the Boiling Plate. Taste for seasoning. Ladle into warm bowls and sprinkle with the rest of the basil and drizzle in some olive oil. Serve with extra balsamic vinegar and ciabatta bread.

conventional cooking:

Pre-heat the oven to 150°C/300°F/gas 2. Roast the tomatoes in the middle of the oven for 35–40 minutes. Cook the soup over a medium heat on the hob.

sweetcorn and cheese chowder

serves 6–8

200g pancetta, cubed

30g butter

30ml olive oil

2 large onions, peeled and finely chopped

50g plain flour

1.4 litres chicken stock

700g potatoes, peeled and cut into 3cm cubes

500g frozen sweetcorn

230ml whipping cream

250g medium Cheddar cheese, grated

1 small bag organic tortilla chips, crushed

salt and pepper

1 Cook the pancetta cubes on the Simmering Plate until crispy, using a saucepan large enough to hold all of the ingredients (a stockpot that fits into the ovens would be perfect).

2 Remove the crispy pancetta and set aside. Pour in the butter and oil, add the chopped onions and cook until they are soft. (If the pot will fit into the Roasting Oven, soften the onions there.)

3 Stir the flour into the fat and season with salt and pepper. Cook for about 3 minutes on the Simmering Plate. Stirring all the time, add the stock and potatoes. Bring up to the boil and transfer to the Simmering Oven for 20 minutes or until the potatoes are tender but still holding their shape.

4 Take the pot out of the oven and add the sweetcorn, whipping cream and three-quarters of the cheese. Bring it back to a gentle simmer and taste for seasoning. Ladle into warmed soup bowls and sprinkle over some crushed tortilla chips, the pancetta and the remaining cheese.

conventional cooking:

Cook on the hob for 20–30 minutes over a medium heat.

bread and tomato soup

Known as *pappa al pomodoro*, for this soup to be delicious you must use delicious tomatoes so choose them carefully – they should smell like tomatoes and be heavy.

serves 6

1 loaf of stale, good-quality sourdough or ciabatta bread

3kg very ripe delicious tomatoes

2–3 garlic cloves, peeled and sliced

100ml good olive oil, plus a little extra

1 large bunch fresh basil, torn

Parmesan cheese, freshly grated

salt and pepper

1 Remove the crust from the loaf and roughly tear the bread into pieces.

2 Skin the tomatoes – put them into a bowl and pour boiling water over them. Leave for a few minutes then, wearing rubber gloves, carefully peel off the skins. Cut in half and scoop out and discard the seeds.

3 Put the garlic and the olive oil into a large saucepan and cook very gently for 2–3 minutes on the Simmering Plate. Take care not to let the garlic burn or go brown.

4 Add the tomatoes. Stir and simmer for about 20 minutes (you can also do this in the Simmering Oven). The tomatoes will become very concentrated. Season with salt and pepper, then add 350ml water and bring up to the boil on the Boiling Plate. Taste. Add the bread and stir to combine well. Add more water if it is too thick.

5 Remove from the heat and add the torn basil leaves. Stir again. Add a good glug of olive oil and stir. Ladle into bowls and serve sprinkled with the Parmesan cheese.

conventional cooking:
Cook as above on the hob.

courgette soup

serves 6

1.5kg courgettes, chopped

1 garlic clove, peeled

1 litre stock

1 tbsp finely chopped fresh mint

1 tbsp torn fresh basil

2 tbsp crème fraîche

50g Parmesan cheese, grated

salt and pepper

1 Soften the courgettes in the olive oil for about 20 minutes in a frying pan on the floor of the Roasting Oven, adding the garlic clove halfway through the cooking.

2 Remove the pan from the oven, add the stock and season with salt and pepper. Bring up to the simmer on the Simmering Plate and gently simmer for about 5 minutes.

3 Take off the heat and liquidise using a blender or food processor. Pour back into the saucepan and add the herbs, crème fraîche and Parmesan, stirring well. Check for seasoning and serve with crusty bread.

conventional cooking:
Cook the courgettes in a frying pan over a medium heat on the hob. Pour in the stock and continue as above, over a medium heat.

bread and tomato soup

chilled broad bean and mint soup

serves 4

1.5kg broad beans, plus a handful for garnish

1 litre good-quality stock

1 garlic clove, peeled

2 tbsp finely chopped fresh mint

1 tbsp torn fresh basil

2 tbsp crème fraîche

50g Parmesan cheese

olive oil, for serving

salt and pepper

1 Have a bowl of iced water ready for blanching. Shell the beans from the tough pod. Bring a pan of water up to the boil on the Boiling Plate and cook the beans in salted boiling water for 2–3 minutes or until they start to wrinkle and they still have a bit of bite to them. Remove the beans with a slotted spoon and plunge them into the iced water immediately. Drain from the iced water, carefully peel off the membrane and put the bright green beans into a bowl. This can be done in advance.

2 Put the stock and garlic into a saucepan, season well and bring it up to a simmer on the Simmering Plate. Gently simmer for about 2 minutes.

3 Add the prepared broad beans (reserving a few for a garnish), then take off the heat and add the herbs and crème fraîche, then liquidise using a blender or food processor. Leave to chill in the fridge.

4 Check the seasoning and serve with a few of the reserved beans, a shaving of the Parmesan, a drizzle of olive oil and crusty bread. (Note: when you are serving something chilled, you must season it well with salt as the taste will dull in the chilling process.)

conventional cooking:
Cook on the hob.

roasted garlic and onion soup

serves 6

500g medium-sized white onions (about 10)

4 whole heads of garlic, unpeeled

3 tbsp olive oil

1.5 litres beef stock

100ml white wine

4 medium potatoes, peeled and chopped

6 slices French bread, toasted

160g Gruyère cheese, grated, for garnish

salt and pepper

1 Cut the onions in half, leaving the outer skin on. Put them into a bowl and add the garlic heads. Pour in about 3 tablespoons of olive oil and toss them together, making sure they are well coated in the oil.

2 Tip into the large Aga roasting tin, place on the Roasting Oven floor and cook for 20 minutes. Stir the onions and garlic, move the tin to the second set of runners and cook for a further 20–25 minutes or until soft and caramelised.

3 Remove the onions and garlic from their skins and put them into a deep saucepan. Add the stock, white wine and potatoes. Bring to the boil on the Boiling Plate, then transfer to the Simmering Oven for 35 minutes or until the potatoes are soft. Whiz the soup in a food processor or with a hand-held blender and taste for seasoning.

4 Ladle into soup bowls and top each one with a toasted slice of baguette and some Gruyère cheese sprinkled over the top.

conventional cooking:
Pre-heat the oven to 220°C/425°F/gas 7 and roast the garlic for about 1 hour. Cook the soup on the hob over a medium heat.

butternut squash and ginger soup with parmesan croûtons

serves 6

1.5kg butternut squash

3 tbsp olive oil

1 leek, sliced thinly

2 garlic cloves, crushed

1 parsnip, peeled and chopped

4cm piece fresh ginger or more to taste, peeled and grated

1 litre vegetable or chicken stock

salt and pepper

FOR THE CROUTONS:

1 stale loaf of ciabatta bread, cut into 2cm cubes

1 tbsp olive oil

Parmesan curls, to garnish (shave curls off a hunk of Parmesan cheese using a potato peeler, allowing 1–3 curls per person)

1 Cut the butternut squash in half. Remove the seeds and any fibres, then slice the halves into quarters. Brush the cut edges of the squash with a tablespoon of the olive oil and sprinkle over some salt and pepper. Roast in a roasting tin on the first or second set of runners in the Roasting Oven for about 20 minutes or until the squash is soft and slightly charred around the edges. Set aside to cool, then scrape away the flesh from the skin and reserve the flesh.

2 While the squash is cooking, heat the remaining oil in a deep pan on the Simmering Plate. Gently cook the leek and garlic until soft. Add the parsnip and ginger. Pour in the stock, bring everything to the boil on the Boiling Plate and cook for about 3–5 minutes, then transfer to the Simmering Oven for 10 minutes or until the parsnip is tender.

3 To make the croûtons, toss the bread cubes in a bowl with the olive oil, making sure they are well coated. Spread on a baking sheet and bake on the first set of runners in the Roasting Oven for 8–10 minutes. Watch them carefully as they burn very easily. Leave to cool on a plate lined with kitchen towel.

4 When it is ready, add the roasted butternut squash to the soup and add salt and pepper as needed. Use a food processor to purée the soup, then return it to the pan until warmed through. Serve with the croûtons and garnish with the Parmesan curls.

conventional cooking:

Cook the soup on the hob over a medium heat. To bake the croûtons, pre-heat the oven to 200°/400°F/gas 6 and continue as above.

crab and coconut soup

1 tbsp sunflower oil

1 medium onion, peeled and minced

pinch of sugar

6cm piece ginger, peeled and cut into very thin matchsticks

1 chilli, deseeded and sliced

1 tsp garam masala or red curry paste

500ml chicken stock

3–4 good pinches saffron

1 tsp sesame oil

2 tbsp fish sauce

400ml coconut milk

275g brown crab meat

1 bunch fresh coriander leaves, chopped but with some left whole for garnish

1 tbsp lime juice (optional)

500g white crab meat

salt and pepper

1 Pour the sunflower oil into a large, deep saucepan and heat up on the Simmering Plate. Add the minced onions and pinch of sugar, and cook until the onions are soft and translucent.

2 Add the ginger, chilli, garam masala or curry paste and stock to the saucepan. Cook for another 2–3 minutes, then add the saffron, sesame oil, fish sauce and coconut milk. Stir in the brown crab meat and cook for another 2–5 minutes.

3 Add the chopped coriander and adjust the seasoning with salt, pepper and lime juice (if using). Bring to a rapid simmer and add the white crab meat. Stir for 1 minute, then serve garnished with the whole coriander leaves.

conventional cooking:
Cook on the hob.

split pea and ham soup

These old-fashioned cuts of meat are coming back into favour due to people who are interested in food buying these cheaper cuts from top-class butchers, and eating them in fab restaurants which are using them with great success.

serves 6–8

350g split green peas

6 peppercorns

1.5kg smoked collar of bacon

3 stalks of celery

3 small carrots, peeled

1 bay leaf

1 large onion, peeled and studded with cloves

1 Rinse the peas in cold water. Wrap the peppercorns in a muslin bag (for easy removal later).

2 Put all the ingredients into a large stockpot that will fit into the Simmering Oven. Cover with cold water and bring up to a boil on the Boiling Plate. Cover and transfer to the Simmering Oven for 2½–3 hours.

3 Transfer the bacon to a plate and discard the celery, carrots, bay leaf, peppercorns and onion. The peas should be soft. Taste the liquid for seasoning – you probably won't need to add any salt.

4 Either use a hand-held blender or food processor to blend the peas so you have a smoothish soup. Reheat if necessary, check the seasoning and serve with croûtons. Serve the bacon separately as a main course.

conventional cooking:
Cook on the hob.

crab and coconut soup

3 starters

rillettes of duck with toasted brioche

serves 4–6

1 duck, weighing about 2.75kg

150g duck fat, cut from the duck

350g pork fat

125g pork fillet, cut into large pieces

1 garlic clove

1 carrot, peeled and cut in half

1 onion, peeled and cut in half

bouquet garni, made of juniper berries, thyme and sage

300ml white wine

1 tbsp pink peppercorns, drained and rinsed

clarified butter (see page 21)

salt and pepper

1 Cut the breasts and thigh meat off the duck and save the carcass for making stock at a later date. Cut as much fat as possible off the duck meat, discarding the skin but cutting the fat into small pieces. Put the duck fat and pork fat into a casserole with 3 tablespoons of water.

2 Put the casserole on the Simmering Plate and bring to a simmer. Transfer it to the Simmering Oven and leave for 30–35 minutes or until all the water has evaporated and the fat has melted.

3 Add the duck meat, pork fillet, garlic, carrot, onion, salt, pepper and bouquet garni. Pour over the white wine and bring to the boil on the Boiling Plate. Cover the casserole with a lid and transfer to the floor of the Simmering Oven for 4 hours.

4 Take the casserole out of the oven and remove the vegetables and bouquet garni. Add the pink peppercorns and cover the casserole with a damp tea towel. Leave to cool in a cool, well-ventilated area.

5 When it is cool enough to handle, shred the meat with your hands and knead it so that the fat and meat is really well mixed. Spoon the rillettes into individual ramekins and cover them with a layer of clarified butter. It is best if you make these 2–3 days in advance. They will keep in the fridge for up to 5 days. Bring the rillettes back to room temperature before eating, and serve with toasted brioche.

conventional cooking:

Cook the duck in a casserole over a medium heat on the hob until the water has evaporated and the fat has melted. Pre-heat the oven to 120°C/250°F/gas ½ and cook for 3–4 hours.

leeks vinaigrette

serves 4

16 baby leeks (4 per person)

1 tbsp toasted pine nuts

1 tsp pink peppercorns, drained and rinsed

FOR THE DRESSING:

1 tbsp red wine vinegar

1 tbsp walnut oil

2 tbsp sunflower oil

1 tsp Dijon mustard

½ tsp sugar

salt and pepper

1 First, make the dressing by whisking the vinegar, oils, mustard, sugar, salt and pepper together.

2 Next, steam the leeks. Put the leeks into an ovenproof dish and add 3 tablespoons of water. Season with salt and pepper and cover with foil. Put the dish on the third set of runners of the Roasting Oven and cook for about 10–12 minutes or until tender.

3 When they are ready, either divide the portions between each plate or pile the leeks onto one large serving platter and drizzle over the dressing, making sure the leeks are all well coated, then sprinkle over the pine nuts and peppercorns. Serve with crusty bread.

conventional cooking:

Pre-heat the oven to 200°C/400°F/gas 6 and bake the leeks for 15–20 minutes or until tender.

tuna pâté with ciabatta crostini and capers

serves 6

175g unsalted butter

4 shallots, peeled and finely sliced

3 anchovy fillets

500g tuna steaks

juice of 2 lemons

zest of 1 lemon

twist of black pepper

1 tbsp fresh flat-leaf parsley

TO SERVE:

12 ciabatta slices

1 garlic clove, peeled

large, good-quality capers

1 Gently heat 15g of the butter in a frying pan on the Simmering Plate and cook the shallots and anchovy fillets until they are soft but not coloured. Remove them from the pan and set aside.

2 Heat another 15–30g of the butter in the same pan and cook the tuna steaks for about 3–4 minutes on each side. Remove them from the pan and let them cool to room temperature.

3 When the shallots and tuna are cool, put them and the rest of the ingredients into a food processor and whiz until very smooth. Taste for seasoning. Place the pâté into a bowl and chill in the refrigerator.

4 When you are ready to serve, toast the ciabatta bread and then rub each half with the clove of garlic. Spoon on some of the pâté and garnish with capers. Serve 2 or 3 slices per person.

conventional cooking:

The tuna can be cooked in a frying pan on the hob over a medium heat.

prawn tempura

serves 6

12–18 raw tiger prawns
sunflower oil, for frying

FOR THE TEMPURA BATTER:
2 free-range egg whites
140g flour, sifted
sparkling water, beer or ice-cold
water

FOR THE DIPPING SAUCE:
2 tbsp soy sauce
1 tbsp rice vinegar
3 spring onions, finely sliced

1 Bring a pan of well salted water up to the boil on the Boiling Plate and blanch the prawns in the boiling water for about 60 seconds. Peel them and set aside.

2 Quickly mix the batter ingredients together – don't be too fussy, you must have a lumpy batter for lightness. Add enough water or beer to make the mixture up to 250ml in total.

3 Mix the dipping sauce ingredients and pour into a bowl.

4 Heat up the sunflower oil in a deepish frying pan on the Boiling Plate – you will find that you will need to move it to the Simmering Plate so it is not too hot. Dip the prawns in the batter and then plunge into the hot oil – they should puff up and turn golden in about 1 minute so don't take your eyes off them. Drain them on a plate lined with kitchen paper. Serve straight away with the dipping sauce and ice-cold beer.

conventional cooking:
Cook on the hob.

prawn tempura

roasted root vegetable salad

serves 6

4 large Desirée potatoes, peeled and cut into wedges

4 parsnips, peeled and cut in half lengthways (or quarters if they are large)

2 bulbs of fennel, trimmed and cut into wedges

4 baby carrots

1 tbsp fresh thyme leaves

olive oil

salt and pepper

1 Put the potato wedges into a bowl of cold water for 10 minutes. Drain them well and pat dry with kitchen paper.

2 Put the potato wedges, parsnips, fennel, carrots, thyme and salt and pepper into a bowl and pour over about 2 tablespoons of olive oil. Toss the vegetables so they are well coated and tip them into an Aga roasting tin.

3 Hang the tin on the second set of runners of the Roasting Oven and roast for 40–45 minutes until the vegetables are charred around the edges and tender. Check after 25 minutes – if the carrots and fennel are cooked, remove them and set aside until the other vegetables are done.

4 When they have finished cooking, remove the vegetables from the tin with a slotted spoon and leave them to cool to room temperature. Arrange the vegetables on plates and serve with individual bowls of rouille (see below) and crusty bread.

conventional cooking:

Pre-heat the oven to 220°C/425°F/gas 7 and roast for 40–45 minutes.

garlic rouille

300g potatoes, peeled and chopped into large chunks

2 garlic cloves, crushed

3 hard-boiled free-range eggs, peeled and roughly chopped

300ml olive oil

pinch of saffron

salt and white pepper

1 Put the potatoes into a saucepan and cover with water. Bring them to the boil on the Boiling Plate and boil for 5 minutes. Drain off all the water, put a lid on the pan and move the pan to the Simmering Oven for 20–25 minutes or until the potatoes are tender.

2 When they are cooked, remove the lid and put the pan into the Roasting Oven for 1 minute to dry the potatoes out slightly.

3 Put a sieve over a large bowl and first rub the potatoes through the sieve, then the hard-boiled eggs. Stir them together until well mixed, then pour in the olive oil a little at a time, stirring constantly to emulsify. Season to taste with saffron, salt and white pepper.

conventional cooking:

Boil the potatoes for 25 minutes over a medium-high heat on the hob. Drain and leave for 5 minutes, then continue as above.

roasted root vegetable salad with garlic rouille

arbroath smokies with pernod and crème fraîche

serves 6

30g butter

1 small onion, peeled and chopped finely

8 Arbroath smokies, skinned, boned and flaked

2 tbsp Pernod

3 tbsp crème fraîche

feathery fronds of a fennel bulb, chopped

salt and pepper

rye bread (see page 275), to serve

1 Put the butter and onion into a large frying pan and cook them on the floor of the Roasting Oven for 10 minutes or until they are soft but not coloured.

2 Transfer the frying pan to the Simmering Plate and add the smokies and Pernod. Cook for a few minutes then add the crème fraîche and cook for 2 more minutes.

3 Sprinkle in the fennel tops, stir and check the seasoning, then spoon into six individual shallow warmed dishes. Serve with buttered rye bread.

conventional cooking:

Cook in a large frying pan on the hob over a medium heat.

flat bread with parma ham and taleggio

serves 6

12 large tortilla breads

olive oil

12 slices Parma ham

1 large bunch of fresh basil leaves

240g Taleggio cheese, sliced thinly

1 bag rocket salad

FOR THE BALSAMIC DRESSING:

1 tbsp aged balsamic vinegar

1 tbsp extra virgin olive oil

2 tbsp olive oil

salt and pepper

1 Take six tortillas and lay them out on a flat surface. Drizzle a small amount of olive oil over each tortilla and lay two slices of ham on the bottom. Divide the basil between them and top each with the sliced Taleggio. Cover with the remaining tortillas and gently press together.

2 Lift the lid of the Simmering Plate and place a round piece of Bake-O-Glide on the hot surface. Wipe with a little olive oil and lay the filled tortillas directly on the hot surface. Cook for about 3–4 minutes on each side or until they are golden and the cheese has melted. Repeat for each tortilla, keeping the cooked ones warm on a warmed plate covered with a clean tea towel.

3 Whisk all the dressing ingredients together.

4 Cut the tortillas into quarters with a pair of scissors and divide the slices between 6 plates. Sprinkle them with salt and black pepper and serve with a rocket salad dressed with balsamic dressing.

conventional cooking:

Heat a frying pan over a medium heat. Wipe the merest hint of oil over the frying pan and cook the tortillas in the pan for 3–4 minutes on each side and serve as above.

oven-baked avocados

serves 2

2 large ripe avocados

2 spring onions, trimmed and sliced

1 tbsp tomato purée

pinch of flaked chillies

1 tbsp fresh basil, shredded

1 garlic clove, peeled and crushed

100g sun-blushed tomatoes

50g black olives, stones removed

1 ball mozzarella, sliced thinly

1 tbsp olive oil

focaccia bread, to serve

salt and pepper

1 Cut the avocados in half, remove the stones and skin, and place in an ovenproof dish and set aside.

2 In a bowl mix the spring onions, tomato purée, flaked chilli, basil, garlic, sun-blushed tomatoes and olives together and check the seasoning.

3 Spoon the mixture into the avocados, cover with the sliced mozzarella and drizzle over the olive oil. Bake on the third set of runners in the Roasting Oven for 10–15 minutes or until the cheese is melted and golden.

conventional cooking:
Pre-heat the oven to 220°C/425°F/gas 7 and bake for 15–20 minutes.

asparagus and mint mini frittatas

serves 6

olive oil

9 large free-range eggs

250g asparagus, blanched and cut into tips and 2cm pieces

100g freshly grated Parmesan cheese

1 heaped tbsp fresh mint, shredded

salt and pepper

1 Brush the insides of a muffin tin with olive oil.

2 Break the eggs into a large bowl and beat lightly. Stir in the rest of the ingredients and pour the egg mixture into the muffin tin. Place the tin on the third set of runners in the Roasting Oven and cook for 10–15 minutes or until the frittatas are puffy and golden.

3 Serve the frittatas straight away or at room temperature, garnished with more Parmesan. Serve with a green salad and cherry tomatoes. These are also great to pack up for a picnic.

conventional cooking:
Pre-heat the oven to 200°C/400°F/gas 6 and continue as above.

grilled tiger prawn and fennel salad

These prawns can be prepared several hours in advance and the dish assembled at the last minute, making this salad a perfect summer dinner party starter.

serves 6

1kg raw tiger prawns, shelled and deveined

1 yellow pepper, roasted, skinned, de-seeded and cut into chunks

1 red pepper, roasted, skinned, de-seeded and cut into chunks

1 large head fennel, trimmed and sliced very thinly

1 head radicchio, torn into medium pieces

1 bag wild rocket

1 heaped tbsp freshly chopped flat-leaf parsley

FOR THE DRESSING:

juice of 1 lemon

3 tbsp light olive oil

sea salt, to taste

pepper

1 In a bowl, whisk all the ingredients for the dressing together until well combined, then set aside.

2 Heat a ridged grill pan in the Roasting Oven. Put the tiger prawns into a bowl, add 2 tablespoons of the dressing and toss well to coat.

3 Take the grill pan out of the Roasting Oven and put onto the Boiling Plate. Cook the prawns in batches (do not overcrowd the pan) for about 2 minutes on each side. If the heat is too intense, transfer the pan to the Simmering Plate. Don't overcook them or they will be tough.

4 Put the cooked prawns into a bowl and add the peppers and fennel. Deglaze the grill pan with some of the dressing and pour over the prawns. Pour over the remaining dressing and leave to cool.

5 When you are ready to serve, arrange the radicchio and rocket on a large platter and put the tiger prawn and pepper salad on top. Garnish with flat-leaf parsley and serve with lots of crusty bread.

conventional cooking:
Pre-heat a grill pan over a high heat until smoking and cook the prawns as above. Turn the heat down if it becomes too hot.

grilled tiger prawn and fennel salad

chicken liver pâté

Pâté is delicious and simple to make. To save time, I make pâtés by pan frying and whizzing in a processor rather than cooking in a bain-marie. Careful seasoning is vital to a good pâté as it is served cold. Chilled foods can stand a little more salt as the taste will dull when cool.

serves 8–10

500g chicken livers, picked over and any green bits removed

milk, for soaking

1 rasher bacon, chopped or cubed

175g unsalted butter

1 red onion, peeled and finely chopped

1 garlic clove, peeled and crushed

1 tsp fresh thyme leaves

2 tbsp Marsala

50–60g clarified butter, melted (see page 21)

salt and pepper

1 Soak the chicken livers in some milk for about 30 minutes. Drain the chicken livers and discard the milk.

2 In a heavy-based frying pan on the Simmering Plate, fry the bacon until cooked but not too crispy. Remove from the pan and set aside.

3 Drain off the fat and melt about a tablespoon of the unsalted butter in the pan on the Simmering Plate. Put the rest of the butter into a bowl and leave to melt at the back of the Aga. Add the onions to the pan and cook on the floor of the Roasting Oven until soft.

4 Transfer the pan to the Simmering Plate and add the drained chicken livers, garlic and thyme leaves. Season with salt and pepper and cook for 5–7 minutes or until the chicken livers are well cooked all the way through.

5 Spoon the mix into a food processor and add the bacon. Deglaze the frying pan on the Simmering Plate with the Marsala, scraping up all the bits from the bottom of the pan. Add this to the food processor bowl along with the rest of the melted butter sitting at the back of the Aga. Blitz the pâté until it is smooth.

6 Check the seasoning again and, using a spatula, turn the pâté out into an earthenware dish. The dish must be big enough to have a 3cm gap at the top so that you can pour in the clarified butter. Leave the pâté to cool for about 30 minutes, then melt the clarified butter and pour over the top of the pâté. Add a few thyme leaves to garnish if you wish.

7 Cool until the butter has set, then cover with cling film and chill in the fridge. It is better to make the pâté a day in advance and let the flavours mingle. Serve with crusty bread, a wedge of lemon and redcurrant jelly.

conventional cooking:
Cook in a frying pan on the hob.

potato pancakes with smoked salmon

makes 10–14

FOR THE PANCAKES:

100g cold, smooth mashed potato with nothing else in it (I use a potato ricer for smooth mash)

1 free-range egg, separated

1 tbsp double cream

1 rounded tbsp self-raising flour

sunflower oil

salt and white pepper

FOR THE TOPPING:

4 tbsp sour cream

1 tbsp chopped fresh chives

150g smoked salmon, cut into strips or chopped

1 lemon

ground black pepper

1 In a large bowl mix the potato, egg yolk, cream, flour and salt and pepper together. Whisk the egg white in a separate bowl until stiff, then gently fold into the potato mix.

2 Open the lid of the Simmering Plate, place a round piece of Bake-O-Glide on it and lightly grease with a piece of kitchen paper dipped in some sunflower oil. Drop spoonfuls of the pancake mix onto the Bake-O-Glide. Cook for 1 minute on each side and remove to a warmed plate. (You can make the pancakes 2 weeks in advance, freeze them and re-heat in the Roasting Oven for 2–3 minutes.)

3 Top each pancake with some sour cream mixed with chives and some smoked salmon strips. Add a squeeze of lemon juice and some freshly ground black pepper.

conventional cooking:

Cook the pancakes in a frying pan on the hob.

baked camembert with walnut bread

serves 6

2 x 220g wooden boxes of ripe, ready-to-eat Camembert

3 ripe pears, cut into quarters

12 organic dates, stones removed

1 loaf of walnut and raisin bread (see page 281), sliced thinly

1 Remove the wrapping from the cheeses and place the cheeses back into the boxes. Discard the box lids.

2 Place the boxes on a baking tray and slide onto the third set of runners in the Roasting Oven for 10–15 minutes or until very soft.

3 While the cheese is in the oven, arrange the fruit and walnut bread on two platters, leaving space in the centres for the cheese boxes. Place a baked cheese on each platter and serve immediately. Scoop out the melted cheese with a spoon.

conventional cooking:
Pre-heat the oven to 200ºC/400ºF/gas 6 and bake for 10–15 minutes or until very soft.

fonduta

serves 6

500g Fontina cheese

300ml full-fat milk

40g Italian butter

4 free-range egg yolks

splash of grappa or truffle oil (or, if you are feeling really flush, shavings of white truffle in season!)

salt and pepper

1 Cut the cheese into small cubes and put in a bowl. Pour over half the milk and leave in a cool place for at least 4 hours.

2 When you are ready to cook the fonduta, put a pan of water on to boil on the Boiling Plate, then move to the Simmering Plate. Cut the butter into cubes, put into a largish heatproof bowl and melt over the pan of simmering water. When it has melted, slowly add the cheese and milk mixture plus the remaining milk to the butter, stirring all the time. Do not let the bowl of water boil and stir the mix constantly. This will take about 8–10 minutes.

3 Add the egg yolks one at a time, taking care not to let the mixture curdle. Don't add the next egg yolk until the first one has been completely absorbed into the cheese. The mix is ready when it looks like thick double cream. Season and serve in one bowl or in individual bowls, topped with a drizzle of truffle oil, the truffle shavings or a tiny splash of grappa. Serve with delicious Italian breads.

conventional cooking:
Cook on the hob.

crab soufflé

There are two tricks to a soufflé. The first is to grease the soufflé dish thickly with butter. To do this, butter it then freeze for about 1 hour, then butter again and repeat up to three times. If you are using cheese in your soufflé, dust with grated cheese at the last stage of buttering and freezing. The other trick is to place the dish on a pre-heated baking tray so that it gets an extra boost of heat as it goes into the oven.

serves 4–6

75g unsalted butter, plus extra for greasing

75g flour

1 tsp mustard powder

450ml milk, warm

1.5kg crab meat (three-quarters white and the remainder brown)

6 free-range eggs, separated

Worcestershire sauce

Tabasco

salt and pepper

1 First, make the roux. Melt the butter in a small saucepan on the Simmering Plate. Add the flour and mustard powder to the butter and stir well with a wooden spoon until it turns into a glossy paste. Gradually pour in the warm milk, a little at a time, stirring or whisking all the time until all the milk is incorporated and you have a smooth, lump-free sauce.

2 Simmer the sauce for 3–5 minutes, whisking occasionally, so that the flour is cooked. Do not let the sauce burn or catch on the bottom. Set aside and cool a little.

3 Mix the crab meat into the roux, then add the egg yolks one at a time. Season with salt, pepper, Worcestershire sauce and Tabasco. (Seasonings need to be strong so that the blandness of the egg whites is balanced by the seasoning.) Cover the surface of the sauce with cling film so that a skin doesn't form. The soufflé can be prepared to this stage in advance.

4 Grease a 1.25 litre soufflé dish with butter (see the tip in the recipe introduction). Place a baking sheet in the Aga to pre-heat.

5 Whisk the egg whites until they form stiff peaks, then whisk a little of the white into the roux to loosen the mix. Using a metal spoon, carefully fold the remaining whites into the roux. Pour into the prepared soufflé dish and place onto the pre-heated baking sheet. Cook in the Roasting Oven for 25–30 minutes until the soufflé has risen and is golden on top. Serve immediately.

conventional cooking:
Pre-heat oven to 190°C/375°F/gas 5 and cook as above.

golden croustades

Croustades can be made in regular-sized muffin tins or mini muffin tins. They are so versatile that you can fill them with almost anything – hot or cold. They can be made a day in advance or frozen for up to 2 weeks.

makes as many as slices in the loaf

1 loaf organic bread, thinly sliced with crusts removed

3–4 tbsp melted butter or olive oil

1 Using a rolling pin, roll out each slice of bread and brush with the butter or oil. Gently press one slice of bread into each section of a muffin tin until all the holes are lined.

2 Bake in the Roasting Oven for 5–8 minutes or until golden brown. Remove from the tins and cool. Fill with your choice of filling.

3 If you want to use them with a hot filling, bake until just beginning to turn brown, then fill with something like a frittata mix (see page 43) and return to the Roasting Oven to bake for a further 5–8 minutes. They are also wonderful holders for baked eggs.

conventional cooking:
Pre-heat the oven to 180°C/350°F/gas 4 and bake for 6–8 minutes or until golden brown.

herbed popovers

These are wonderful with crème fraîche and smoked salmon. If you make them in a mini muffin tin, they can be filled and used as a base for canapés.

makes 6

vegetable oil, for coating the muffin tin

165g plain flour

½ tsp salt

3 free-range eggs

250ml milk

1 tbsp vegetable oil

1 heaped tbsp chopped fresh herbs of your choice, e.g. chives, dill, basil, etc.

1 Lightly grease a 6-hole muffin tin with some oil and place it in the Roasting Oven while you make up the batter.

2 Sift the flour into a large bowl, then add the remaining ingredients and mix well so there are no lumps.

3 Remove the tin from the oven and ladle in the batter. Bake on the third set of runners in the Roasting Oven for 15–20 minutes or until golden and puffed up.

4 Remove from the oven and immediately prick each popover with a knife to let the steam escape. Return to the oven and bake for another 5 minutes, then serve straight away.

conventional cooking:
Pre-heat the oven to 200°C/400°F/gas 6 and bake the popovers as above.

4 poultry & game

Chicken is the 'Little Black Dress' of the kitchen! I could eat it every day and find it the most versatile meat to cook – nothing beats a good roast chicken. Naturally low in fat, game such as pheasant and woodcock is a healthy and full-flavoured option when simply cooked, and it is its seasonality that makes it so special and eagerly awaited.

roast chicken

This method is for roasting chicken and all poultry except large turkeys (see method opposite). Line the roasting tin with Bake-O-Glide. Cut an onion in half (use two for a large chicken) and place the chicken on top of the onion. Stuff the cavity of the chicken with herbs, onion or lemon and season with salt and pepper. Rub over butter or oil or lay strips of bacon over the chicken, then rub in more salt and pepper. Slide the tin onto the lowest set of runners in the Roasting Oven and set the timer (see right). Check halfway through cooking and cover the chicken with foil if it is browning too quickly. To test if the chicken is thoroughly cooked, pierce the thigh with a skewer; if the juices run clear, it is cooked. If they are pink or red, the chicken is not ready so cook for a little longer. Rest the chicken for 15 minutes before carving.

Approximate timings for roasting a whole chicken:
900g chicken (small): 35–45 minutes
1.5kg chicken (medium): 45–60 minutes
2kg chicken (large): 1½–1¾ hours
3kg chicken (very large): 2 hours

roast pheasant

Line the roasting tin with Bake-O-Glide. Place the bird or birds in the tin and generously rub with butter or lard (or even cover with the paper that the butter is wrapped in) and season with salt and pepper. If you wish, cover the breasts with bacon. Stuff the cavity of the pheasant with half an onion or apple and season with salt and pepper. Slide the tin onto the third set of runners of the Roasting Oven and set the timer for 45–50 minutes. Halfway through cooking, baste. To test if the pheasant is cooked, pierce the thigh with a skewer; if the juices run clear, it is cooked. Serve with bread sauce, game chips and fried breadcrumbs. Be careful not to overcook game. As the fat content is lower, it does have a tendency to dry out.

roast partridge, grouse, woodcock, snipe and quail

Cook as for pheasant (above) but adjust the cooking times and accompaniments.
partridge: Roast for 30–35 minutes and serve with quince cheese or redcurrant jelly.
grouse: Roast for 20–30 minutes and serve on croûtes of fried bread spread with the pan-fried liver of the grouse if you are lucky enough to have it.
woodcock, snipe and quail: Roast for 12–15 minutes. Serve woodcock and snipe on croûtes (as for grouse). Quail is such a versatile bird that it can be served in almost any way you wish. On average, allow 1½ birds per person.

roast turkey

The Aga can accommodate a turkey weighing up to 12.5kg and I recommend using the Aga turkey roasting tin. There are two methods of roasting turkey: the slow roasting method, which can be done overnight, and the conventional (or fast roasting) method. The advantage of the slow roasting method is that you don't have to worry about the turkey and the Roasting Oven will be available for cooking all the traditional trimmings.

The timings given here are approximate and very much depend on the size of the bird. Cooking time may have to be increased for older Agas if you use the slow roasting method.

The conventional method of cooking the turkey will use up quite a lot of heat, so planning and preparation are very important.

preparing a fresh turkey

Wash the turkey well with water and pat dry with kitchen towel. Stuff only the neck end of the bird, put a couple of onions into the body cavity and season well with salt and black pepper. Place the turkey into the roasting tin. Do not truss the bird. Generously brush melted clarified butter all over the bird (see page 21). Season with salt. The secret of a succulent golden bird is all in the basting. Leave the pot of clarified butter at the back of the Aga so that it is within easy reach for basting every 30 minutes or so if cooking the bird conventionally.

slow roasting method

Place the roasting tin directly on the floor of the Roasting Oven and cook for about 1 hour or until the turkey is browned. A larger turkey may take longer to brown. It is essential to give the turkey a real blast of heat for a good amount of time for food safety. When it is browned, baste with the clarified butter, cover loosely with foil and move to the Simmering Oven for the following times:

3.6–4.5kg: 3–6 hours
5–7.25kg: 5–8½ hours
7.25–9kg: 8½–11 hours
9–11kg: 11–13½ hours
11–12.8kg: 13½–15½ hours
All times are approximate.

conventional or fast roasting method

Place the roasting tin on the floor of the Roasting Oven. After about 1 hour, or when the turkey is browned, cover loosely with foil and cook for the following times:

3.6–4.5kg: 1¾–2 hours
5–7.25kg: 2–2½ hours
7.25–9kg: 2½–3 hours
9–11kg: 3½–4½ hours
11–12.8kg: 4½–5½ hours
All times are approximate.

The turkey is done when the thigh juices run clear when pierced with a skewer. Rest the turkey for at least 20 minutes. A large bird will stay hot for a long time and can withstand a long resting time, so take this into consideration when working out your cooking timetable.

When using the conventional roasting method, you can start cooking the turkey breast side down, turning it breast side up about 45 minutes before the end of the cooking time. This way of cooking the turkey ensures the breast meat will not be dry.

christmas cooking timetable

Christmas doesn't have to be a hectic rush with all preparation left to the last minute. With a large glass of wine, a deep breath and a little planning, this timetable will guide you through the Christmas holidays.

Early December: Order fresh turkey. If you are buying a frozen turkey, do it now. It is best to allow 4–5 days for it to thaw so having it to hand will be an advantage. Make and freeze the mince pies.

One week before Christmas: Start to defrost turkey at the back of the fridge. Write shopping lists and purchase all non-perishables. Buy milk in cartons and freeze in case of emergency.

Two days before Christmas: Make cranberry sauce (see page 292) and store in the fridge. For stuffings and bread sauce you will need stale bread. Cut and cube it now and lay it out on a baking tray in a single layer.

Christmas Eve:

Morning: Collect fresh turkey. Buy fresh fruit and vegetables. Prepare giblet gravy. Defrost mince pies.

Afternoon: Prepare stuffings. Leave well covered in a cool place, but not in the refrigerator, as they shouldn't be too cold when you stuff the turkey.

Prepare vegetables. Peel potatoes and put in cold water in the fridge. Prepare other vegetables and store in polythene bags and refrigerate. Or start the 'get ahead vegetables' off – make the roast potatoes and blanch the other vegetables (see page 154).

Make bread sauce (see page 169) and store in the fridge, taking care to cover the surface with cling film.

Before you retire to bed: Take turkey out of the fridge to allow it to come to room temperature. Do the same with the stuffing and butter so that it softens for the morning. If you are cooking a turkey using the overnight method (see page 53), calculate the timings and start cooking it. With all the newly created space, fill up the fridge with wines, mineral water, etc.

christmas day

Aga owners are always worried about running out of heat so to prevent this, write out a preparation schedule and a cooking timetable. This timetable is based on a 7kg turkey, to be served at 2pm.

7:30am Stuff the turkey.

8:15am Put the turkey in the oven and baste with melted butter every 30 minutes. If you are using the Warming Oven in a 4-oven Aga, put in the required plates and serving dishes.

11:30am Prepare bacon rolls and chipolatas. Re-heat bread sauce and place it in a jug with butter on top to melt over the surface, keep warm.

12:00 Start steaming the Christmas pudding. Bring to the boil on the Boiling Plate, then transfer to the Simmering Oven for 3 hours.

12:45pm If you are cooking your vegetables conventionally, do roast potatoes and prepare saucepans of boiling water for any other vegetables.

1:15pm Remove turkey from oven, cover loosely with foil and let it rest. Make gravy (see page 171) and keep it warm.

1:30pm Check chipolatas and bacon rolls, remove and keep warm. Put in 'get ahead' roast potatoes.

1:45pm Put sprouts on to cook or put in 'get ahead' blanched vegetables. While they are cooking, transfer the other food into serving dishes and carve the turkey. Check Christmas pudding.

2:00pm Serve Christmas lunch.

christmas turkey

The stuffing for this recipe is made from the legs of the turkey.

serves 12–14

7kg turkey (size depends on how many people you intend to serve; remove gizzard and use for stock)

2 medium onions, peeled and chopped

1 garlic clove, peeled and crushed

175g vacuum-packed chestnuts, chopped

2 tbsp chopped fresh sage, plus 6 sprigs whole fresh sage leaves

salt and pepper

2 free-range eggs per 500g of minced turkey meat (see step 1)

a good handful of fresh herbs – sage, bay or other large leaf herbs, left whole and in good condition

4 tbsp unsalted butter, for basting

1 First, remove both legs and bone them (if possible, get your butcher to do this), making sure all the sinews are removed. Open out the boned legs and cut off about a quarter of the inside meat (the meat is mostly in flaps and is easy to cut away). Be very careful not to tear the skin. Mince the leg meat in a food processor, weigh and set aside.

2 Sweat the onions and garlic in a frying pan on the Simmering Plate until soft. In a large bowl, combine the minced leg meat, onions, garlic, chestnuts, chopped sage, salt and pepper and the eggs. Lay out the sage sprigs on a large piece of greased foil, then put the prepared legs skin side down on top. Divide the stuffing between the legs, then carefully roll up the legs, twisting the ends of the foil tightly. Set aside until ready to cook.

3 Gently loosen the breast skin away from the meat with your fingers, taking great care not to tear the skin. Lift the skin carefully and arrange the herb leaves underneath the skin in a pretty pattern. Refrigerate until ready to cook. All of the above can be done the day before.

4 When you are ready to cook the turkey, melt about 4 tablespoons of unsalted butter in a bowl and keep near the oven with a pastry brush so that you are ready to baste the breast.

5 Cook the legs and breast in the Roasting Oven, on the last set of runners or wherever the roasting tin fits, for about 1¾ hours, basting the breasts with butter every 15 minutes or so. Check the turkey breast after 1½ hours to see if it is cooked – insert a skewer and if the juices run clear it is done, if not put it back into the oven for another 15 minutes and check again. The legs will need the full 1¾ hours. Check to see if they are cooked by inserting the skewer. If the breast skin starts to burn, cover with a piece of foil.

6 Let the cooked turkey rest for at least 20 minutes before carving. Make the gravy and serve with Cranberry and Walnut Sauce (see page 292).

conventional cooking:
See page 53 for conventional roasting times.

stir-fried chicken with soba noodles

serves 4

40ml groundnut oil

1 garlic clove, peeld and crushed

8cm piece of fresh ginger, peeled and cut into strips

2 chicken breasts, skinned and cut into thin strips

10–12 shiitake mushrooms, sliced

300g broccoli, cut into spears

1 small bunch spring onions, trimmed and cut into diagonal chunks

½ tbsp rice vinegar

50ml soy sauce

240ml chicken stock

½ tsp brown sugar

½ tbsp cornflour, mixed with 1 tbsp water to form a thin paste

½ tsp sesame oil

500g soba noodles, cooked (or substitute cooked linguine or spaghetti)

sesame seeds, to garnish

1 Put a large bowl into the Simmering Oven to warm.

2 Heat three-quarters of the groundnut oil in a wok on the Simmering Plate. Add the garlic and half the ginger. Cook gently to infuse the oil with the flavourings. When the garlic and ginger turn brown, remove them with a slotted spoon and discard.

3 Transfer the wok to the Boiling Plate and quickly brown the chicken pieces. Add the mushrooms, broccoli, spring onions and the rest of the ginger. Cook for 3–4 minutes, stirring the chicken and vegetables constantly.

4 Add the vinegar, soy sauce, stock, sugar and cornflour paste. Bring to the boil and cook for 2 minutes or until the sauce starts to thicken. Take the bowl out of the Simmering Oven; transfer the chicken and vegetables to the warmed bowl and set aside.

5 Add the rest of the groundnut oil and the sesame oil to the wok and heat the noodles through, adding a little of the sauce from the bowl of chicken. Divide the noodles between warmed serving bowls and top with the chicken and vegetables. Garnish with a sprinkling of sesame seeds.

conventional cooking:

Use a wok over a high heat and cook as above.

stir-fried chicken with soba noodles

chicken roasted on freshly baked focaccia bread

We have a brilliant team at The George Hotel. Our chef, Kevin Mangeolles, is a constant inspiration and his passion and knowledge about food are enviable. This is a dish he devised for one of my cookery demonstrations as he thought it would be a perfect Aga recipe and, as usual, he was right!

serves 2 generously

1 quantity of focaccia bread dough (see page 274)

olive oil

1kg free-range chicken, trimmed (ask your butcher to prepare it for you)

1 tbsp fresh rosemary leaves

salt

2 garlic cloves, peeled and sliced

6 cherry tomatoes

1 Roll the bread dough into a long sausage shape, set aside. Line a frying pan large enough to hold the chicken and bread with greaseproof paper and set aside.

2 Heat some olive oil in another pan on the Boiling Plate until smoking. Season the chicken with salt and seal the chicken in the hot pan. Place the sealed chicken in the prepared frying pan and wrap the dough around it so it looks like a life-saving ring. Drizzle over some more olive oil and scatter the rosemary, some salt and the garlic over the chicken and the dough.

3 Bake for 40 minutes on the fourth set of runners in the Roasting Oven. After 40 minutes, take the chicken out and scatter over the cherry tomatoes. Cook for a further 10 minutes, test to see if the chicken is done, then remove chicken from the oven, rest for 10 minutes and serve with a green salad.

conventional cooking:

This chicken dish cannot be cooked successfully in a conventional oven.

herb roasted chicken with quince jelly, thyme and rosemary sauce

serves 4

2 red onions, peeled and halved

50g butter, softened

1 tbsp fresh thyme, chopped

1 tbsp fresh rosemary, chopped

1 garlic clove, peeled and crushed

juice and zest of 1 unwaxed lemon

salt and pepper

1 large chicken, free-range if possible

FOR THE SAUCE:

2 tbsp quince jelly

2 tbsp mature red wine vinegar or balsamic vinegar

2 tbsp freshly chopped thyme

2 tbsp freshly chopped rosemary

salt and pepper

1 Put the halved onions into a roasting tin, cut side down, and set aside.

2 Put the softened butter into a bowl and add the herbs, garlic, lemon juice and zest, salt and pepper, then mash with a fork to combine.

3 Gently ease off the skin of the chicken breast with your fingers, taking care not to tear the skin. Lift the loosened skin and spread the herb butter mix underneath. Place the chicken on the onions and cook on the third set of runners in the Roasting Oven for 1 hour or until the leg juices run clear. Cover with foil if the top is browning too much. When the chicken is cooked, let it rest for 10–15 minutes before serving with the red onions and sauce.

4 To make the sauce, whisk the quince jelly, vinegar and 1–2 tablespoons of water in a saucepan on the Simmering Plate until melted and simmer for about 2 minutes. Take off the heat and add the herbs and salt and pepper. Check the seasoning, pour into a jug and set aside until you are ready to serve the chicken. (If the sauce is too thick, thin down with a little water.)

conventional cooking:

Pre-heat the oven to 200°C/400°F/gas 6 and cook the chicken for 1½–1¾ hours or until the juices run clear. Cook the sauce in a saucepan over a gentle heat on the hob.

thai green chicken

serves 6

6 chicken breasts or 12 thighs, skinned

2 tbsp grapeseed oil

2 shallots, peeled and finely chopped

2–3 lemongrass stalks, finely sliced

2 garlic cloves, peeled and crushed

6 spring onions

juice and zest of 2 limes

2 shredded kaffir lime leaves

2 tsp coriander seeds, roasted and ground

2 tsp ground cumin

4cm piece of ginger, grated

3 red chillies, deseeded and thinly sliced

2 tsp fish sauce

1 tbsp torn fresh basil

1 tbsp freshly chopped coriander

1 tsp peanut butter

400ml coconut milk

1 tbsp chopped cashew nuts, for garnish

1 Put the chicken into a large bowl and set aside.

2 Heat up a large wok on the Boiling Plate and add the oil. Next quickly fry, in this order, the shallots, lemongrass and garlic. Add everything else except for the coconut milk, chicken and cashew nuts. Take the spices and herbs off the heat, then pour in the coconut milk. Let the sauce cool.

3 Pour the sauce over the chicken, cover with cling film and marinate in the fridge for a minimum of 2 hours – the longer the better.

4 When you are ready to cook the chicken, transfer it to a large ovenproof dish with the marinade and slide it onto the third set of runners in the Roasting Oven for 25 minutes. Stir it, then cover with foil and cook for another 25 minutes. The coconut milk will probably split but it won't affect the taste. Garnish the chicken with more fresh herbs and the chopped cashew nuts, and serve with jasmine rice.

conventional cooking:

Pre-heat the oven to 200°C/400°F/gas 6 and cook as above.

thai green chicken

chicken in marsala wine with oranges and shallots

1 tsp cardamom seeds, removed from their outer pods

1 tsp coriander seeds

30g flour

8 chicken pieces (either a whole jointed chicken or breasts cut in half)

2 tbsp olive oil

150g pancetta, cubed

16 shallots, peeled

300ml marsala wine

300ml orange juice

1 tbsp sherry vinegar

1 stick cinnamon

6 garlic cloves, peeled

1 orange, cut into thick slices

1 heaped tbsp crème fraîche

salt and pepper

1 First, dry fry the cardamom and coriander seeds in a frying pan on the Simmering Plate, then crush in a pestle and mortar.

2 Season the flour with salt, pepper and the spices. Mix together well. Coat each piece of chicken with the flour and set aside.

3 In a shallow casserole dish on the Simmering Plate or floor of the Roasting Oven, heat the olive oil and cook the pancetta, then add the chicken and shallots and cook until they are all a nutty brown colour. Add any of the leftover flour, then pour in the marsala wine, orange juice, vinegar, cinnamon stick, garlic and orange slices.

4 Stir and bring to the boil on the Boiling Plate, then transfer to the Simmering Oven for 1½–2 hours, uncovered. It is ready when the juices run clear from the chicken. Stir in the crème fraîche and serve with wild rice and a green salad.

conventional cooking:

Pre-heat the oven to 150°C/300°F/gas 2 and cook for 2–2½ hours as above.

casseroled chicken legs with tarragon and crème fraîche

serves 4

30g flour

4 chicken legs, skinned

1 tbsp sunflower oil

knob of butter

1 shallot, peeled and finely chopped

1 garlic clove, peeled and crushed

2 flat field mushrooms, finely chopped

100ml chicken stock

50ml white wine

4 tbsp Dijon mustard

1 heaped tbsp fresh tarragon leaves, roughly chopped

140ml crème fraîche

salt and pepper

1 Season the flour with salt and pepper, then coat each chicken leg in it.

2 Heat a frying pan on the floor of the Roasting Oven and melt the sunflower oil and butter. Brown the chicken legs in the oil and butter on the Roasting Oven floor and set aside. Do not discard the oil.

3 Fry the shallot, garlic and mushrooms in the frying pan on the Simmering Plate until they are soft. Add any leftover flour and stir in the stock and wine. Bring to the boil and stir in the mustard and the tarragon leaves. Remove from the heat.

4 Arrange the chicken legs in a lidded casserole and pour the mustard sauce over the top, cover and cook on the third set of runners in the Roasting Oven for 30 minutes, then transfer the casserole to the Simmering Oven for 2–2½ hours or until the chicken is cooked and tender.

5 Remove the chicken legs to a warmed plate and reduce the sauce on the Simmering Plate until it has thickened a little. Whisk in the crème fraîche and check the seasoning. Serve with rice and garnish with some more tarragon leaves.

conventional cooking:
Pre-heat the oven to 150°C/300°F/gas 2 and cook for 2 hours as above.

maple-glazed turkey with orange and herb stuffing

serves 8–10

5.5kg turkey

1 whole orange

1 onion, peeled

FOR THE GLAZE:

200ml maple syrup

80g Dijon mustard

50g butter

2 tbsp Worcestershire sauce

FOR THE STUFFING:

1 day-old 'country-style' loaf, cut into cubes

4 heaped tbsp freshly chopped parsley

1 onion, peeled and chopped

zest of 3 oranges

1 tbsp fresh thyme leaves

65g butter, softened

2 large free-range eggs, lightly beaten

120ml orange juice

80ml water

salt and pepper

1 First make the stuffing. Tip all the ingredients into a large bowl and mix together really well. Add more orange juice if it is too dry – all breads are different and you will have to judge the moistness – the mixture should hold together without being too loose. Butter a large casserole and fill with the stuffing. Cover with foil and bake on the third set of runners in the Roasting Oven for 40–45 minutes or until cooked.

2 Cut the orange and onion in half. Season the inside of the turkey with salt and pepper. Push the orange and onion into the turkey. Mix the glaze ingredients together and set aside.

3 Cook the turkey according to your usual method (see page 53). I always baste my turkey with melted butter and cover it with foil for the first 3½ hours of cooking. For this size of bird allow about 4–4½ hours. If you stuff the bird, it will probably take an extra hour. Only stuff the neck end of the bird.

4 Remove the foil and pour over the maple glaze 30 minutes before the end of the cooking time.

conventional cooking:

To cook the stuffing, pre-heat the oven to 190°C/375°F/gas 5 and bake for 45–50 minutes.

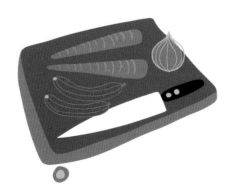

turkey burgers with tomato confit

You can make the tomato confit in advance and store it in a covered bowl or jar in the fridge for up to one week. It makes a delicious accompaniment to so many things; serve it warm or at room temperature.

serves 4

FOR THE BURGERS:

900g minced turkey

½ tbsp fresh thyme leaves

3 spring onions, white part only, very finely chopped

1 tbsp Worcestershire sauce

1 tbsp tomato purée

salt and pepper

FOR THE TOMATO CONFIT:

1kg ripe vine tomatoes, cut in half

6 garlic cloves, peeled and sliced thinly

100g fresh sourdough breadcrumbs

1 tbsp fresh flat-leaf parsley, chopped

3 tbsp olive oil

4 soft round wholewheat burger buns, to serve

mayonnaise, to serve

curly endive, to garnish

1 In a large bowl mix all the burger ingredients together by hand, making sure they are all well combined. Shape the meat into four round patties, place on a piece of greaseproof paper and refrigerate for an hour.

2 To make the confit, put the tomatoes, cut side up, in an Aga roasting tin. Scatter the garlic slices over them and season with salt and pepper. Mix together the breadcrumbs and parsley and cover the tomatoes with them. Drizzle over the olive oil. Slide the tin onto the second set of runners in the Roasting Oven and bake for 45–60 minutes or until soft and sizzling. Transfer to a bowl and set aside.

3 To cook the burgers, heat a frying pan or Aga grill pan on the floor of the Roasting Oven until it is very hot and smoking. Put the burgers into it and put the pan back onto the Roasting Oven floor and cook for 8 minutes on each side.

4 Toast the burger buns using the Aga toaster; spread a little mayonnaise on the bottom half of each bun and add a little of the curly endive. Put the turkey burgers on top and spoon on some of the tomato confit. Serve with coleslaw.

conventional cooking:

To cook the confit, pre-heat the oven to 200°C/400°F/gas 6 and cook as above. To cook the burgers, pre-heat a grill pan and cook the burgers under a medium heat.

crispy duck pancakes with plum sauce

This is a really easy way to cook Peking Duck at home, and I've yet to meet anyone who doesn't like it. Children love the sweet-sour flavour and adore assembling and rolling up the duck pancakes – it makes eating such fun! Buy the pancakes ready made from an oriental grocer or supermarket.

serves 4 as a main
course; 6 as a starter

2.3kg oven-ready duck, dry plucked if possible

50ml plum brandy or ordinary brandy

1 tbsp Chinese 5-spice powder

80ml honey

1 tbsp soy sauce

1 tsp sesame oil

4cm piece ginger, peeled and cut into strips

200ml hoisin sauce or plum sauce

½ a cucumber, peeled and cut into 5cm thin strips

1 bunch spring onions, trimmed, cut into 5cm long strips and separated

2 x 250g packs of Chinese pancakes

1 Deal with the duck first. You can prepare this the day before and reheat if you wish. Put the duck into a colander and pour over a kettle of boiling water to help loosen the fat. Drain the duck and dry really well with kitchen paper inside and out. Brush the duck with the brandy (alcohol helps to dry out the skin, giving a crispier finish).

2 Hang the duck up by its wings with a plate underneath in a place where there is a cool breeze (the air helps to keep the duck really dry). If this isn't possible, put it uncovered into the fridge. This can be done a day in advance, but it must be left hanging for a minimum of 6 hours.

3 When you are ready to cook the duck, place a piece of Bake-O-Glide in the half-size roasting tin and then put in the grill rack. Put the duck on the grill rack. Rub the 5-spice powder all over the bird and brush on the honey and soy sauce. Slide the tin onto the third set of runners in the Roasting Oven and cook for 1 hour, then transfer to the Simmering Oven for a further hour or until the duck is cooked and the skin is crispy (this can take up to 2 hours). You want to end up with the meat falling away from the bones and really crispy skin.

4 While the duck is cooking, gently heat up the sesame oil and the ginger strips in a large saucepan and cook for 2 minutes on the Simmering Plate. Don't burn the ginger. Remove the ginger strips and add the hoisin sauce or plum sauce and heat through. Set the sauce aside to cool.

5 When the duck has finished cooking, remove it from the oven and allow to rest for 5–10 minutes, then shred all the meat away from the carcass, cut up the skin and keep warm.

6 Follow the cooking instructions on the packaging for the pancakes and serve the shredded duck with the pancakes, cucumber and spring onion strips and the sauce. Spread some sauce over a pancake and top with some duck, spring onions and cucumber strips, roll up tightly and eat.

conventional cooking:
Pre-heat the oven to 200°C/400°F/gas 6 and start the duck off for about an hour, then turn down the temperature to 180°C/350°F/gas 4 and cook for another hour or so until the duck is tender.

crispy duck pancakes with plum sauce

spatchcock poussins with parsley and pinenut dressing

serves 6

6 butterflied spatchcock poussins (ask your butcher to prepare them)

FOR THE DRESSING:

40g raisins

juice of ½ a lemon

100ml olive oil

2 tbsp freshly chopped flat-leaf parsley

60g lightly toasted pine nuts

salt and pepper

1 First, make the dressing. Put the raisins into a bowl and soak them in boiling water for 5 minutes, then drain. Whisk the lemon juice and oil together in a small bowl. Add the raisins, parsley and pine nuts and season with salt and pepper. Set aside. If you make this ahead of time, leave out the pinenuts until you are ready to serve. This dressing should be served at room temperature.

2 Heat a griddle pan in the Roasting Oven until it is smoking. Transfer the pan to the Boiling Plate and seal the poussins in the pan on both sides. You are aiming for charred grill marks on the birds. If the pan is too hot, transfer it to the Simmering Plate.

3 When you have sealed all the birds, put them on a baking tray, season with salt, and cook in the Roasting Oven for 10–15 minutes, or until they are cooked through. When they are done, leave them to rest for about 10 minutes. (Any of the juices that are left in the pan or tray should be poured into the dressing.)

4 Serve the poussins with the pine nut dressing spooned over the top.

conventional cooking:

Heat the griddle pan on the hob and pre-heat the oven to 200°C/400°F/gas 6. Seal the poussins in the griddle pan on the hob, then place them in the pre-heated oven and continue as above. Timings may vary a little so check the birds after 15 minutes – they may need a few minutes more.

pheasant sausages

serves 4

100g butter, on the cold side of room temperature

1kg minced pheasant meat, well chilled

200g shallots, peeled and finely diced

1 tsp fresh thyme leaves

75g vacuum-packed chestnuts, chopped

salt and pepper

1 Beat the butter into the pheasant meat and the other ingredients in a large bowl. Do this as quickly as possible as you want to keep the mixture as cold as possible.

2 Lay out two 40cm pieces of cling film on a work surface. Pile about 2 tablespoons of the meat onto the cling film and shape into a sausage shape. Roll up the sausage in the cling film, tightly twisting the ends together so that the sausage is tightly bound. Repeat until all of the mixture is used. Chill the sausages for 3–4 hours.

3 To cook, bring a large pan of water to the boil on the Boiling Plate, then drop the cling film-wrapped sausages into the water and cook at a simmer for 3–5 minutes or until the sausages are cooked. Remove the cling film and serve with braised red cabbage and mashed potatoes.

conventional cooking:

Boil the water on the hob and proceed as above.

curried pheasant with apples and sultanas

serves 4

40g butter

2 tbsp grapeseed oil

2 large apples, peeled, cored, sliced into rings and dipped in lemon juice to prevent discolouring

30g unrefined golden caster sugar

15g sultanas, soaked in hot water to cover

4 pheasant breasts

1 shallot, peeled and finely chopped

1 tbsp mild curry powder

1 tsp tomato purée

30ml game or chicken stock

30ml dry cider

2 tbsp crème fraîche

salt and pepper

1 Heat half the butter and 1 teaspoon of the oil in a frying pan on the Simmering Plate. Add the apple rings and sprinkle over the sugar. Fry the apples until they have caramelised in the sugar, then toss in the drained sultanas. Set aside and keep warm at the back of the Aga.

2 In a clean frying pan, add the remaining butter and oil and brown the pheasant breasts quickly on the Boiling Plate. Transfer them to a roasting tin and roast on the third set of runners in the Roasting Oven for about 10 minutes. Don't overcook them or they will dry out.

3 Meanwhile, make the sauce. Pour off all but 1 tablespoon of the fat left in the frying pan and fry the shallot on the Simmering Plate until it is very soft and starting to caramelise. Add the curry powder and tomato purée and cook for about 1 minute.

4 Next, pour in the stock and the cider and stir vigorously, scraping up all the caramelised bits from the bottom of the pan. Bring the sauce to the boil and reduce until it is quite thick. Season with salt and pepper. Stir in the crème fraîche. Check the seasoning.

5 When the breasts are done, cover them with foil, making sure that you rest them for at least 10 minutes in a warm place. Put a few apple rings and sultanas on each plate and pop a pheasant breast on top, then pour over a little sauce and serve with basmati rice. Hand round any remaining sauce separately.

conventional cooking:
Pre-heat the oven to 220°C/425°F/gas 7 and proceed as above.

serves 6

6 large ripe figs, cut into quarters

icing sugar, for dusting

12 shallots

6 oven-ready partridges

salt and pepper

clarified butter, about ½ a teacup full (see page 21)

100ml Madeira

600ml home-made game stock

1 tbsp butter

345g foie gras, cubed into 2cm pieces

1 First make the oven-dried figs. Spread out the fig quarters on a baking tray and dust lightly with icing sugar. Place them on the third set of runners in the Simmering Oven and bake for about 30 minutes, or until dried but still supple. This can be done in advance and kept in an airtight container.

2 Cut the shallots in half and place them cut side down in a roasting tin. Season the inside of the partridges with salt and put the birds on top of the shallots. Brush over a little clarified butter and season the birds with salt and pepper. Cook on the third set of runners in the Roasting Oven for 20–25 minutes.

3 When they are cooked, take the tin out of the oven and remove the partridges (but not the shallots) to a warmed platter, cover with foil and let the birds rest for 15 minutes before serving.

4 While they are resting (which is imperative), finish the sauce. Take the roasting tin and deglaze with the Madeira. Add the game stock, bring to the boil and reduce until it has halved in volume. Remove the shallots with a slotted spoon and discard. While it is reducing, season the foie gras with salt, and in a pre-heated pan add some clarified butter. Whisk in the butter. Sauté the foie gras on the Boiling Plate until it is brown on all sides. This should take about 1½ minutes – don't overcook it. Remove with a slotted spoon to a warm plate and set aside. Check the sauce for seasoning.

5 When you are ready to serve, add the foie gras and figs to the sauce for about 1 minute, just to heat through. Place each partridge on a warmed plate and spoon over the sauce.

conventional cooking:
Bake the figs in the oven at 190°C/375°F/gas 5. Roast the partridges in an oven pre-heated to 220°C/425°F/gas 7.

pan-fried pigeon breasts with maltaise sauce

serves 6

2–3 tbsp flour
12 pigeon breasts (2 per person)
clarified butter (see page 21)
1 orange, segmented
watercress to garnish
salt and pepper

FOR THE MALTAISE SAUCE:
2 large free-range egg yolks
juice of ½ a lemon
1 tbsp water
salt and white pepper
250g unsalted butter, cut into cubes
juice and zest of 1 organic orange

1 To make the sauce, place the egg yolks, lemon juice, water, salt and pepper in a bowl over a pan of simmering water (do not let the bowl come into contact with the water) and whisk until the mix leaves a ribbon trail. Do this on the Simmering Plate. Whisking constantly, drop in the cubes of butter one at a time – don't drop in the next cube until the previous one has been absorbed. This will take some time.

2 Meanwhile, in another small pan, reduce the juice of the orange together with the zest by half. When all the butter is used and you have a thick velvety sauce, add the reduced orange juice and zest. Taste for seasoning. Keep the sauce warm at the side of the Aga.

3 Season the flour with salt and pepper and put it on to a flattish plate. Dust the pigeon breasts in it and shake off the excess.

4 Heat a heavy frying pan in the Roasting Oven until it is searingly hot. Remove it from the oven and continue on the Simmering or Boiling Plate. Melt about a tablespoon of clarified butter in it and fry the pigeon breasts in batches for 2 minutes each side or longer, to your liking.

5 Drain the meat on kitchen paper and rest for 5 minutes in a warm place.

6 Slice the breasts and arrange on a warm plate. Spoon over some of the sauce and garnish with watercress and an orange segment.

conventional cooking:
Cook on the hob.

rabbit with garlic and lemon zest with tagliatelle

serves 6

4 tbsp olive oil

60g white sourdough breadcrumbs

knob of butter

1kg rabbit, cut into pieces (ask your butcher or game dealer to do this for you)

2 garlic cloves, peeled and sliced thinly

500g tagliatelle

juice of ½ a lemon and the zest of 1 lemon

1 heaped tbsp freshly chopped rosemary

salt

1 Put a frying pan on the Simmering Plate and heat up about half the olive oil. Add the breadcrumbs and fry until they are golden. Drain them on kitchen paper and set aside.

2 In the same pan, heat the remaining oil with the butter. Add the rabbit pieces and garlic, then transfer to the floor of the Roasting Oven until they are cooked through and browned on all sides (this should take about 10 minutes). If necessary, add more olive oil so that the pan is not dry.

3 Meanwhile, bring a large pan of salted water to the boil on the Boiling Plate. Add the pasta and cook until it is *al dente*. Drain it, leaving a little of the water in the bottom so the pasta doesn't stick together.

4 When the rabbit is cooked, transfer it to the Simmering Plate and add the lemon juice and zest, rosemary and a little more olive oil if it needs it. Toss the rabbit in the pasta and arrange on warm plates, topping the rabbit and pasta with the fried breadcrumbs and a little more lemon zest for garnish.

conventional cooking:

This dish can be cooked in a large frying pan entirely on the hob.

rabbit with garlic and lemon zest with tagliatelle

game pie

It is best to make this pie a couple of days in advance to let the flavours develop. When game is not in season, replace it with pork. The chicken stock needs to be home made from a chicken carcass and reduced. It mustn't be too thin – aim for a loose jelly consistency. You can either make this pie in a traditional raised pie mould or use a 20.5cm round cake tin with a removable base and deep sides.

serves 6

FOR THE PASTRY:

450g plain flour

1 tsp salt

225g butter

2 large free-range egg yolks

70–85ml ice cold water

FOR THE PIE FILLING:

sunflower oil

knob of butter

250g pheasant breasts, cut into chunks

200g lean veal, cubed

100g pigeon or chicken, cubed

85g pancetta, cubed

2–3 tbsp brandy, for deglazing

85g pork back fat, cubed

fresh thyme

1 free-range egg, beaten

500–600ml good-quality home-made chicken stock

salt and pepper

1 First make the pastry. Sift the flour and salt into a food processor bowl. Add the butter and pulse for a few seconds so the butter is rubbed into the flour, then add the yolks. Slowly add the water a little at a time (you may not need all of it) until it forms a dough. Wrap in cling film and refrigerate overnight.

2 Heat up about a tablespoon of oil and the butter in a large pan. Brown all the meat, including the pancetta, a batch at a time so they truly brown (don't overload the pan). Move the browned meat to a plate and deglaze the pan with the brandy, scraping up the caramelised bits. Set aside.

3 Roll the pastry out into a circle about 3cm thick. Grease a deep 20.5cm round cake tin with a removable base or a game pie mould. Cut a triangular 'slice' out of the pastry and set aside. Cone the rest of the pastry and fit it into the tin, letting the pastry overhang the sides. Press it well into the sides.

4 Spoon in the browned meat and pork fat, sprinkle over the thyme leaves and season with salt and pepper. Pour in any juices from the deglazed pan.

5 Roll out the triangle to make a lid. Cover the meat with the lid and fold in the overhanging pastry to meet the lid top so the filling is sealed in. Brush the top with beaten egg and make a generous-sized hole in the centre to allow steam to escape, and to fill with the stock after it has been cooked.

6 Bake the pie on the grid shelf on the floor of the Roasting Oven with the Cold Plain Shelf above for 15–20 minutes until the crust is set and starts to colour. For 4-oven Aga owners, bake in the Baking Oven for 20–25 minutes.

7 Move to the Simmering Oven for 1½–2 hours or until the meat is cooked (check by using a meat thermometer). If it colours too quickly, cover with foil.

8 Remove the pie from the oven and carefully pour the stock in through the hole in the pastry lid. (You may not need all the stock.)

9 Cool the pie completely before turning it out of the mould or tin.

conventional cooking:

Pre-heat the oven to 190°C/375°F/gas 5 and bake the pie for 25–30 minutes until the crust is set and starts to colour. Reduce the temperature to 180°C/350°F/gas 4 and cook the pie for a further 1–1½ hours or until the meat is cooked. You can check by using a meat thermometer. If the pie browns too quickly, cover the top with foil. Cool the pie completely before turning it out.

venison and chestnut casserole

serves 4-6

8 juniper berries

800g venison, cubed

3cm piece of ginger, peeled and grated

1 garlic clove, peeled and crushed

5 tbsp sunflower oil

100ml red wine

50g flour

knob of butter

1 large carrot, peeled and finely chopped

½ an onion, peeled and finely chopped

250g vacuum-packed chestnuts

salt and pepper

1 Put the juniper berries into a mortar and crack them open with a pestle to release their aroma. Put the venison, berries, ginger, garlic, 3 tablespoons of oil and wine into a freezer bag and marinate the meat overnight in the fridge.

2 Season the flour with salt and pepper and remove the meat from the marinade, shaking off the excess liquid, and coat each piece in the flour.

3 Heat 2 tablespoons of the oil and the knob of butter in a large casserole dish on the floor of the Roasting Oven and brown each piece of venison. Don't overcrowd the pan. When the meat has all been browned, add the carrot and onion to the pan and cook until they take on some colour, either on the Simmering Plate or on the Roasting Oven floor.

4 When they are ready, add any excess flour to the pan and scrape up all the caramelised bits, then add the meat, chestnuts and finally the marinade juices. Bring it all up to the boil on the Boiling Plate and then transfer to the Simmering Oven for 2 hours or until it is tender. This can all be done the day before you want to serve it as casseroles often taste better reheated the next day. When you are ready to serve, reheat in the Roasting Oven for 30–60 minutes or until it is really hot, then serve with mashed potatoes.

conventional cooking:

Pre-heat the oven to 150°C/300°F/gas 2 and cook for 2–3 hours as above.

5 meat

Roasting a joint of meat in the Aga is easy and the radiant heat locks in the flavour, making it a truly different eating experience altogether. For meats like lamb and pork, you can use the slow roasting method or cook it conventionally. For good cuts of meat, veal and beef, I suggest using the fast roasting method.

slow roasting method

Prepare the joint for cooking. Cut a couple of onions in half and put them into a tin lined with Bake-O-Glide. Put the joint on top of the onions and then slide the tin onto the fourth set of runners of the Roasting Oven for 30–40 minutes or until it begins to brown. Then transfer it to the Simmering Oven for approximately double the amount of conventional cooking time. Weigh the joint before cooking to calculate the timings.

conventional fast roasting method

Prepare joint as above and calculate the roasting time according to the cut and type of meat. When it has finished cooking, rest for 15–20 minutes before carving.

beef

Rare: 12 minutes per 450g

Medium: 15 minutes per 450g

Well done: 20 minutes per 450g

lamb

Pink in the middle: 15 minutes per 450g

Well done: 20 minutes per 450g

pork

25 minutes per 450g

veal

15 minutes per 450g

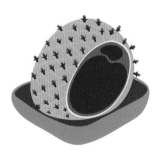

fillet of beef

This method of cooking a whole fillet of beef gives you a beautifully rare middle.

For 900g fillet, put about 2 tablespoons of dripping in the large roasting tin and place it on the Roasting Oven floor. When the fat is smoking, take the tin out, put it on the Boiling Plate and seal the meat on all sides. The fat will splatter so you will need a damp cloth nearby. Remove the excess fat, then hang the tin on the third set of runners in the Roasting Oven. Cook for no more than 15–20 minutes. When the cooking time is up, take the fillet out of the oven and remove from the tin. Do not wash the tin. Wrap the meat very tightly in cling film, twisting the ends for a really snug fit. Put the fillet onto a plate and leave it to rest for at least 20 minutes on top of the protected Simmering Plate. To serve the meat, remove the cling film, put the meat back into the tin and put the tin on the Roasting Oven floor for 8–10 minutes, just to heat it through. Serve it straight away.

calves' liver and bacon

serves 4

sunflower oil

4 slices back bacon

50g butter

1 onion, peeled and thinly sliced

splash of ketchup

2 tbsp flour

salt

16 x 225g slices of calves' liver (all the tubes, membrane and veins must be removed)

1 Pour about a tablespoon of oil into a heavy-bottomed frying pan and place the pan on the floor of the Roasting Oven. When it is very hot, remove the pan and fry the bacon on the Simmering Plate until it is crispy around the edges. Remove the bacon and set aside on a warmed plate.

2 Add a knob of butter to the fat and when it foams, add the onion slices and fry until soft on the floor of the Roasting Oven. Add a squeeze of ketchup and stir well. Spoon onto the plate with the bacon. Wipe out the pan and pour in fresh oil.

3 Spoon the flour onto a plate and season with salt. Dust the liver slices in the seasoned flour and add a knob of butter to the pan. Heat this until hot on the Boiling Plate, then fry the slices of calves' liver for a few minutes per side, depending on how thick they are. Divide the liver among four plates and top each piece with some onions and a slice of bacon.

conventional cooking:
Cook on the hob in a frying pan.

the ultimate roasted rib of beef

The quality of the meat is of paramount importance; it is worth buying well-hung meat from a really good old-fashioned, top-quality butcher. Look for Aberdeen Angus – it's hard to beat! The cooking times for rare, medium and well-done meat are on page 76.

The cooking times for rare, medium and well-done meat are on page 76.

serves 6–8

1 tbsp beef dripping

3kg forerib of beef on the bone

3 onions, unpeeled unless they are dirty, cut in half

salt and pepper

FOR THE GRAVY:

1½ tbsp flour

1 glass red wine

1 litre stock or vegetable cooking water

1 Put the dripping into the large roasting tin and melt in the Roasting Oven until it is smoking. Transfer the tin to the Boiling Plate and seal the joint of beef in the dripping, making sure all the sides of the meat are browned. Set the meat aside.

2 Place the onions in the tin, cut side down. Stand the meat on top of the onions and season with some salt and pepper. Hang the tin on the third set of runners of the Roasting Oven and cook for about 1¾ hours for rare beef. Adjust the time to suit your taste.

3 Rest the meat for at least 15 minutes in a warm place (the Warming Plate if you have a 4-oven Aga or next to a 2-oven Aga), covered loosely with foil.

4 While the meat is resting, you can make the gravy. Spoon away all but 2 tablespoons of fat from the tin. Do not remove the onions. Sprinkle in the flour and stir well so it absorbs all the fat. Pour in the wine and bring to the boil until it has almost evaporated, then pour in either stock or water (the quantity depends how thick you like your gravy). Bring the gravy up to a rapid simmer on the Simmering Plate and let it cook there for about 5 minutes. Taste, season and reduce until it has reached the required consistency. Strain it into a jug and keep warm at the back of the Aga or in the Simmering Oven.

conventional cooking:

Pre-heat the oven to 220°C/425°F/gas 7 and cook as above.

braised beef

All casseroles taste much better if made one day in advance and then re-heated before serving.

serves 6–8

1 litre red wine

200ml port

1.2kg braising steak, cut into large cubes

2 sprigs of fresh thyme, leaves removed from the stalks and stalks discarded

3 red onions, peeled and quartered

1 tbsp flour

1 tbsp mustard powder

100g beef dripping

salt and pepper

1 Bring the wine and the port up to the boil for 2 minutes in a saucepan on the Boiling Plate, then cool. Put the beef cubes, thyme and onions into a large plastic bag, then pour over the cooled wine and port. Marinate in the fridge for 24 hours.

2 When you are ready to cook the beef, remove it from the marinade. Reserve the marinade. Put the flour and mustard powder into a large bowl and season with salt and pepper. Toss the beef cubes in the flour mix until they are well coated.

3 Melt the dripping in a casserole and brown the meat on the floor of the Roasting Oven. You will have to do this in batches so as not to overcrowd the pan and so the meat browns on all sides. When all of the meat is browned, tip in any remaining flour-mustard mix and stir so that the fat absorbs the flour. Put the meat back into the casserole and pour over the marinade.

4 Cover the casserole and bring this to the boil on the Boiling Plate, then transfer to the Roasting Oven for 40 minutes. Transfer the casserole either to the Baking Oven if you have one and cook for 4 hours, or to the Simmering Oven and cook for 5–6 hours or until the meat is tender. Serve with mashed potato.

conventional cooking:

Once the meat has been browned, bring it to the boil as above, then transfer to an oven pre-heated to 150°C/300°F/gas 2 and cook for 2–3 hours or until tender.

chilli

olive oil

2kg good-quality minced beef

500g chorizo sausage, skin removed and chopped

6–8 red onions, peeled and finely chopped

6–8 garlic cloves, peeled and crushed

6–8 400g tins of plum tomatoes (or 4 very large tins)

6 red peppers, deseeded and chopped into pieces

2 hot chilli peppers, seeds left in for added heat (or removed for a milder heat), chopped

cayenne pepper to taste

½ tsp ground cumin

2 tins of organic kidney beans in water, drained

salt and pepper

TO SERVE:

pita bread toasted and roughly torn into strips or tortilla chips

sour cream

chopped spring onions

grated mature Cheddar cheese

1 Heat up about 100ml olive oil in a large pan and brown the minced meat and chorizo sausage on the Simmering or Boiling Plate. You may need to do this in batches. It is important not to overcrowd the pan as you want the meat to brown not steam. Remove the meat to another dish.

2 If necessary, add more oil to the pan, then fry the onions until they are soft but not coloured. Add the garlic, tomatoes, peppers, chilli, and spices. Cook for about 1 minute.

3 Tip the meat back in and bring the sauce up to the boil, then simmer for about 1 hour in the Simmering Oven. Taste for seasoning, then add the beans. Return to the Simmering Oven and cook for a further 20–30 minutes.

4 Serve in large bowls with pita strips or tortilla chips, sour cream, chopped spring onions and grated Cheddar cheese.

conventional cooking:

Brown the meat on the hob. Prepare the sauce on the hob. Pre-heat the oven to 200ºC/400ºF/gas 6 and cook as above.

chilli

spaghetti bolognese

This sauce originated in Bologna and is a classic. In Italy it is traditionally served with shorter pasta or tagliatelle, but America partnered it with spaghetti and a whole new dish was born! It is a thick and meaty sauce that can be used for lasagne as well. This sauce freezes well.

serves 6–8

2 tbsp olive oil

3 medium sweet onions (red ones are fine), peeled and finely chopped

3 celery stalks, finely diced

2 carrots, finely diced

500g minced beef

250g minced veal

250g minced pork

200g chicken livers, finely chopped

150ml white wine

500ml passata (sieved tomatoes)

500ml chicken stock

2 bay leaves

a good grating of nutmeg (optional)

salt and pepper

1 You will need a very large pan for this. Put the grid shelf onto the floor of the Roasting Oven. Heat up the olive oil in the pan on the Simmering Plate, add the onions, then transfer to the Roasting Oven grid shelf. Soften the onions for about 10–15 minutes – do not let them colour or burn.

2 Remove from the oven and put the pan back on to the Simmering Plate. Add the celery and carrots and cook for a few minutes. Add the beef, veal and pork and cook for 10 minutes, breaking it up with a wooden spoon. You can do this on the Roasting Oven floor or, if you are not going to cook anything else for a while, on the Boiling and Simmering Plates.

3 Add the chicken livers and cook for another few minutes. Pour in the wine, passata and stock. Season with salt and pepper and add the bay leaves and nutmeg, if using. Bring up to the simmer and then transfer to the Simmering Oven for 2–2½ hours, stirring every hour or so. Do not cover. You should end up with a meaty thick sauce. Adjust the seasoning and serve with pasta.

conventional cooking:
Cook the sauce and pasta on the hob.

brisket of beef with mustard sauce

Brisket needs long, slow cooking. It's great served with potatoes and carrots tossed with lots of butter and parsley.

serves 6

50–60g dripping

1.5kg brisket of beef

1 large onion, peeled and cut into 3 thick slices

1 pig's trotter, split in half

175ml beef stock

salt and pepper

MUSTARD SAUCE:

50g butter

50g flour

500ml hot beef stock, made from the brisket

1 round tbsp mustard powder

1 level tbsp sugar

3 tbsp cider or white wine vinegar

salt and pepper

1 Put the dripping into a large casserole with a tightly fitting lid and heat on the Boiling Plate until it is very hot. Add the brisket and seal on all sides, then season the meat with salt and pepper. Remove the meat from the pot.

2 Add the onion (skin still on) to the bottom of the pot and put the brisket on top (use the onion as a trivet) and add the pig's trotter.

3 Put the casserole into the Roasting Oven and cook for 20 minutes, then add the beef stock. Bring up to the boil on the Boiling Plate. Cover with the lid and transfer to the Simmering Oven. Cook for 2–3 hours or until the meat is tender.

4 To make the sauce, melt the butter in a small pan on the Simmering Plate. Add the flour and stir briskly to make a roux. Add the hot stock a little at a time, whisking constantly. The sauce should be thick and glossy. Simmer for 2–3 minutes. Season with salt and pepper.

5 In a separate bowl, whisk together the mustard powder, sugar and vinegar, then stir into the sauce and cook for another minute. Taste for seasoning and serve with the meat.

conventional cooking:

Simmer very gently on the hob. Check the liquid levels and add more stock if necessary. Alternatively, cook as above in an oven pre-heated to 150°C/300°C/gas 2.

beef stroganoff

As I have Austro-Hungarian blood, I like to add a teaspoon of paprika and serve my stroganoff with wide noodles such as fettuccine, but rice is delicious too. The key is to prepare as much as possible in advance. The beef will need to be cooked at the last minute and under no circumstances should you overload the pan with beef as it will stew and become tough rather than melt in the mouth. Use a large frying pan so that you have lots of room to fry the beef strips without them steaming.

serves 4

2 tbsp sunflower oil

50g butter

1 medium onion, peeled and sliced very thinly

1 tsp sweet smoked paprika (optional)

200g button mushrooms, sliced thinly

150ml red wine

350g fillet of beef, cut into strips 6 x 2cm

1 tbsp flour

2–3 tbsp brandy

100ml double cream

100ml sour cream or crème fraîche

sea salt and freshly ground black pepper

1 Heat up half the sunflower oil and half the butter in the frying pan on the Simmering Plate.

2 Add the onions and fry until they are soft and translucent. Add the paprika, if using, and the mushrooms and cook for a minute. Add the red wine and cook and reduce for 3 minutes or until you only have 2 tablespoons of liquor left. Remove the onion-mushroom mix to a bowl and set aside. (This can be done up to 6 hours in advance.)

3 Dust the beef strips in flour – simply put the flour onto a plate and dip the beef strips into it, shaking off the excess.

4 Heat the remaining oil and butter on the Boiling Plate in the same frying pan (no need to wash it) as hot as you can, and fry the beef very quickly so that it is still pink in the middle – this will take a minute or so. Do this in batches and remove the beef to a warmed plate.

5 When you have cooked all the beef, deglaze the pan with the brandy and set it alight. When the flames have gone, add the onion-mushroom mix and heat through again, then add both the creams and season with salt and pepper. Taste. If the sauce is too thin, continue cooking it over a high heat to reduce.

6 When it is ready, add the beef strips and stir so that they are coated with the sauce and serve with noodles or rice.

conventional cooking:
Cook on the hob.

cottage pie

The best meat to use for cottage pie is mince made from a pre-roasted meat. I particularly like mince made from braised beef. If you don't have braised beef, you can use topside or silverside. Buy it from the butcher and have him mince it in front of you or take it home and mince it yourself. Don't use pre-packed mince from the supermarket. A friend of mine always adds a handful of raisins which adds a sweetness to the dish – give it a try if you wish.

serves 6

750g minced cooked beef (see above)

1 tbsp dripping

1 onion, peeled and finely chopped

1 carrot, peeled and finely chopped

1 tbsp Worcestershire sauce

1 tbsp tomato ketchup

325ml meat juice – ideally leftover gravy topped up with water to required amount, or use stock

1 tbsp flour

750g mashed potato, for the topping

salt and pepper

1 If using raw beef mince (rather than mince made from roasted meat), brown it well in a heavy-based frying pan in a little extra dripping.

2 Melt the tablespoon of dripping in a large pan on the Boiling or Simmering Plate and brown the onion and carrot. Add the flour and stir well to absorb the fat. Mix in the meat, sauces and gravy and then check the seasoning. Bring the meat to a simmer for a few minutes, then tip the meat into a pie dish and cool slightly.

3 Spread the mashed potato over the top and rough the surface up with a fork. This can be cooked immediately, frozen in this state or refrigerated until ready to cook. If you wish, dot a few pieces of butter over the surface before cooking.

4 Place the dish on the third set of runners in the Roasting Oven and cook for 30–40 minutes. If the top browns too quickly, use the Cold Plain Shelf. Serve with peas, and more Worcestershire sauce and ketchup.

conventional cooking:
Pre-heat the oven to 180°C/350°F/gas 4, and cook as above for 35–45 minutes.

steak sandwich with oven chips

This is more than just a sandwich – it's a whole mood! See page 157 for Aga oven chips.

serves 4

4 x 150g rib eye steaks, beaten out so they are thin

4 slices rye bread, toasted

4 free-range eggs

FOR THE WELSH RAREBIT SAUCE:

50g butter

230g extra mature Cheddar cheese

150ml Guinness or stout

1 tsp mustard powder

2 free-range egg yolks, slightly beaten

½ tbsp Worcestershire sauce

1 To make the Welsh rarebit sauce, melt the butter in a saucepan on the Simmering Plate; add the cheese, stir, then add the stout slowly, stirring all the time until the mix is smooth. Stirring constantly, add the mustard powder, egg yolks and Worcestershire sauce and cook until the sauce is thick and glossy. Check for seasoning. Do not let the cheese mix boil or bubble or it will become lumpy. Set aside.

2 Heat the Aga grill pan on the floor of the Roasting Oven until it is very hot. Remove the pan from the oven and put it on the Boiling Plate. Lay the steaks in the pan and cook to your liking, about 1–2 minutes each side. Set aside and keep warm.

3 Line the half-size Aga baking tray with Bake-O-Glide. Spread the Welsh rarebit mix on the toast and place on the baking tray. Slide the tray onto the first set of runners in the Roasting Oven for about 2 minutes or until it starts to bubble.

4 While the rarebit is in the oven, fry the eggs on the Simmering Plate (either grease the surface or use a pre-cut round disc of Bake-O-Glide).

5 To assemble the sandwich, remove the rarebit from the oven, put the steak on it, then top the steak with the fried egg. Eat immediately.

conventional cooking:

Cook the sauce over a gentle heat on the hob. Fry the steaks and eggs in a frying pan on the hob.

traditional cornish pasties

makes 6

FOR THE SAVOURY PASTRY
342g plain flour
226g butter, cold and cubed
1 free-range egg, from the fridge
salt and pepper

FOR THE FILLING:
sunflower oil
200g really good-quality steak, such as rib eye, finely cubed
1 onion, peeled and finely minced
1–2 tbsp beef stock or water
1 large potato, peeled and finely cubed
grating of fresh horseradish or 1 tsp of mustard (optional)
1 free-range egg yolk, beaten, for egg wash
salt and pepper

1 To make the pastry, put everything into a food processor and pulse until it comes together to form a ball. Add a little water only if it is crumbly. Wrap in cling film and rest in the fridge for at least an hour. Bring to room temperature and roll out.

2 To make the filling, heat up a little oil in a frying pan on the Simmering Plate and quickly brown the steak cubes – this should only take 1–2 minutes. Remove them to a bowl. Add the onion to the pan and soften for a few minutes. Add the onion to the beef. Add the beef stock or water to the pan and scrape up all the bits. Pour that over the meat and onions, then add the potatoes to the bowl and mix together. Stir in the horseradish or mustard, if using, and check the seasoning.

3 To make the pasties, roll out the pastry and using a 20cm plate, cut out 6 circles – you may want to do this in batches. Put some of the filing into the centre of the circle, brush the egg wash around the edge of the pastry and bring two sides of the pastry together so that it forms a semicircle. 'Crimp' the edges of the pastry together with your fingers to make a well-sealed, wavy edge across the top. Transfer the pasties to a baking tray lined with Bake-O-Glide and brush with the remaining egg wash. Refrigerate for 10–15 minutes.

4 Bake the pasties on the fourth set of runners in the Roasting Oven for 15–20 minutes, then transfer to the Simmering Oven for a further 40–60 minutes. Cool on a wire rack and serve.

conventional cooking:
Pre-heat the oven to 180°C/350°F/gas 4 and bake for 30–35 minutes.

steamed steak, mushroom and horseradish pudding

If possible, use organic mushrooms as they have more flavour.

serves 6

FOR THE SUET PASTRY:

350g self-raising flour

175g suet

cold water, to bind

salt

FOR THE FILLING:

1 large onion, peeled and sliced

½ tbsp sunflower oil

1 tsp unrefined golden caster sugar

knob of butter

1 tbsp flour

600g chuck steak, cut into cubes

185g button mushrooms, cut in half if they are big.

2 tbsp freshly grated horseradish (or bought in a jar if fresh is not available)

beef stock

salt and pepper

1 First make the pastry. Grease a 1.5 litre china pudding basin. Sieve the flour into a roomy bowl and then add the suet and a pinch of salt, mixing it in using cutting motions with a knife. Slowly add the water until you have a firmish dough. Wrap the dough in cling film and let it rest in the fridge for 30 minutes. When the pastry is ready, dust a surface with flour and roll it into a large circle, about 1cm thick. Cut a wedge of about one-third from the circle for the lid. Carefully lift the remaining pastry and shape into a cone and fit into the pudding basin. Make a circle shape out of the reserved pastry for the lid and set aside.

2 While the pastry is resting, caramelise the onions. Put the sliced onions into a bowl and pour in the oil and sugar. Season with the salt and pepper and mix well, then tip into the half-size roasting tin, add the knob of butter and put the tin on to the floor of the Roasting Oven for about 20 minutes, stirring halfway through cooking. The onions should be soft and slightly charred around the edges and golden brown. Drain them and set aside. This can be done in advance.

3 Put the flour into a bowl, season with salt and pepper and toss the steak pieces in it. Add the mushrooms, horseradish and onion to the bowl and stir well to mix. Spoon the meat mix into the pudding basin and pour in enough beef stock just to cover the meat and season with more salt and pepper.

4 Dampen the edges of the pastry with water and place the lid on top, sealing it well. Using two sheets of foil, butter the sheet that will be closest to the pastry and cover the top of the pudding with it, making a pleat on the top to allow for expansion. Tie with string, making a handle for easy removal.

5 If you have a cake baker, use it for steaming or put a trivet into a large pot with a lid and stand the pudding on the trivet. Pour boiling water into the pot so that it comes halfway up the sides of the basin and bring the water back to the boil on the Boiling Plate. Cover with the lid and move to the Roasting Oven for 30 minutes, then transfer to the Simmering Oven for a further 5–6 hours.

6 When the pudding is cooked, remove it from the steamer and let it rest for 10 minutes before turning out. Cut into wedges and serve.

conventional cooking:

Place the pudding on a trivet in a deep saucepan. Pour in enough boiling water to come halfway up the side of the pan and bring to the boil. Turn down the heat to a simmer and steam the pudding for 2½–3 hours, checking the pan from time to time and topping up with boiling water if necessary.

braised lamb with prunes and apricots

This is a great dish because you can put it in first thing in the morning and forget about it.

3 tbsp olive oil

2kg trimmed lamb neck fillets, cut into 2cm chunks

2 large onions, peeled and cut into segments

2 tbsp flour

100ml red wine

350ml vegetable or chicken stock

120g chopped dried apricots

120g chopped dried prunes

salt and pepper

1 Heat 2 tablespoons of oil in a large casserole on the Simmering Plate until it is smoking, then add the lamb and brown in batches until it is all lightly coloured. Tip the meat onto a plate and set aside. (Alternatively, you can brown the meat in a shallow baking tray at the top of the Roasting Oven and then transfer the tray, without turning the meat, to the floor of the Roasting Oven.)

2 Add the remaining oil to the casserole and fry the onions until charred around the edges. Sprinkle in the flour and make sure it coats all of the onion mix and soaks up all the fat. Pour in the wine and then the stock a little at a time, whisking until it is all in and there are no lumps.

3 Add the apricots, prunes, salt and pepper and lamb and bring to the boil. Cover with a lid and transfer to the floor of the Simmering Oven. Cook for 2½–3 hours minimum or leave it in the Aga until you get home.

conventional cooking:
Pre-heat the oven to 140°C/275°F/gas 1 and cook for 2½–3½ hours.

herb-crusted loin of lamb

serves 6

1 x 150g loin fillet per person, trimmed

FOR THE HERB CRUST:

½ an onion, peeled and cut in quarters

2 rashers of smoked streaky bacon, cut into pieces

1 garlic clove, peeled

1 tbsp fresh basil

1 tbsp fresh mint

3 tbsp soft white breadcrumbs

2 tbsp grated Parmesan cheese

2 tbsp butter, softened

salt and pepper

1 Trim the fillets of any fat and make them all roughly the same size.

2 Put all the herb crust ingredients into the bowl of a food processor and combine until thoroughly mixed together. Press the mixture on top of each fillet and place on a baking sheet lined with Bake-O-Glide. At this stage the fillets can be left in the fridge, covered, until you want to cook them.

3 Cook the fillets on the second set of runners in the Roasting Oven for 12–15 minutes, depending on how rare/well done you like them. Serve on a bed of mashed potatoes with courgettes sautéed in basil and mint.

conventional cooking:

Pre-heat oven to 220°C/425°F/gas 7 and continue as above.

gigot boulangère

This is simply lamb cooked on potatoes. The Aga cooks this dish to perfection.

serves 6

olive oil

1.8kg potatoes, peeled and sliced thinly

2 onions, peeled and finely sliced

1 tbsp fresh rosemary, chopped, plus some sprigs to push into the meat

100ml white wine

4 cloves garlic

2.4kg leg of lamb

salt and pepper

1 Line the large roasting tin with Bake-O-Glide. Drizzle a little olive oil onto the bottom and layer the potato slices, onion, chopped rosemary and salt and pepper into the tin. Pour over the white wine.

2 Cut the garlic into slivers and push them and the rosemary sprigs into the leg of lamb, making slits with a sharp knife.

3 Lay the lamb on top of the potatoes and rub in some olive oil and salt and pepper all over the lamb. Hang the tin on the third set of runners in the Roasting Oven and cook for 45 minutes. Transfer to the Simmering Oven for 3–4 hours or until the lamb is tender. Serve with the juices from the tin.

conventional cooking:

Pre-heat the oven to 200°C/400°F/gas 6 and cook the potatoes for 1–1½ hours. Place the lamb on top of the potatoes and cook the lamb for 18 minutes per 500g, depending on how well done you like your meat (about 1½ hours). Rest the meat for 10 minutes before serving.

persian slow-roasted shoulder of lamb

This is a delicious dish that captures the aromatic essence of Middle Eastern cooking. Serve it with a rice pilaff (see page 166) and home-made yoghurt and mint sauce.

serves 6

1 tsp coriander seeds

½ tsp cumin seeds

4 cardamom pods

2kg shoulder of lamb, with bone in

350ml Greek yoghurt

juice and zest of 2 limes

2 garlic cloves, peeled and crushed

1 heaped tbsp freshly chopped mint

1 tbsp olive oil

salt

1 First dry fry the coriander seeds, cumin and cardamom pods in a frying pan on the Simmering Plate for 2 minutes. Tip the spices into a pestle and mortar and crush to release the flavours.

2 Place the lamb in a shallow dish or a large sealable plastic bag (I prefer the bag method). Mix together the yoghurt, lime juice and zest, crushed garlic and mint, then rub well into the lamb. Pour over the oil and cover the dish or close the bag. Leave to marinate overnight in the fridge. Turn meat occasionally in the marinade. If you forget to do this the night before, the minimum marinating time is 1 hour.

3 When you are ready to cook the lamb, season it with salt and place it in the small Aga roasting tin. Pour over all the marinade juices. Place the tin on the third set of runners in the Roasting Oven and cook for 1 hour, then transfer to the third set of runners in the Simmering Oven for 2–3 hours, basting occasionally, until the meat is tender and succulent.

4 Remove the lamb from the oven and let it rest for 10–15 minutes before carving. Pour the pan juices into a blender and whiz until smooth (the reason for this is that the yoghurt will 'split' so it looks better when whizzed up!). Check the seasoning and serve this sauce with the lamb.

conventional cooking:

Pre-heat the oven to 180°C/350°F/gas 4 and roast for 3–4 hours. Check the meat after 3 hours – the lamb should be very tender. Rest the lamb for 15 minutes before serving.

persian slow-roasted shoulder of lamb

shepherd's pie

This dish must be made with minced lamb from a roasted joint – if you use other mince it just isn't the same. This is the ultimate 'left-over' recipe loved by everyone.

serves 6

1 tbsp sunflower oil or clarified butter (see page 21)

1 carrot, peeled and finely chopped

1 onion, peeled and finely chopped

½ tsp freshly chopped rosemary

1 garlic clove (optional as this depends how much garlic was used with the roasted joint)

1 tbsp flour

750g minced roasted lamb

1 tbsp Worcestershire sauce

1 tbsp tomato ketchup

325ml meat juice (ideally leftover gravy topped up to required amount, or you can use stock)

salt and pepper

FOR THE TOPPING:

750g mashed potato (see page 156)

1 Melt the fat in a large pan on the Simmering Plate and brown the carrot and onion. Add the rosemary and garlic, then add the flour and stir well to absorb the fat.

2 Mix in the meat, sauces and gravy and then check for seasoning. Bring the meat up to a simmer, then tip the meat into a pie dish and leave to cool slightly.

3 Spread the mashed potato over the top and rough the surface up with a fork. This can be cooked immediately, frozen in this state or refrigerated until ready to cook. If you wish, dot a few pieces of butter over the surface before cooking.

4 Place the dish on the third set of runners in the Roasting Oven and cook for 30–40 minutes. If the top browns too quickly, use the Cold Plain Shelf. Serve with peas, and more Worcestershire sauce and ketchup.

conventional cooking:

Pre-heat oven to 200°C/400°F/gas 6 and cook for 45–60 minutes.

grilled chump chops

serves 4

4 lamb or pork chump chops
1 clove garlic, peeled
60g soft butter
1 tbsp freshly chopped parsley
1 lemon, preferably organic
salt and pepper

1 Heat the Aga grill pan on the floor of the Roasting Oven until it is very hot.
2 While the pan is heating up, rub each chop with the garlic and season with salt and pepper. Place the grill pan on the Boiling Plate and put in the chops. Transfer to the floor of the Roasting Oven for 3–4 minutes (pork will take a little longer), then turn the chops over and cook for a further 3–4 minutes.
3 Crush the garlic and mash it into the butter with the parsley and season with the juice and zest of the lemon and salt and pepper.
4 When the chops are cooked, take the grill pan out of the oven and put a small knob of the garlic butter on each chop. Rest for 5 minutes and serve with a green salad and crusty bread.

conventional cooking:
Heat a grill pan on the hob and cook the entire dish on the hob.

grilled pork chops with honey and meaux mustard

serves 4

4 pork chops
½ tbsp mild olive oil
½ an onion, peeled and very finely chopped
60ml cider
1 tbsp honey
1 tbsp Meaux mustard
80ml crème fraîche
salt and pepper

1 Heat the Aga grill pan on the floor of the Roasting Oven until it smokes. Season the pork chops with salt and pepper.
2 Take the grill pan out of the oven and put it on the Boiling Plate. Add the chops and put the pan back on the Roasting Oven floor for 4–5 minutes (this depends on how thick the chops are). Turn the chops and cook for a further 4–5 minutes. When they are cooked, transfer them to a warmed plate, cover and rest.
3 While the chops are cooking you can start the sauce. Heat up the oil in a frying pan on the Simmering Plate and cook the onion until soft and starting to caramelise around the edges. Add the cider and cook for 1 minute to burn off the alcohol. Stir in the honey, mustard and crème fraîche. Add any pan juices left in the grill pan and check for seasoning. Bubble the sauce up for 2 minutes and serve with the pork chops. Oven chips are great with these chops (see page 157).

conventional cooking:
Pre-heat a grill pan over a high heat until smoking and cook the chops as above. To cook the mustard sauce, use a frying pan set over a medium heat and continue as above.

oven-roasted spare ribs

Allow a minimum of 450g ribs per person if you want to feed lots of people.

serves 6

2.7kg pork spare ribs, unseparated

FOR THE SAUCE:
5cm piece of fresh ginger, grated
2 garlic cloves, peeled
80ml honey
120ml hoisin sauce
1 tsp Chinese 5-spice powder
2 tbsp soy sauce
1 tbsp brown sugar
1 tbsp Chinese rice wine

1 Mix all of the sauce ingredients in a large bowl. Add the ribs and marinate in the sauce in the fridge for a minimum of 1 hour, or longer if possible.

2 Drain the ribs from the marinade, reserving the sauce. Line the large roasting tin with Bake-O-Glide and lay the ribs in the tin. Hang the tin on the fourth set of runners in the Roasting Oven and bake for 40 minutes.

3 Pour the sauce into a saucepan and bring to the boil on the Boiling Plate. When the ribs have been in for 40 minutes, pour the sauce over them and transfer them to the Simmering Oven for 1–2 hours or until the meat is tender. Serve hot with finger bowls and lots of napkins!

conventional cooking:
Pre-heat the oven to 220°C/425°F/gas 7 and cook the marinated ribs for 1 hour. Turn down the heat to 150°C/300°F/gas 2. Pour over the boiled sauce and cook the ribs for 2–2½ hours.

balsamic pork roast

serves 6

2.5kg boned pork loin, rind and fat removed
2 red onions, peeled and quartered
50g butter
1 tbsp olive oil
1 tbsp fresh thyme leaves
350ml balsamic vinegar
50ml red wine
salt and pepper

1 Pre-heat an Aga cast-iron grill pan on the floor of the Roasting Oven. Remove the pan from the oven and place it on the Boiling Plate. Seal the pork on all sides.

2 Put the onion, butter, olive oil and thyme into the large roasting tin. Place the pork in the tin and add the balsamic vinegar, making sure the meat is well coated in the onion/vinegar mixture. Slide the tin onto the third set of runners of the Roasting Oven and roast the pork for 45–50 minutes, turning the pork in the juices halfway through cooking. Check that the pork is cooked right through.

3 When the meat is ready, place the pork on a warm dish and leave to rest while you de-glaze the roasting tin with the red wine. Put the tin directly onto the Simmering Plate and pour in the red wine. Reduce the pan juices for 4–5 minutes. Check the seasoning. Slice the pork thinly and serve accompanied by the onion balsamic jus.

conventional cooking:
Pre-heat the oven to 200°C/400°F/gas 6 and roast the pork for 1–1¼ hours.

oven-roasted spare ribs

crackling roast pork

The secret to getting the crackling really crispy is to start off with very dry skin. If you are keeping the skin on the joint, leave it in the fridge for 24 hours, patted dry with a piece of kitchen paper and uncovered. Score it with a very sharp knife so that the cuts are only 1cm apart.

serves 6–8

3kg leg of pork on the bone
100g lard
salt
3 onions

FOR THE GRAVY:
1½ tbsp flour
100ml cider
1 litre stock or cooking water
from vegetables
1 tsp apple jelly
salt and pepper

1 On the day before, remove the rind/skin from the pork leg with a sharp knife. Leave the skin to dry out overnight in the fridge, as above.

2 To cook, slice the pork rind/skin into strips about 2cm thick. Melt the lard in the half-size roasting tin in the Simmering Oven and add the pork skin strips to the fat. Cook in the Simmering Oven for 3–4 hours or until it is translucent.

3 Move the tin to the second set of runners in the Roasting Oven and cook for 40–60 minutes. It should be crisp and twisted into curly shapes. Drain on kitchen paper and sprinkle liberally with salt. Store at the side of the Aga until ready to use. This can be made the day before if you like.

4 Score the fat left on the meat and cut the onions in half. Line the large roasting tin with Bake-O-Glide and stand the pork on top of the onions, cut side down, and cook for 2½–3 hours on the fourth set of runners in the Roasting Oven or until done. Cover the meat loosely with foil and rest for 15 minutes. (My preferred method for cooking this dish is to cook the pork for 45–60 minutes in the Roasting Oven, then transfer it to the Simmering Oven for 3–4 hours or until done.)

5 While the meat is resting, make the gravy. Spoon away all but 2 tablespoons of fat from the tin. Do not remove the onions. Sprinkle in the flour and stir well so it absorbs all the fat. Pour in the cider and bring to the boil on the Boiling Plate until it has almost evaporated, then pour in the stock or vegetable water (the quantity depends on how thick you like your gravy). Add the apple jelly to give a hint of sweetness. Bring the gravy to a rapid simmer on the Simmering Plate and let it cook for about 5 minutes. Taste, season and reduce until it has reached the required consistency. Strain it into a jug and keep warm at the back of the Aga or in the Simmering Oven. Serve the pork with the gravy and crackling.

conventional cooking:

To cook the rind, pre-heat the oven to 150°C/300°F/gas 2 and cook as in step 2. Then turn up the heat to 220°C/425°F/gas 7 and continue as in step 3. Roast the pork in an oven pre-heated to 220°C/425°F/gas 7 for 2½–3 hours.

baked gammon with parsley sauce

serves 6

900g piece of gammon or collar of bacon

FOR THE GLAZE:
2–4 tbsp brown sugar
2–4 tbsp English mustard powder

1 Soak the gammon in cold water overnight, ideally changing the water twice.

2 Remove the ham from the soaking water and drain. Lay two long pieces of foil in the large roasting tin, one lengthways, one widthways to form a cross (you need enough foil so that the ham will sit in a tent of foil). Bring the foil up around the ham, leaving enough room for air to circulate around the joint. Hang the tin on the fourth set of runners in the Roasting Oven and bake for 18 minutes per 450g (a 5.5kg ham will take approximately 4 hours). Alternatively, bake for 20 minutes per 450g in the Baking Oven. The ham is done when the juices run clear when a skewer is inserted to the thickest part of the ham.

3 Work out when the final 30 minutes of cooking time is left and remove the joint from the oven, pull back the foil and remove the skin – it will be very hot so protect your hands. Score the fat. Mix together the mustard and sugar. Press the mixture into the fat, using it all up. Hang the tin on the third set of runners in the Roasting Oven and bake for 30 minutes or until it is nicely coloured and glazed. Eat the ham hot, or allow to cool and eat cold. Serve with the parsley sauce (see below).

conventional cooking:

Prepare the ham as above. To cook, pre–heat the oven to 180°C/350°F/gas 4 and cook the ham for 20 minutes per 450g. Before the final 30 minutes of cooking, turn the heat up to its highest setting (at least 220°C/425°F/gas 7), remove the foil cover and continue as above.

parsley sauce

makes about 350ml

5–6 stalks fresh flat-leaf parsley (chop the stalks in half and finely chop the leaves)
piece of organic lemon peel
425ml warm milk
40g butter
20g plain flour
squeeze of lemon juice
salt and pepper

1 Put the parsley stalks and the lemon peel into the milk and heat on the Simmering Plate. When it comes up to the boil, take it off the heat and infuse for about 10 minutes. Strain the milk.

2 Melt the butter in a small saucepan on the Simmering Plate. Add the flour to the butter and stir well with a wooden spoon until it turns into a glossy paste. Gradually pour in the warm milk, a little at a time, stirring or whisking all the time until all the milk is incorporated and you have a smooth, lump-free sauce. Simmer the sauce for 3–5 minutes, whisking occasionally, so that the flour is cooked. Do not let the sauce burn or catch on the bottom.

3 Add the chopped parsley leaves, a squeeze of lemon juice and season to taste. Cover the surface of the sauce with cling film so a skin doesn't form.

conventional cooking:

Cook on the hob.

glazed ham for a crowd

Cooking a whole ham on the bone does take time but nothing tastes better than your own glazed ham and it will keep for ages. For the best flavour, buy an organic ham on the bone. Soak the ham in cold water. Ask the supplier what they recommend, as the soaking time will depend on how much salt is used when curing it. I usually use a plastic bucket or washing-up bowl, depending how big the ham is. I also change the water halfway through the soaking time. There are two cooking options: boil and bake or bake only. Eat the ham either hot or cold.

5.5–6kg ham will feed about 20 people
6.5–7.5kg ham will feed about 30 people

To boil and bake:

1 Remove the ham from the soaking water and place it in a pot big enough to hold the ham yet still able to fit into the Simmering Oven. Cover the ham with fresh cold water and bring to the boil on the Boiling Plate. Transfer it to the Simmering Plate and simmer for 20–30 minutes.

2 Transfer the ham to the Simmering Oven for about 5 hours for a 5.5–6kg ham or 6–6½ hours for a 6.5–7.5kg ham. It is done when the juices run clear when a skewer is put through the thickest part.

3 Remove the ham from the water, peel off the skin and score the fat. Put the ham into the large roasting tin and push 20–30 whole cloves into the fat. Mix together 3–4 tablespoons of English mustard and 3–4 tablespoons of brown sugar. Press the sugar and mustard into the fat.

4 Hang the tin on the fourth set of runners of the Roasting Oven and bake the ham for 20–30 minutes or until it is nicely coloured and glazed.

To bake:

1 Remove the ham from the soaking water and drain. Lay two long pieces of foil in the large roasting tin, one lengthways, one widthways, to form a cross. You need enough foil to allow the ham to sit in a tent of foil. Bring the foil up around the ham, leaving enough room for air to circulate.

2 Hang the tin on the fourth set of runners in the Roasting Oven and bake for 20 minutes per 450g (a 5.5kg ham will take about 4 hours). The ham is done when the juices run clear when a skewer is inserted to the thickest part.

3 Remove the joint from the oven 30 minutes before the end of the cooking time, pull back the foil and remove the skin – it will be very hot so protect your hands. Score the fat and push 20–30 whole cloves into the fat and mix together 3–4 tablespoons of English mustard and 3–4 tablespoons of brown sugar. Press the sugar and mustard into the fat.

4 Hang the tin on the fourth set of runners of the Roasting Oven and bake the ham for 30 minutes or until nicely coloured and glazed.

conventional cooking:

Prepare the ham as above. Pre-heat the oven to 180°C/350°F/gas 4. Cook for 20 minutes per 450g. For the final 30 minutes, turn the oven to its highest setting (at least 220°C/425°F/gas 7), remove the foil and continue as above.

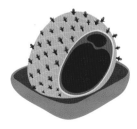

glazed ham

veal cutlets with sage, thyme and garlic butter

serves 4

200g flour, seasoned with salt and pepper

3 large free-range eggs, beaten

300g fresh white breadcrumbs

4 French-trimmed veal cutlets

clarified butter (see page 21)

2 lemons, halved

FOR THE SAGE, THYME AND GARLIC BUTTER:

250g soft butter

2 garlic cloves, peeled and crushed

1 tbsp fresh sage leaves, finely chopped

1 tbsp fresh thyme leaves

1 First make the butter. Mash the butter with the garlic and the herbs really well in a bowl. Spoon the butter along the middle of a piece of greaseproof paper. Roll it up to form a sausage shape and twist the ends. Refrigerate for at least 1 hour or until firm.

2 Place a frying pan on the floor of the Roasting Oven to heat up. Meanwhile, put the flour into a shallow bowl or on a plate and do the same with the beaten eggs and the breadcrumbs. Dip the veal cutlets first into the flour, then the egg, then the breadcrumbs. Repeat this so that each cutlet has a double coating of breadcrumbs.

3 Remove the frying pan when it is smoking and melt enough of the clarified butter to shallow fry the cutlets on the Simmering Plate. When it is ready, add the cutlets to the pan and transfer to the Roasting Oven floor for 8 minutes each side. Drain on kitchen paper, put on a warm plate and rest in the Simmering Oven for 10 minutes.

4 Cut the herb butter into four rounds. Remove the veal from the Simmering Oven. Put a slice of butter on each cutlet and return the veal to the Roasting Oven for about 1 minute or until the butter starts to melt. Serve each cutlet with half a lemon.

conventional cooking:
Heat the grill pan until smoking and cook as above on the hob.

rack of veal with spring leeks

serves 6

4 shallots, peeled

1 garlic clove, peeled

2 tbsp fresh rosemary

2 tbsp fresh thyme

3 tbsp butter

3 tbsp freshly grated Parmesan cheese

6 tbsp fresh breadcrumbs

1 or 2 racks of veal, allowing for 2 ribs per person, with the thick skin and most of the fat removed

1kg baby leeks, trimmed and washed

olive oil

salt and pepper

1 Throw the shallots, garlic, herbs, butter, and salt and pepper into the bowl of a food processor. Whiz until everything is thoroughly chopped and combined. Remove the blade and mix in the Parmesan and the breadcrumbs. Press the mixture on to the veal racks.

2 Put the baby leeks on a shallow baking tray, drizzle with some olive oil and season with salt and pepper. Place the veal on top of the leeks.

3 Slide the tray on to the third set of runners in the Roasting Oven and cook for 20–30 minutes or until golden and crusty. Serve with the leeks and creamy mashed potatoes.

conventional cooking:

Pre-heat the oven to 180°C/350°F/gas 4 and cook for 15–20 minutes, or until cooked to your liking.

old-fashioned meatloaf

serves 6

FOR THE MEATLOAF:

250g minced pork

250g minced beef

250g minced veal

2 large free-range eggs

100ml tomato ketchup

2 tbsp Worcestershire sauce

2 level tsp mustard powder

1 large onion, peeled and very finely chopped

4 tbsp fresh breadcrumbs, from a day-old country loaf

1 tbsp fresh flat-leaf parsley, chopped

salt and pepper

FOR THE TOPPING:

3 tbsp tomato ketchup

2½ tsp mustard powder

2 tbsp brown sugar

6–8 rashers pancetta or smoked streaky bacon

1 In a large bowl mix all the meatloaf ingredients, using your hands to knead until thoroughly combined. Shape the meat mixture into a long loaf so that it will fit into the half-size Aga roasting tin. The mix should be wet enough to hold together.

2 Put the half-size Aga grill rack into the half-size Aga roasting tin and place the meatloaf on it.

3 To make the topping, mix together the ketchup, mustard powder and sugar. Brush it onto the meatloaf and arrange the pancetta slices over it.

4 Cook the meatloaf on the fourth set of runners in the Roasting Oven for 45–60 minutes. If the top is browning too quickly, slide the Cold Plain Shelf in on the second set of runners after about 30 minutes or so. Serve in slices with plenty of mashed potatoes, peas and tomato ketchup.

conventional cooking:

Pre-heat the oven to 200°C/400°F/gas 6 and bake for 1–1½ hours.

bacon and egg pie

300g bacon, cut into cubes or large strips

6 hard-boiled free-range eggs, cut in half

80g Cheddar cheese, grated

1 free-range egg, beaten

FOR THE SAVOURY PASTRY:

340g plain flour

225g butter, softened

1 large free-range egg

salt and pepper

FOR THE CHEESE SAUCE:

15g butter

15g plain flour

300ml milk, warmed

50g mature Cheddar cheese, grated

pinch of mustard powder

salt and pepper

1 Make the pastry in a food processor or by hand. Process the flour with the butter until the mixture resembles coarse breadcrumbs. Add the egg and season. Process until the dough just comes together. Tip it out onto a floured surface and knead lightly until smooth. Wrap in a plastic bag and rest in the refrigerator for 1 hour.

2 Make the cheese sauce. Melt the butter in a saucepan on the Simmering Plate. Stirring constantly with a wooden spoon, add the flour. Cook for 2 minutes. Do not allow the mix to brown. Gradually add the milk little by little, stirring constantly to prevent lumps forming. Continue to cook until the sauce comes to the boil and thickens. Add the cheese and mustard. Stir until it has melted and check for seasoning. Simmer for 2–3 minutes. Set aside to cool.

3 Fry the bacon in a pan on the Simmering Plate until it is crispy around the edges. Drain on kitchen paper.

4 Divide the pastry in half. Roll it out so you have a piece to line a 20-cm pie dish and a piece to cover the pie.

5 Put the boiled egg halves, cut side down, and the bacon into the bottom of the pie dish. Pour over the cheese sauce and scatter over the grated cheese. Roll on the pastry lid, making a slit in the middle. Brush the top with the beaten egg.

6 Put the grid shelf on the fourth set of runners in the Roasting Oven and cook the pie for 20–30 minutes. Slide the Cold Plain shelf onto the second set of runners if the top is browning too fast. Then transfer to the floor of the Roasting Oven for 5 minutes. Remove the pie from the oven and let it cool. For 4-oven Aga owners, use the Baking Oven as above, then transfer the pie to the Roasting Oven floor for the final 5–10 minutes. Serve at room temperature with a green salad.

conventional cooking:

Pre-heat the oven to 190°C/375°F/gas 5 and bake in the middle of the oven for 35–40 minutes.

sausages and mash

serves 6

900g potatoes, peeled and cut in half

80g butter

150ml crème fraîche, double cream or sour cream

12 sausages

salt and pepper

1 Put the potatoes into a saucepan, pour in water to cover, bring to the boil on the Boiling Plate and boil for 3 minutes. Take the pan off the Boiling Plate and drain off all the water. Replace the lid and transfer to the Simmering Oven for 20–30 minutes.

2 When the potatoes are tender, break them up with a knife and mash in the butter and crème fraîche. Season with lots of salt and pepper. If they are too stiff, add more crème fraîche or a little milk.

3 While the potatoes are cooking, put the half-size grill rack into the half-size roasting tin and lay the sausages on top. Slide the tin onto the highest set of runners in the Roasting Oven and cook the sausages for 20–30 minutes, turning halfway through cooking so they are coloured on all sides.

4 When the sausages are ready, serve with the mashed potatoes and some gravy (see page 171).

conventional cooking:

Cook the sausages in a frying pan on the hob.

sausages with apples and smoked applewood cheese

serves 6

12 good-quality sausages

4 tbsp apple sauce

2 red apples, cored and thinly sliced into rings

125g smoked applewood cheese or Montgomery Cheddar cheese, grated

handful of breadcrumbs

1 Line a shallow baking tin with Bake-O-Glide and place the sausages on it. Do not prick them. Slide the tin onto the top set of runners in the Roasting Oven and cook for 8–10 minutes.

2 Remove the tin from the oven and slice the sausages open lengthways. Spoon the apple sauce over the split sausages and spread the apple rings on top. Scatter over the cheese and breadcrumbs.

3 Return the tin to the first or second set of runners in the Roasting Oven and continue to cook for another 8–10 minutes or until the cheese has melted and starts to brown on top. Serve with mashed potatoes.

conventional cooking:

Pre-heat the oven to 180°C/350°F/gas 4 and cook as above.

italian sausages and peppers

Italian sausages are delicious and can be purchased from good Italian delicatessens.

serves 6

12 fennel sausages

3 red peppers

1 green pepper

2 yellow peppers

3–4 large onions, peeled and thickly sliced

olive oil

1 tsp sugar

2 tomatoes, seeded and skinned

2 garlic cloves, peeled and crushed

salt and pepper

1 Put the sausages into a shallow baking tray lined with Bake-O-Glide and drizzle a little olive oil over. Slide them onto the first or second set of runners in the Roasting Oven and cook for 15–20 minutes, turning halfway so that they brown evenly all over and are thoroughly cooked.

2 Deseed the peppers and cut them into wedges. Toss the sliced onions in a little olive oil and the sugar.

3 Heat about 2 tablespoons of olive oil in a large deep frying pan on the Simmering Plate. Add the onions and cook for 5 minutes, then add the peppers. Stir frequently, then add the tomatoes and garlic when the onions and peppers start to soften. The onions and peppers need to be soft and slightly charred. You can also do this on the floor of the Roasting Oven.

4 When the peppers and onions are ready, add them to the pan containing the sausages and stir everything together well. Season with salt and pepper and if necessary pour in a little water and bubble up to loosen the bits on the bottom of the pan. Serve with ciabatta bread to mop up all the juices.

conventional cooking:
Cook on the hob in a frying pan over a medium heat.

toad in the hole

The jury is still out about whether one should or shouldn't let the batter stand for a few hours. To get ahead, I make my batter the day before; if I'm pushed for time, it stands for as long as it takes the fat to get up to temperature – the choice is up to you. Whatever you do, don't prick the sausages!

serves 4

8 sausages
60g dripping
salt and pepper

FOR THE BATTER:
3 free-range eggs
175g plain flour
175ml milk
110ml water
salt and pepper

FOR THE ROASTED ONION
GRAVY:
2 medium onions, peeled and sliced
1 tsp sugar
1 tbsp sunflower oil
1 rounded tbsp flour
1 tbsp Worcestershire sauce
1 tbsp Dijon mustard
1 tsp apple jelly
1 tsp freshly chopped sage
1 litre chicken stock
salt and pepper

1 First make the batter. Whisk the eggs, then sift in the flour and whisk, then slowly add the milk and water, whisking continuously. Season with salt and pepper. Set aside.

2 Put the half-size grill rack into the half-size roasting tin and lay the sausages on top. Slide the tin onto the highest set of runners in the Roasting Oven and cook the sausages for 20 minutes, turning halfway through cooking so they are coloured on all sides.

3 Remove the sausages and the grill rack from the tin. Put the dripping into the tin and heat it up in the Roasting Oven until it is smoking hot. Move the tin to the Simmering Plate. Put the sausages back in the tin, then pour in the batter. Hang the tin on the third set of runners of the Roasting Oven and cook for 30–40 minutes or until the batter has risen and is golden brown.

4 To make the gravy, toss the onions with the sugar and oil in a large bowl. Line a roasting tin with Bake-O-Glide and scatter over the onions. Slide the tin onto the highest set of runners in the Roasting Oven and roast the onions for 10 minutes, then move to the floor of the Roasting Oven for another 5 minutes or until they are golden and caramelised. Remove the tin from the oven to the Simmering Plate and sprinkle in the flour and stir it well to absorb all of the fat. Add the Worcestershire sauce, mustard, jelly and sage, then add the stock little by little, stirring constantly. Season, then cook for 4–5 minutes on the Simmering Plate. Pour into a warmed jug and serve.

conventional cooking:

Cook the sausages in the usual way. Pre-heat the oven to 220°C/425°F/gas 7 and cook for 40–45 minutes. To make the gravy, pre-heat the oven to 200°C/400°F/gas 6 and roast the onions for 15–20 minutes or until they are caramelised, then finish off the gravy on the hob.

savoury roulade

FOR THE ROULADE:

500ml full-fat milk

50g butter

50g plain flour

4 free-range eggs, separated

salt and pepper

50g Parmesan cheese, finely grated

FOR THE FILLING:

200ml cream cheese

150ml crème fraîche

150g cubed pancetta, cooked until crispy and drained

100g Parmesan cheese, plus about 60g really finely grated Parmesan for dusting

1 tbsp fresh parsley, chopped

50g sun-dried tomatoes, chopped

1 tbsp toasted pine nuts

salt and pepper

1 Line a shallow baking tray with Bake-O-Glide and set aside.

2 To make the roulade, heat up the milk in a saucepan on the Simmering Plate and set aside. Melt the butter in a saucepan on the Simmering Plate and stir in the flour. Whisk in the warm milk little by little until it is all used and you have a smooth sauce. Cook for 2 minutes. Take it off the heat and beat in the egg yolks one at a time, then season with salt. Whisk the egg whites until very stiff, then fold them and the Parmesan into the sauce using a metal spoon.

3 Pour the mix on to the Bake-O-Glide lined tray and spread into the shape of the tray. Slide the tray onto the third set of runners in the Simmering Oven (for 4-oven Aga owners, use the middle runners) and bake for 30–40 minutes. Remove from the oven and cover with a large piece of greaseproof paper and a clean, damp tea towel. Leave it to cool completely. (You can make the roulade up to 24 hours in advance and assemble on the day you want to serve it.)

4 To make the filling, beat the cream cheese and the crème fraîche together in a bowl, then fold in the rest of the ingredients.

5 When you are ready to assemble the roulade, remove the tea towel and tear off the greaseproof paper. Put a large, clean sheet of greaseproof paper on a work surface and sprinkle over the rest of the Parmesan cheese. Invert the roulade onto it. Spread the filling over the roulade. Roll up the roulade lengthways, using the greaseproof paper to help you roll it up. Roll it onto a serving plate.

conventional cooking:

Pre-heat the oven to 180°C/350°F/gas 4 and bake for 15–20 minutes.

salami, olive and mozzarella calzone

serves 4 for lunch

1 quantity pizza dough
(see page 143)

olive oil

120g salami, sliced

100g pepperoni, sliced

30–40g oil-marinated black
olives, pitted

8 sun-dried tomatoes

150g ball buffalo mozzarella
cheese

1 Prepare the pizza dough to step 5 (see page 143) and drizzle with olive oil.

2 Lay the salami and pepperoni over the dough base, leaving a 4cm gap around the edge. Scatter over the olives and sun-dried tomatoes. Tear the mozzarella into chunks and place on top. Roll the dough up, tuck in the ends and place on the baking tray with the seam underneath. Let it rise for 30 minutes near the Aga.

3 Put the baking tray directly onto the floor of the Roasting Oven and cook for 20–25 minutes or until puffed up and golden.

4 Remove from the oven and cool a little before slicing and serving. This is great for picnics.

conventional cooking:

Pre-heat the oven to its highest setting. If you have a pizza stone, use it according to the manufacturer's instructions. Bake for 25–30 minutes, as above.

cheat's calzone

The quantities of salami and mozzarella for the filling can vary according to what you have in the fridge.

serves 4

1 tbsp freshly chopped oregano

1 tbsp freshly chopped chives

juice of ½ a lemon

3 tbsp sunflower oil

salt and pepper

1 ciabatta loaf or French stick

1 packet salami

1 ball mozzarella cheese

6–8 sun-dried tomatoes

1 To make the dressing, whisk together the oregano, chives, lemon juice, sunflower oil and salt and pepper.

2 Split open the bread and remove some of the dough from the middle. Spread the dressing over the bread and then layer the salami, cheese and sun-dried tomatoes on the bottom half, repeating the layers until all the ingredients are used up.

3 Cover with the top half of the bread and then wrap the loaf very tightly in cling film. Press it down with tins or other heavy objects and refrigerate overnight.

4 When you are ready to serve, remove the cling film, re-wrap in foil and place it in the Roasting Oven for about 10 minutes until the cheese starts to ooze, then serve straight away.

conventional cooking:

Pre-heat the oven to 200ºC/400ºF/gas 6 and bake the calzone as above.

salami, olive and mozzarella calzone

6 fish & seafood

The Aga is perfect for cooking fish as it locks in the juices at the same time as crisping up the skin. One of the amazing things about the Aga is that fish can easily be cooked in the same oven as, say, a fruit tart without the transference of smell or taste.

poaching fish

For a whole fish, such as a salmon, use the conventional fish kettle method. Make a court bouillon by filling a fish kettle with water, herbs, peppercorns and lemon halves, then put in the whole fish. Bring to the boil on the Boiling Plate (if the kettle is large, use the Simmering Plate as well). As soon as it has boiled for 5 minutes, remove the kettle from the heat and leave the fish to cool in the liquid. This method cooks fish really well and you can forget about it while it cools.

oven-steamed fish

Steaming fish in the Aga is really easy. Lay a large piece of foil in a shallow tin and butter the inside of the foil. Lay the fish on the foil and season with herbs, lemons, salt and pepper. Spoon over 1 tablespoon of white wine or water, and then wrap up the foil into a loose parcel, fully sealed but with enough room for steam at the top. Slide the tin onto the third set of runners of the Roasting Oven and cook for 10–12 minutes or until the fish is cooked to your liking. Owners of 4-oven Agas can also use the Baking Oven, although the fish will take slightly longer to cook.

frying fish in the roasting oven

Pour about 2–3cm of sunflower oil into a heavy-based shallow pan. Place the pan on the floor of the Roasting Oven and heat until smoking. Batter the fish or coat in breadcrumbs. Remove the pan from the oven, add the fish to the pan and return to the Roasting Oven floor. Fry for a few minutes on each side in the pan or until the batter or breadcrumbs are golden.

salmon wrapped in brioche

serves 8

2 x 900g salmon fillets, skinned and boned

½ tbsp semolina

FOR THE BRIOCHE:

60g fresh yeast

150ml milk, at blood temperature

500g '00' pasta flour

1 tsp salt

100g butter, melted

2 free-range eggs, beaten

FOR THE HERB RISOTTO:

1 onion, peeled and finely chopped

olive oil

100g arborio rice

100ml white wine

400ml vegetable stock

zest and juice of 1 lemon

2 tbsp fresh tarragon, chopped

1 tbsp dill, chopped

knob of butter

salt and pepper

1 Make the brioche dough the day before or make well ahead and freeze. Crumble the yeast into the milk and set aside for about 5 minutes. Put the flour and salt into a mixer with the dough hook in place and then add the yeast, melted butter and beaten eggs. Mix for about 10 minutes on high speed or until the dough is smooth and silky. You may need to add more flour if the dough is too sticky or a little more liquid if it is too stiff.

2 Grease the inside of a large bowl and then pop the dough into it. Cover with a clean damp tea towel and leave next to the side of the Aga to rise for 1–1½ hours or until it has doubled in size.

3 Knock it back when it has risen and then put it into a plastic bag or back into the bowl, wrap it with cling film and place it in the fridge overnight or for at least 6 hours (freeze it at this stage if you wish).

4 The risotto can also be made up to a day ahead. Soften the onion in a little oil in a frying pan and cook on the floor of the Roasting Oven until it is soft. Move the frying pan to the Simmering Plate and add the rice, stirring to coat every grain in the onion and oil and cook for 2 minutes or until it starts to colour.

5 Pour in the white wine and cook, stirring constantly, until it has almost all evaporated. Add the stock and season with salt and pepper. Give it another good stir and move the pan to the grid shelf on the third set of runners of the Roasting Oven for 20 minutes. Halfway through cooking, stir again.

6 When the time is up, remove the frying pan from the oven and if it is still too liquidy, cook it off on the Simmering Plate until it is still loose but not sloppy. Add the lemon juice and zest, dill and the knob of butter. Check for seasoning. Set aside to cool, then refrigerate until it is required.

7 When you are ready to assemble and cook the whole dish, bring the dough up to room temperature and roll it out on a board into a large rectangle. Line a shallow baking sheet with Bake-O-Glide and lay the brioche dough on top. Sprinkle on a little of the semolina, then lay the first salmon fillet along the centre of the dough. Season with salt and pepper, then spread the risotto on top of the fillet.

8 Lay the second fillet on top of the risotto. Brush the pastry with milk and wrap up the salmon/risotto like a parcel, long side up and over, then short sides, using the milk as 'glue'. Turn the parcel so the seam is underneath. Using a sharp knife, make six slashes on the top.

9 Put the parcel on the fourth set of runners in the Roasting Oven. Cook for 20 minutes, then slide the Cold Plain Shelf onto the second set of runners. Continue cooking for a further 20–25 minutes or until it is golden on top.

conventional cooking:
Pre-heat the oven to 190°C/375°F/gas 5 and bake as above.

fillet of salmon with a basil, bacon and sourdough crust

Today most of the salmon we buy is farmed and can taste rather bland. To liven it up, add this crunchy crust to make it into a dish perfect for a dinner party or a family supper.

serves 4

4 x 175g salmon fillets

4 tbsp fresh sourdough breadcrumbs

1 tbsp freshly chopped basil

1 tbsp freshly chopped flat-leaf parsley

2 rashers smoked bacon, finely chopped

2 tbsp olive oil

salt and pepper

1 Put the salmon fillets onto a lightly greased baking tray (or onto a piece of Bake-O-Glide). Combine the rest of the ingredients in a bowl and spoon on top of the salmon, pressing it on firmly.

2 Cook the salmon on the floor of the Roasting Oven for 5 minutes, then move it to the top of the Roasting Oven for a further 5–8 minutes. Serve with boiled new potatoes and green beans tossed in a lemon and olive oil dressing.

conventional cooking:

Pre-heat the oven to 200°C/400°F/gas 6 and bake the fish for 10–12 minutes, then place the fish under a very hot, pre-heated grill for 2 minutes or until the topping is golden and crispy.

crab and chilli pasties

makes 6

1–2 tbsp groundnut oil

4 carrots, washed and grated

3cm fresh ginger, peeled and grated

3 spring onions, finely sliced

1 heaped tbsp freshly chopped coriander, plus more for garnish

1 bird's eye chilli, deseeded and finely sliced

1 tbsp fish sauce

1 tsp sesame oil

250g white crab meat, cooked and shredded

1 free-range egg yolk, beaten for egg wash

500g puff pastry

1 Put 1 tablespoon of oil into a frying pan and place the pan on the Roasting Oven floor. When smoking, transfer the pan to the Boiling Plate and quickly stir-fry the carrots, ginger, onions, coriander, chilli, fish sauce, sesame oil and crab meat for 2–3 minutes. If the heat is too high, transfer to the Simmering Plate. (This stage can be done up to 3 days in advance and refrigerated.)

2 To make the pasties, roll out the pastry and using a 20cm plate, cut out 6 circles. Put some of the filing into the centre of the circle, brush the egg wash around the edge of the pastry and bring two sides of the pastry together to form a semicircle. 'Crimp' the edges of the pastry together with your fingers to make a well-sealed, wavy edge across the top. Transfer the pasties to a baking tray lined with Bake-O-Glide and brush with the remaining egg wash. Refrigerate for 10–15 minutes.

3 Bake the pasties on the fourth set of runners in the Roasting Oven for 20–25 minutes. If they brown too quickly, slide the Cold Plain Shelf above. Cool on a wire rack and serve.

conventional cooking:

Pre-heat the oven to 180°C/350°F/gas 4 and bake for 25–30 minutes or until golden brown.

fillet of salmon with a basil, bacon and sourdough crust

hot open salmon sandwich

serves 4

4 salmon fillets, not too thick

grapeseed oil

4 slices rye bread

1 bag washed and prepared wild rocket leaves

salt and pepper

FOR THE SAUCE:

2 tbsp Dijon mustard

3 tbsp brown sugar

1 tsp grapeseed oil

1 tbsp freshly chopped dill

1 Put an Aga grill pan on the floor of the Roasting Oven to heat up.

2 Meanwhile, make the sauce. Put the mustard powder, sugar, oil and 2½ tablespoons of water into a bowl and mix well. Stir in the chopped dill. Set aside.

3 Brush the salmon fillets with a little oil and season with salt and pepper. When the grill pan is smoking, put it on the Boiling Plate and lay the salmon in the pan. Put the pan back on the floor of the Roasting oven and cook for another 3–4 minutes. When the salmon is cooked, take the pan out and set aside.

4 Toast the bread in the Aga toaster and put one slice on each plate. Top each slice with rocket and put a salmon fillet on the rocket. Drizzle over some sauce and serve.

conventional cooking:

Heat a grill pan on top of a hob until smoking and cook as above.

trout with pine nuts

serves 6

3 tbsp flour

salt and pepper

6 fresh trout, gutted and rinsed

237ml milk

160g butter

1 tsp grapeseed oil

1 tbsp sunflower oil

2 tbsp fresh flat-leaf parsley, chopped

3 tbsp chopped roasted pine nuts (or hazelnuts)

zest and juice of 1 lemon

1 Season the flour with some salt and pepper and spoon it on to a flat dish. Dip the trout into the milk and then into the flour. Coat well, shaking off the excess.

2 Heat 60g of the butter and the grapeseed oil until frothing in a large frying pan on the Simmering Plate, then add as many trout as the pan will take (do not overcrowd the pan). Transfer the pan to the Roasting Oven floor and fry the trout in batches for about 3–5 minutes each side until crispy (add more butter if necessary). Check the fish to make sure the butter does not burn. Set aside on a serving dish and keep warm.

3 Heat the sunflower oil in a clean pan on the Simmering Plate until hot, add the remaining butter, parsley, pine nuts, lemon juice, zest and salt and pepper. Cook for 1 minute, then pour over the trout and serve.

conventional cooking:

Cook in a frying pan on the hob.

hot open salmon sandwich

hot asian tuna salad

serves 6

8cm piece fresh ginger, peeled and cut into thin strips

3 garlic cloves, peeled and thinly sliced

6 spring onions, trimmed and sliced

6 x 250g tuna steaks

2 tbsp fish sauce

4 tbsp soy sauce

3 tbsp Chinese rice wine vinegar

sesame seed oil

6 heads bok choy

1 tbsp oyster sauce

1 Line the large roasting tin with foil – you will be wrapping the fish up so allow for that. Scatter half of the ginger, garlic and spring onions onto the foil. Place the tuna steaks on top, then scatter over the remaining ginger, garlic and spring onions.

2 Evenly spoon over the fish sauce, soy sauce and rice vinegar. Sparingly drizzle a tiny amount of sesame oil over, then spread the bok choy over the tuna and spoon on the oyster sauce.

3 Close the foil so that the fish is well sealed in and bake on the third set of runners of the Roasting Oven for 15 minutes or on the third set of runners of the Baking Oven for 20–25 minutes. Remove from the oven and serve the tuna on top of the bok choy and spoon over the sauce. This is good accompanied by rice.

conventional cooking:

Pre-heat the oven to 200°C/400°F/gas 6 and cook as above.

sea bass baked with green beans and anchovies

serves 6

350g green beans, tailed and blanched

47.5g tin anchovies

6 x 225g sea bass fillets, boned

juice of 3 lemons

zest of 1 lemon

1 heaped tbsp fennel tops, roughly chopped

15–20 vine cherry tomatoes

olive oil

salt and pepper

1 Blanch the green beans in boiling salted water until tender. Plunge them into iced water and drain.

2 Put a sheet of Bake-O-Glide in the large shallow baking tray and spread out the beans, put the anchovies and their oil over the beans, then lay the sea bass fillets on top of the anchovies and beans. Squeeze the lemon juice over the fish and sprinkle the zest and fennel tops over. Push the tomatoes into the gaps and drizzle the whole thing with olive oil and season with salt and pepper.

3 Slide the baking tray onto the second set of runners in the Roasting Oven and bake the fish for 10–15 minutes. Serve with garlic mayonnaise and crusty bread.

conventional cooking:

Pre-heat the oven to 200°C/400°F/gas 6 and bake the fish in the centre of the oven for 15 minutes or until done.

hot asian tuna salad

moules marinières

3kg fresh mussels

1 tbsp sunflower oil

50g butter

2 large onions or 6 large shallots, peeled and chopped

3 garlic cloves, chopped finely

200ml white wine

100ml water

50ml double cream

large bunch of fresh flat-leaf parsley, chopped

salt and pepper

1 Clean the mussels in cold running water and pull off their 'beards' – the stringy bits that hang from them. Put them into a large bowl of cold water. If any of the mussels are cracked or still open after they are washed, tap them – if they still don't close, throw them away.

2 Place the oil and butter in a large heavy casserole with a lid and heat on the Simmering Plate until really hot – you might have to move it to the Boiling Plate to achieve this.

3 Add the onions/shallots, garlic, white wine and water to the casserole and simmer for about 8–10 minutes or until the onions are soft and the liquid has reduced a little. You can do this on the floor of the Roasting Oven if you are worried about losing heat.

4 Drain the mussels, add them to the casserole and move to the Boiling Plate to bring up to the boil. Put the lid on the casserole and, shaking the pan from time to time, cook the mussels for about 5 minutes.

5 Place a colander over a bowl, tip the mussels into the colander (reserving the liquid), then set aside and keep warm. Pour the liquid from the mussels back into the casserole, add the double cream and season with salt and pepper. Bring up to the boil on the Boiling Plate for 2 minutes, then add the parsley and tip the mussels back in. Serve with lots of crusty bread and finger bowls.

conventional cooking:
Cook on the hob.

smoked fish pie

serves 6–8

650g smoked finnan haddock

450ml milk

½ an onion, peeled and quartered

2 heaped tbsp fresh flat-leaf parsley, chopped

2 kippers, skinned, boned and flaked into pieces

250g smoked salmon trimmings, chopped into bite-sized pieces

5 cornichons, chopped

3 free-range eggs, hard-boiled, peeled and cut into wedges

zest and juice of 1 lemon, preferably organic

30g butter

30g flour

30ml double cream

salt and pepper

FOR THE MASHED POTATO TOPPING:

900g potatoes

generous knob of butter

100ml sour cream or crème fraîche

30g Gruyère cheese, grated

salt and pepper

1 Put the potatoes into a saucepan of salted water on the Boiling Plate. Boil for 3–4 minutes then drain off all the water, cover with a lid and move to the Simmering Oven for 30–45 minutes.

2 Lay the haddock in the large roasting tin and pour over the milk. Season with pepper and add the chopped onion. If you have any parsley stalks, throw them in too. Slide the tin onto the second set of runners in the Roasting Oven and cook for 10 minutes.

3 Put the flaked kippers and smoked salmon trimmings into a large deep-sided ovenproof dish, and add the cornichons, egg, parsley and lemon zest.

4 When the haddock is cooked, remove the fish from the milky liquid and strain it into a jug and reserve. When the haddock is cool enough to handle, skin and flake it into the ovenproof dish with the other fish.

5 Make the sauce. Melt the butter in a saucepan on the Simmering Plate and add the flour, stirring all the time. When all the flour has been absorbed into the butter, slowly add the strained milk little by little, stirring constantly. When all the milk has been used, add the lemon juice. You should have a smooth white sauce. Pour in the cream and a little salt and pepper (not too much salt as the fish is salty). Simmer the white sauce on the Simmering Plate for 3–4 minutes so that it is slightly thick and glossy.

6 When it is ready, pour it over the fish, mixing it all in well so that everything is coated with the sauce. Do this gently to avoid breaking up the flakes of fish. Set aside.

7 Make the mashed potato topping. When the potatoes are done, remove them from the oven and put them through a potato ricer or mash them by hand or use an electric hand whisk until they are creamy and fluffy. Beat in the butter and sour cream or crème fraîche and season.

8 Spread the potatoes over the fish, then sprinkle over the cheese. The pie can be made to this point 24 hours in advance and refrigerated. When you are ready to cook, put the pie into the large roasting tin and slide onto the fourth set of runners in the Roasting Oven and cook for 35–40 minutes. The top of the pie should be crispy and enticingly browned. (If the top is browning too much, slide the Cold Plain Shelf onto the second set of runners.) Serve with peas.

conventional cooking:

Pre-heat the oven to 180°C/350°F/gas 4 and cook the pie for 40–45 minutes or until done.

crab spring rolls with lemon oil

makes 10 small rolls

FOR THE SPRING ROLLS:

2 tbsp sunflower oil

4 carrots, washed and grated

3cm fresh ginger, peeled and grated

3 spring onions, trimmed and finely sliced

1 heaped tbsp freshly chopped coriander, plus more for garnish

1 bird's eye chilli, de-seeded and finely sliced

1 tbsp fish sauce

1 tsp sesame oil

250g white crab meat, cooked and shredded

500g packet spring roll pastry, in sheets

1 free-range egg yolk, beaten

FOR THE LEMON OIL:

peel of 1 whole unwaxed lemon

2 stalks lemongrass

250ml grapeseed oil

1 First make the lemon oil. Peel the skin off the lemon and put it into a saucepan, then split the lemongrass and put that in. Pour the oil over the lemon skin and lemongrass.

2 Bring to the boil on the Boiling Plate, then transfer to the Simmering Oven for 30 minutes. Remove from the oven and cover with cling film. Stand at room temperature overnight. Strain into a jar and use. The oil will last for about 1 month when stored in the refrigerator.

3 To make the spring rolls, put 1 tablespoon of the sunflower oil into a frying pan and place the pan on the floor of the Roasting Oven. When smoking, transfer the pan to the Boiling Plate and quickly stir-fry the carrots, ginger, onions, coriander, chilli, fish sauce, sesame oil and crab meat for 2–3 minutes. If the heat is too high, transfer to the Simmering Plate. (This can be done up to 3 days in advance if you wish.)

4 Put the remaining sunflower oil into a frying pan and place it on the floor of the Roasting Oven until hot and smoking.

5 Lay the spring roll pastry out on a flat surface. Cut the sheets in half and brush with beaten egg yolk all around the edges. Place a teaspoon of the crab mix 4cm from the top of the pastry, fold the pastry over the mix tightly to remove all the air, then carry on rolling it up. Secure the end with a little more egg so it acts as 'glue'.

6 When the spring rolls are complete, take the frying pan out of the oven, add the spring rolls and 'fry' them on the floor of the Roasting Oven in batches, adding more oil if necessary (don't forget to bring the oil up to temperature when adding more). One tablespoon of oil is all that is needed per batch. The rolls will be cooked as soon as they are brown and crispy on the outside. Serve them on a bed of salad with a little lemon oil drizzled over the top.

conventional cooking:

Prepare the crab rolls as above. Using a deep fat fryer, fry the rolls in batches for 2–3 minutes or until they are golden and crispy.

crab and cod kedgeree

This is a great dish for large numbers as it is easy to make.

serves 6–8

300g basmati rice

590ml stock or water

300g cod

460ml milk

1 tbsp sunflower oil

1 onion, peeled and chopped

30g clarified butter (see page 21)

2 tsp madras curry powder

300g crab meat, cooked

2 tbsp fresh flat-leaf parsley, chopped

4 free-range eggs, hard-boiled, peeled and cut into quarters

1 Put the rice into a saucepan with a lid and pour in the stock or water. Bring the rice to the boil on the Boiling Plate; cover with the lid and then move the saucepan to the floor of the Simmering Oven for 20 minutes.

2 Lay the cod in the large roasting tin and pour over the milk. Slide the tin onto the first set of runners in the Roasting Oven and cook for 5–8 minutes. Remove the cod from the liquid. Discard the milk and skin, and flake the cod into large pieces.

3 Put the sunflower oil into a frying pan and add the chopped onion. Place the frying pan on the floor of the Roasting Oven and fry the onions for 5–8 minutes until they are soft and starting to char around the edges. Remove from the pan with a slotted spoon and set aside.

4 In the same frying pan, melt the clarified butter and add the curry powder and stir for a few minutes. Add the crab meat and cod and cook until heated through.

5 Remove the rice from the Simmering Oven and add the fish, onions and parsley. Season to taste and mix gently to avoid breaking up the flakes of fish. Transfer the kedgeree to a warmed serving dish, top with the hard-boiled eggs and sprinkle over a little more parsley.

conventional cooking:

Cook the rice conventionally on the hob. The fish can be cooked in a frying pan over a medium heat for 6–8 minutes. The dish can be finished off on the hob as above.

cod with garlic shrimps

serves 4

2 slices smoked bacon, cut into strips

100g unsalted butter

2 garlic cloves, peeled and crushed

zest and juice of 1 organic lemon

1 tbsp freshly chopped parsley

100g shrimps or chopped prawns

4 x 180g cod fillets

salt

1 Line a shallow baking tray with Bake-O-Glide. Slide the tray into the Roasting Oven to heat up.

2 Fry the bacon in a pan on the Simmering Plate or on the floor of the Roasting Oven until crispy. Drain and set aside.

3 Beat the butter in a bowl with the crushed garlic, very little salt if any, half of the lemon zest plus a squeeze of juice and the parsley. Mix in the shrimps or prawns and the bacon. Spread the top of the cod fillets with this mixture.

4 Remove the tray from the oven and place the cod fillets on the tray. Slide the tray back on to the floor of the Roasting Oven and cook for about 8–10 minutes or until the cod is cooked – this depends on how thick it is. Serve with the tray juices poured over and with buttery mashed potatoes.

conventional cooking:
Pre-heat the oven to 180°C/350°F/gas 4 and cook for 12–15 minutes as above.

roast cod with lemon and rosemary vinaigrette

serves 6

6 x 225g cod fillets

30g butter

FOR THE VINAIGRETTE:

juice and zest of 2 unwaxed lemons

1 tbsp lemon oil (see page 122)

6 tbsp mild olive oil

1 tbsp fresh rosemary leaves, finely chopped

salt and pepper

1 Whisk up the lemon juice, lemon oil, olive oil, rosemary, salt and pepper in a bowl and set aside.

2 Line the large roasting tin with Bake-O-Glide and lay the cod fillets on it. Spoon 1 tablespoon of the vinaigrette over each piece of cod. Slide the tin onto the first set of runners in the Roasting Oven and cook for 5–7 minutes, depending on how thick the cod is. Move the tin to the floor of the Roasting Oven and cook for a further 3–5 minutes.

3 When the fish is cooked, carefully lift it out, place on a warm plate and cover to keep warm.

4 To complete the sauce, put the roasting tin on the Simmering Plate and pour in the remaining vinaigrette and the lemon zest and whisk in the butter. Reduce for 1 minute, whisking all the time, and pour over the cod. Serve with rice or pasta.

conventional cooking:
Pre-heat the oven to 200°C/400°F/gas 6 and roast the cod in the middle of the oven for 8–12 minutes.

pancetta-wrapped prawns

serves 6

18 king prawns, de-veined and shelled

18 slices pancetta

olive oil

butter

brandy

1 Soak 18 cocktail sticks in water before using them.

2 Wrap each king prawn in a slice of pancetta and secure in place with a cocktail stick.

3 Heat some olive oil and a little butter in a frying pan on the Boiling Plate. When it is sizzling, sauté the prawns in batches, then transfer to a plate and keep warm until they are all cooked. If the Boiling Plate is too fierce, move the pan to the Simmering Plate.

4 De-glaze the pan with a slug of brandy and pour over the prawns. Serve with rice.

conventional cooking:

Cook on the hob.

prawn and pumpkin curry

serves 4

1 tsp cumin seeds

1 tsp coriander seeds

3 cardamom pods, split open and seeds removed

½ tsp ground turmeric

1 tbsp clarified butter (see page 21)

2 onions, peeled and chopped

3 garlic cloves, peeled and crushed

3cm piece of ginger, peeled and grated

1 bird's eye chilli, de-seeded and finely sliced

900g pumpkin, peeled and chopped into 3cm chunks

400ml tin coconut milk

1kg tiger prawns, peeled and de-veined

1 large bunch fresh coriander, roughly chopped

salt

1 Dry fry the spices in a frying pan on the Simmering Plate, then pound them to a powder with a pestle in a mortar.

2 Pour the clarified butter into a deep saucepan with a lid and put it on the Roasting Oven floor to melt. Add the onions, cover and cook for about 10 minutes until soft.

3 Transfer it to the Simmering Plate and add the spices, salt, garlic, ginger and chilli and cook for 1 minute to release the flavours. Add the pumpkin pieces and coconut milk and bring up to a rapid simmer. Transfer to the Simmering Oven, uncovered, for 20–25 minutes or until the pumpkin is tender.

4 Bring it back to the Simmering Plate and reduce for 2–3 minutes. Stir in the prawns and cook for 3–4 minutes or until they are just cooked. Take the pan off the heat, add the coriander and check for seasoning. Serve with basmati rice.

conventional cooking:

Start the cooking on the hob over a medium heat, then turn it down to a very low heat to simmer for 30–35 minutes.

scallops with peas à la française

serves 4

550g frozen peas, or podded if using fresh

1 little gem lettuce

40g butter

1 level tbsp granulated sugar

4 spring onions, trimmed and sliced

1 large bunch fresh mint

120ml crème fraîche

1 tbsp lemon juice

zest of 1 unwaxed lemon

1 rounded tsp unrefined golden caster sugar

2 tbsp grapeseed oil

1 tbsp olive oil

12 plump shucked scallops, corals removed, rinsed and drained

a little olive oil for brushing

salt and pepper

1 First make the pea purée. Put the peas, lettuce, butter, granulated sugar, spring onions, half the mint, crème fraîche and salt and pepper into a saucepan with a lid. Bring it to a rapid simmer on the Simmering Plate, then transfer to the Simmering Oven for 15–20 minutes or until it is tender.

2 Put the pea mixture into a blender and whiz it up until smooth or sieve it. Set it aside and keep warm either at the back of the Aga or in the Warming or Simmering Oven.

3 Place the Aga grill pan on the floor of the Roasting Oven to heat up.

4 Put the lemon juice, zest, caster sugar, the remaining mint, salt and pepper into a bowl and whisk until the sugar has dissolved, then whisk in the oils to make a vinaigrette.

5 Remove the hot grill pan from the Roasting Oven and put it on the Simmering Plate. Brush each scallop with a little olive oil and sear each one in the grill pan. Cook on each side for about 1–2 minutes, depending how thick they are. Do not overcrowd the pan. When they are cooked, place them on a warmed plate and cover loosely.

6 Dollop a large spoonful of the pea purée in the centre of each plate and arrange the scallops on top. Drizzle over the vinaigrette and serve.

conventional cooking:

Cook the pea purée on the hob top over a gentle heat. Pre-heat a grill pan until it is smoking and cook the scallops as above.

scallops with peas à la française

7 vegetarian

alsatian potato torte

serves 4–6

15g unsalted butter, cut into cubes, plus a little more for greasing the dish

750g waxy potatoes, peeled

2 fat garlic cloves, peeled and thinly sliced

2 tsp caraway seeds or cumin

250g Munster cheese, sliced

175ml double cream

500g pack puff pastry

1 free-range egg yolk

salt and pepper

1 Grease an ovenproof dish with some of the butter.

2 Cook the potatoes in a saucepan of boiling water on the Boiling Plate for about 8 minutes. Drain and slice.

3 Build up layers in the prepared dish in the following order: potatoes, garlic, salt, pepper, caraway or cumin seeds, Munster cheese, cream. Repeat until all the ingredients are used up.

4 Roll out the pastry and top the potatoes with it, tucking in the pastry. Brush the top with a beaten egg yolk. Slide a grid shelf onto the fourth set of runners in the Roasting Oven and place the dish on the shelf. Cook for 45–50 minutes or until the pastry is puffed up and golden. Slide the Cold Plain Shelf onto the second set of runners 20 minutes into the cooking time.

5 Cut the potato torte into slices and serve warm with a green salad with French dressing.

conventional cooking:

Pre-heat the oven to 200°C/400°F/gas 6 and bake in the middle of the oven for 40–45 minutes.

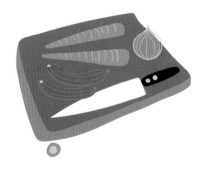

free-form roasted vegetable pie

Don't be alarmed if the pastry crust of this rustic-style pie crumbles and some patching up is required. However, whatever you do, try not to over-work the dough.

serves 4 generously

FOR THE PIE CRUST:

340g plain flour

225g cold butter

80g Parmesan cheese, grated

1 large free-range egg

1 tbsp water

salt and pepper

FOR THE ROASTED VEGETABLES:

2 red onions, peeled and cut into segments

2 garlic cloves, whole, not peeled

2 red peppers, deseeded and sliced into large pieces

2 yellow peppers, deseeded and sliced into large pieces

1 small tin anchovy fillets in olive oil, drained with the oil reserved

2 tbsp mixed fresh herbs (such as flat-leaf parsley, tarragon and thyme)

50g black olives, pitted

1 free-range egg yolk, beaten

30g Parmesan cheese, grated

1 Make the pastry in a food processor or by hand. Process the flour with the butter until the mixture resembles coarse breadcrumbs. Add the cheese and egg, then season. Process with the water until the dough just comes together. Tip it out onto a floured surface and knead lightly until smooth. Wrap in a plastic bag and rest in the refrigerator for 1 hour.

2 Put the onions, garlic cloves and peppers into a bowl and pour over the reserved oil from the anchovy fillets. Season with salt and pepper and toss it all together to coat everything well. (If you need a bit more oil, pour in some olive oil.)

3 Spread the vegetables out onto a shallow Aga baking tray and hang it on the first set of runners in the Roasting Oven for 20 minutes, then move it to the floor of the oven for a further 20 minutes or until the vegetables are soft and charred around the edges. Set aside to cool. This can be done 24 hours in advance.

4 When you are ready to assemble the pie, roll out the pastry on a lightly floured surface to a thickness of 5mm. Carefully transfer the pastry to a 25-cm pie dish and let the excess dough hang over the sides. Spoon in the roasted vegetables and herbs. Squeeze out the garlic from their papery cases over the peppers, then scatter over the olives and anchovies. Fold in the sides of the pastry dough, leaving the centre of the pie exposed. Brush with a little beaten egg and sprinkle over the grated Parmesan cheese.

5 Bake for 20 minutes on the floor of the Roasting Oven, then move it to the fourth set of runners for a further 15 minutes. If the pastry browns too quickly, slide the Cold Plain Shelf onto the third set of runners.

conventional cooking:
Pre-heat the oven to 200°C/400°F/gas 6 and bake in the middle of the oven for 35–40 minutes.

baked eggs in beefsteak tomatoes

per person:

1 large firm, slightly under-ripe beefsteak tomato

1 tbsp melted butter

1 medium free-range egg

1 tbsp double cream

1 tsp finely chopped fresh tarragon

salt and pepper

1 Cut the top of the tomato off about one-quarter of the way down from the stem end and carefully scoop out the seeds. Try not to break or split the tomato. Brush the inside of the tomato with the melted butter and season with a little salt and pepper.

2 Break the egg into the buttered tomato, season with salt and pepper. Pour over the double cream, sprinkle in the tarragon and set the tomato on a baking tray.

3 Slide the tray onto the third set of runners in the Roasting Oven and cook for 5–8 minutes or until the egg is cooked. (The key thing to watch out for is if the tomato is too ripe, it may split during baking.)

4 Remove from the oven and place the baked tomato on a dish with a few chicory leaves. Garnish with some more fresh tarragon leaves if desired and serve with warm bread.

conventional cooking:

Pre-heat the oven to 200°C/400°F/gas 6 and bake for about 8–10 minutes.

savoury egg meringue

Another delicious way to serve this dish is to add a slice of ham or smoked salmon beneath the meringue or to replace the grated cheese with snipped chives.

per person:

1 slice brioche or other similar bread

butter

1 large free-range egg, separated

30g mature Cheddar cheese, finely grated

salt and pepper

1 Toast the brioche using the Aga toaster and spread with butter. Put the toast on a shallow Aga baking tray. Make a dent in the centre of the toast and carefully slide the yolk into it.

2 In a very clean bowl, beat the egg white until stiff. Fold in the cheese and season with salt and pepper. Carefully spoon the egg white over the egg yolk and the top of the toast completely, so that all you can see is a fluffy white mass.

3 Slide the baking tray onto the third set of runners of the Roasting Oven and cook for about 5–7 minutes or until the meringue is starting to brown and rising a little. Serve straight away.

conventional cooking:

Pre-heat the oven to 220°C/425°F/gas 7 and cook for 7–8 minutes.

baked eggs in beefsteak tomatoes

parmigiano, thyme and rosemary risotto

Simple, fresh ingredients and good stock are essential to make risotto, and there can be no quicker way to make stock than in an Aga – see page 28 for instructions. For a vegetarian stock, use a selection of root vegetables in place of the meat bones.

serves 6

olive oil

1 onion, peeled and finely chopped

1 garlic clove, peeled and finely chopped

500g arborio rice

1 glass white wine

1 litre stock, warmed

200g Parmigiano Reggiano cheese, grated

generous knob of butter

½ tbsp freshly chopped rosemary

½ tbsp fresh thyme

salt and pepper

1 Put a tablespoon of olive oil into a heavy-bottomed frying pan and place it on the floor of the Roasting Oven to heat up. When it is hot, take out the pan and add the onion and put back on the Roasting Oven floor for about 10 minutes to soften.

2 When the onion is ready, place the pan on the Simmering Plate and add salt and pepper, the garlic and rice. Stirring constantly, coat the rice in the onion and oil mixture until the rice becomes translucent.

3 Pour in the wine and stir until it is almost all evaporated, then add the stock. Stir and bring to the boil, then place the pan on the Simmering Oven floor for 15–20 minutes.

4 When the liquid has nearly all been absorbed and the rice is tender but still has a bit of a bite, take the pan out of the oven and stir in the Parmigiano cheese, a knob of butter and the fresh herbs. Check the seasoning and serve with a green salad.

conventional cooking:

Pre-heat the oven to 150°C/300°F/gas 2 and when all of the stock has been added to the rice, place the pan in the centre of the oven and cook for 30 minutes.

wild mushroom risotto with crispy sage leaves

Wild mushrooms are a great treat in the autumn and if you live near an area where you can collect them, find out the picking rules from your local forest rangers. I always advise people to go gathering with an expert as results can be fatal from just one wrong mushroom. Always buy or gather only what you need for one meal – mushrooms should be eaten as fresh as possible as they are living fungi and decompose quickly. Do not put mushrooms in plastic; keep them in an open basket or a brown paper bag as the air should circulate around them. Do not choose mushrooms with black spots or bruises. Before cooking them, use a soft natural bristle brush to brush any dirt from the surface or gills. Wipe them with a damp cloth – do not submerge them in water as they can easily become waterlogged.

serves 6

sunflower oil

6 large fresh sage leaves

olive oil

1 onion, peeled and finely chopped

450g wild mushrooms, such as porcini, chanterelle, oyster or trompette, sliced

1 garlic clove, peeled and finely chopped

1 sprig fresh thyme, leaves stripped

500g arborio risotto rice

1 glass white wine

1 litre stock, warmed

200g Parmesan cheese, grated

generous knob of butter

1 tbsp chopped fresh herbs – choose your favourites

salt and pepper

1 Heat some sunflower oil in a shallow frying pan on the floor of the Roasting Oven until the oil starts to smoke. Drop in the sage leaves, fry until crispy, then drain on kitchen paper and set aside.

2 Put 1 tablespoon of olive oil into a heavy-bottomed frying pan and place it on the floor of the Roasting Oven to heat up. When it is hot, add the onion and mushrooms and put it back on the Roasting Oven floor to soften them.

3 When the onion and mushrooms are ready, place the pan on the Simmering Plate and add salt and pepper, the garlic, thyme leaves and risotto rice. Stirring all the time, coat the rice in the onion and oil mixture until the rice is translucent. Pour in the wine and stir until it has almost all evaporated, then add all the stock and stir. Bring to the boil, then place the pan on the fourth set of runners in the Roasting Oven for 20–25 minutes. When the liquid has nearly all been absorbed and the rice is tender but still has a bit of a bite, take the pan out of the oven and stir in the Parmesan, a knob of butter and the fresh herbs.

4 Check the seasoning and serve each portion of risotto with a fried sage leaf on top.

conventional cooking:

Fry the sage leaves and the onion and mushrooms on the hob. Cook the risotto on the hob.

Note:

If you use dried mushrooms in this recipe, soak them in boiling water for about 10 minutes or until soft, then strain, reserving the liquid to use with or instead of the stock.

baked root vegetable crumble with cucumber dressing

serves 4

3 medium parsnips, peeled and cut into chunks

3 red onions, peeled and quartered

3 carrots, peeled and cut into chunks

1 large fennel head, cut into quarters

1 sweet potato, peeled and chopped into large chunks

60g pancetta, cubed (optional, if cooking for non-vegetarians)

butter, for greasing dish

olive oil

2 sprigs fresh thyme, stalks removed

salt and pepper

FOR THE CRUMBLE TOPPING:

180g ciabatta breadcrumbs

1 tsp fresh thyme leaves

zest of ½ lemon

120g butter

60g feta cheese, crumbled

40g haloumi cheese, cubed

FOR THE DRESSING:

½ a cucumber, peeled, deseeded and chopped into small cubes

pinch of sugar

1 tsp white wine vinegar

1 bunch fresh mint

1 bunch fresh dill

200ml Greek yoghurt

1 Put the prepared vegetables into a saucepan of water and boil for 5 minutes on the Boiling Plate. Drain off the water and tip the vegetables and the cubed pancetta (if using) into a buttered ovenproof dish. Drizzle over some olive oil and season with salt, pepper and the thyme leaves.

2 Make the crumble topping. Put the breadcrumbs into a large bowl and add salt, pepper, thyme leaves and lemon zest. Rub in the butter. Top the root vegetables with the crumble, then scatter over the cheeses.

3 Put the crumble onto the fourth set of runners in the Roasting Oven and bake for about 40–45 minutes. Place the Cold Plain Shelf on the second set of runners after 20–25 minutes.

4 While the crumble is cooking, make the dressing. Put the chopped cucumber, salt, pepper, sugar and white wine vinegar into a bowl and leave to stand for 5–10 minutes. Drain off any excess liquid, then add the herbs and yoghurt and mix well. Remove the crumble from the oven and serve with the dressing and a green salad.

conventional cooking:
Pre-heat the oven to 200°C/400°F/gas 6 and bake for 45–60 minutes.

baked root vegetable crumble with cucumber dressing

cheese and rice soufflé

serves 4

2 tbsp butter, plus more for greasing

3 tbsp flour

100ml milk

4 free-range egg yolks

225g Cheddar cheese, grated

pinch of cayenne pepper

pinch of salt

50g cooked rice

4 free-range egg whites, stiffly beaten

1 Grease a large soufflé dish with butter.

2 Make a roux by melting the butter in a small saucepan on the Simmering Plate, then add the flour and stir well. Add the milk slowly, whisking until smooth. Next add the egg yolks and cheese and stir until the cheese has melted. Stir in the cayenne pepper, salt and rice. Mix well and remove from the heat.

3 Fold in the egg whites very gently, then pour into the soufflé dish. Place the dish on the baking tray.

4 With the grid shelf on the floor of the Roasting Oven and the Cold Plain Shelf on the second set of runners, place the dish on the grid shelf and cook for 30–35 minutes until well risen and golden on top. Serve immediately.

conventional cooking:

Pre-heat the oven to 200°C/400°F/gas 6 and cook for 30–35 minutes.

macaroni cheese

serves 6

500g macaroni

butter

700ml double cream

1 shallot, peeled and minced or grated on a microplane grater

500g mature Cheddar cheese, grated

dash of Worcestershire sauce

½ tsp English mustard powder

200g Parmesan cheese, grated

150g dried breadcrumbs, made from good bread

salt and pepper

1 Cook the pasta in a large pan of plenty of salted water on the Boiling or Simmering Plate until it is tender but still has a bite to it. Drain and tip into a shallow buttered ovenproof dish.

2 Pour the cream into a saucepan, add the minced shallot and bring up to the boil on the Boiling Plate. Move to the Simmering Plate and add the Cheddar, a dash of Worcestershire sauce and the mustard powder. Stir until it has melted. Check the seasoning.

3 Pour the sauce over the pasta and stir well to make sure it is all coated. Sprinkle over the Parmesan, then the breadcrumbs. Put the dish on the third set of runners in the Roasting Oven and bake for 25–30 minutes or until the top is golden and bubbling.

conventional cooking:

Make the sauce on the hob. Pre-heat the oven to 180°C/350°F/gas 4 and cook for 30–35 minutes.

lasagne

serves 6

olive oil

2 onions, peeled and finely chopped

3 large tins of good-quality Italian plum tomatoes (about 2kg in total)

450g ricotta cheese

80g Parmesan cheese, finely grated, plus 1 tbsp for topping

500g mozzarella cheese, grated, plus 2 tbsp for topping

1 free-range egg

freshly grated nutmeg

1 bunch fresh basil, torn

butter, for greasing

18–20 sheets of fresh lasagne sheets

salt and pepper

1 Heat up a tablespoon of olive oil in a heavy-bottomed saucepan and fry the onions until soft on the floor of the Roasting Oven. Add the tomatoes and season with salt and pepper. Bring up to the boil on the Boiling Plate, then transfer to the Simmering Oven until the mixture has reduced to about 1 litre – this will take 45–60 minutes.

2 Put the cheeses, egg, grating of nutmeg and basil into a bowl, season with salt and pepper and mix together.

3 Grease a deep-sided ovenproof dish with some butter. Put a ladleful of the tomato sauce on to the bottom of the dish and spread it out. Lay three sheets of pasta on the sauce, overlapping slightly. Pour over some more sauce and scatter with some of the cheese mix. Repeat this until all the lasagne sheets, sauce and cheese are used up ending with a layer of pasta.

4 Sprinkle the rest of the mozzarella and Parmesan over the pasta for the topping. You can freeze the dish at this point or prepare it up it this stage two days before and refrigerate.

5 To cook, bring the lasagne to room temperature and slide it onto the third set of runners in the Roasting Oven for 25–30 minutes or until it is bubbling and brown on top. Serve with lots of hot garlic bread and a green salad of Romaine lettuce.

conventional cooking:

Cook the onions and tomatoes on the hob. Pre-heat the oven to 200ºC/400ºF/gas 6 and cook as above.

fettuccine alfredo

250ml double cream

50g butter

500g fettuccine

100g Parmesan cheese, freshly grated

salt and pepper

1 Put the cream and butter into a large casserole and gently warm on the Simmering Plate for only a minute or until the cream and butter have melted and thickened. Stir and remove from the heat and set aside.

2 Bring a large pan of water to a rapid boil and add a good amount of salt to the water. Cook the pasta according to the instructions and drain.

3 When the pasta is ready, drain and toss the fettuccine in the butter and cream sauce, adding the Parmesan and continuing to toss until the pasta is coated with the sauce. Season with salt and pepper and serve immediately.

conventional cooking:
Cook on the hob.

lemon spaghetti

This recipe is all about taste – the quantities given are guidelines and depend on the strength of your ingredients.

serves 6

500g spaghetti

juice of 4 large organic lemons

zest of 2 large organic lemons

125–150ml olive oil

180g Parmesan cheese, freshly grated, plus more for serving

1 bunch (or a small pot) fresh basil leaves

salt and pepper

1 Bring a large pan of water to a rapid boil on the Boiling Plate and add a good amount of salt to the water. Cook the pasta according to the instructions and drain.

2 Whisk the lemon juice and half of the zest with the olive oil. Stir in the Parmesan. Season with salt and pepper and taste to adjust – if it needs more lemon juice or olive oil or cheese, then add.

3 When the pasta is ready, drain it, tip into a serving bowl and pour over the lemon sauce. Fold in the basil leaves and remaining zest. Serve straight away with more Parmesan sprinkled over the top.

conventional cooking:
Cook on the hob.

baked leek and squash frittata

You will need a deep dish for this frittata – my tarte tatin dish is perfect!

serves 4–6

2 large leeks, washed and sliced

olive oil

7 free-range eggs

**425g tin puréed pumpkin, or
purée your own**

60ml crème fraîche

½ tbsp fresh rosemary, chopped

60g toasted pine nuts

salt and pepper

1 Put the leeks on a baking tray and drizzle with a little olive oil. Slide the tray onto the first set of runners in the Roasting Oven and bake for about 10 minutes or until they are soft.

2 Grease the tarte tatin dish with some more olive oil and set aside.

3 In a large jug mix together the eggs, pumpkin, crème fraîche, rosemary, and some salt and pepper. Fold in the leeks and pine nuts and pour into the greased tarte tatin dish.

4 Bake on the grid shelf on the third set of runners in the Roasting Oven for about 10 minutes or until set. For 4-oven Aga owners, put the grid shelf on the third set of runners in the Baking Oven and bake for about 15 minutes.

5 Remove from the oven and serve the frittata either straight away or at room temperature. Cut into thick wedges and serve with a green salad and a drizzle of pumpkin oil.

conventional cooking:

Pre-heat the oven to 200°C/400°F/gas 6 and bake the leeks for 10 minutes. Turn the temperature down to 180°C/350°F/gas 4 and bake the frittata for 10–15 minutes or until set.

tomato and gruyère tart

This recipe can also be made as four individual tarts by cutting the pastry into smaller circles and placing on a shallow tray lined with Bake-O-Glide.

serves 4

butter, for greasing

500g good-quality store-bought puff pastry

1 tbsp Dijon mustard

250g Gruyère cheese, grated

1 bunch fresh basil

3 large vine-ripened tomatoes, very thinly sliced

salt and pepper

1 Lightly butter a 20.5 cm tart tin with a removable base.

2 Roll out the puff pastry and line the tart tin.

3 Spread the mustard over the base of the pastry, then sprinkle over the cheese. Scatter half of the basil leaves over the cheese, then top with the tomato slices. Season with salt and pepper.

4 Bake the tart on the floor of the Roasting Oven for 25–30 minutes or until puffed up and golden. Slide the Cold Plain Shelf in directly over the tart about 10 minutes into the baking time.

5 Remove the tart from the oven and stand on a cooling rack for 15 minutes. Remove from the tart tin and scatter over the remaining basil leaves. Serve warm or at room temperature with a watercress salad.

conventional cooking:
Pre-heat the oven to 190ºC/375ºF/gas 5 and bake for 20–25 minutes.

tomato and gruyère tart

roasted vegetable tarte tatin

serves 4–6

FOR THE PIE CRUST:

342g plain flour

226g butter, softened

80g Parmesan cheese, grated

1 large free-range egg

salt and pepper

FOR THE ROASTED VEGETABLES:

2–3 parsnips, peeled and cut into thick log shapes

2–3 carrots, peeled and cut like the parsnips

2 red onions, peeled and quartered

1 tbsp olive oil

1 tbsp unrefined golden caster sugar

2 tbsp fresh rosemary, chopped

salt and pepper

FOR THE GLAZE:

1 tbsp butter

1 tsp balsamic vinegar

1 tbsp pomegranate molasses (see page 298)

1 free-range egg yolk, beaten

1 Make the pastry in a food processor or by hand. Process the flour with the butter until the mixture resembles coarse breadcrumbs. Add the salt, pepper, cheese and egg. Process until the dough just comes together. Tip it out on to a floured surface and knead lightly until smooth. Wrap in a plastic bag and rest in the fridge for 1 hour.

2 Meanwhile, place the parsnips and carrots in a saucepan of water and bring to the boil on the Boiling Plate. Drain off all the water, then transfer to the Simmering Oven and cook for about 12 minutes. They need to be just cooked and not too soft.

3 When ready, put the carrots, parsnips and onions into a bowl and pour over the olive oil. Add the sugar and rosemary, season and toss together to coat everything well. Spread the vegetables out on a shallow Aga baking tray and roast on the first set of runners in the Roasting Oven for 15–20 minutes. Move the tray to the floor of the Roasting Oven for a further 15–20 minutes or until the vegetables are charred around the edges. Set aside to cool. (This can be done 24 hours in advance if you wish.)

4 When you are ready to assemble the tarte tatin, put the butter, balsamic vinegar and pomegranate molasses into the tarte tatin tin. Place it on the Simmering Plate until it has all melted and cook for about 2 minutes. Take off the heat and assemble the vegetables around the bottom of the tin.

5 Roll out the pastry on a lightly floured surface to a thickness of 5mm. Drape the pastry over the vegetables and tuck in excess pastry loosely around the side, leaving a little space so that air can escape. Brush the top of the pastry with a little beaten egg yolk.

6 Bake on the floor of the Roasting Oven for 35–40 minutes, sliding the Cold Plain Shelf onto the third set of runners after 20 minutes.

conventional cooking:

Cook the carrots and parsnips on the hob. Pre-heat the oven to 200°C/400°F/gas 6 and bake the tarte for 40–45 minutes.

roasted beetroot pizza

makes 2 pizzas

1 quantity pizza dough (see below)

FOR THE TOPPING:
10 baby beetroot
olive oil
balsamic vinegar
125g ball buffalo mozzarella cheese, grated or thinly sliced
100g Taleggio cheese, thinly sliced
½ tbsp fresh thyme
½ tbsp fresh rosemary, chopped
salt and pepper

1 Cut the beetroot in half and put on a baking tray. Drizzle over some olive oil and balsamic vinegar, and season with salt and pepper. Slide on to the second set of runners in the Roasting Oven and roast for 15–20 minutes or until slightly charred and softish.

2 When you are ready to assemble the pizza, turn a large baking tray upside down and line with Bake-O-Glide. Pull half the pizza dough on the Bake-O-Glide into a circle. Scatter the base of the dough with half the mozzarella, then spread over half the roasted beetroot. Top the beetroot with half the Taleggio slices and herbs.

3 Carefully slide the Bake-O-Glide directly onto the floor of the Roasting Oven, pulling the upturned baking tray away as you do so. Bake the pizza for about 12 minutes or until puffed up and golden. Repeat for the second pizza. I like to make one pizza and share it while it is hot, and cook the next one while we are eating.

conventional cooking:

Pre-heat the oven to 200°C/400°F/gas 6 and roast the beetroot as above. To cook the pizza, pre-heat the oven to its highest setting. If you have a pizza stone, use it according to the manufacturer's instructions. Bake for 25–30 minutes.

pizza dough

makes 2 pizzas

40g fresh yeast
125ml milk, at room temperature
175ml hand-hot water
300g '00' flour
40g strong plain flour
3g salt
olive oil, for greasing the bowl

1 Prove the yeast with the milk and water by crumbling yeast into the liquid and leaving for 10 minutes.

2 Mix the yeast with the sifted flours and salt and knead for 10 minutes. The dough should be sticky.

3 Knead for a further 10 minutes, adding more flour if necessary. Whatever happens, do not end up with stable dough! It should be threatening to stick to the sides of the bowl. Let it rise in an oiled bowl set close to the Aga or another warm place for about 1 hour or until doubled in size.

4 Shape the dough into a pizza shape – pull and stretch, but do not roll.

5 Let it rise for about 10 minutes, then add your chosen toppings and bake (see above).

pumpkin and taleggio calzone

serves 4 for lunch, 6 for a starter

FOR THE DOUGH:

40g fresh yeast

125ml milk, at room temperature

175ml hand-hot water

300g '00' flour

40g strong plain flour

3g salt

olive oil, for greasing the bowl

FOR THE FILLING:

500g pumpkin, peeled and deseeded

olive oil

100g Parma ham, sliced very thinly

150g Taleggio cheese, sliced

100g mozzarella, sliced

50g sun-dried tomatoes, chopped

100g wild rocket leaves

salt and pepper

1 Prove the yeast with the milk and water by crumbling yeast into the liquid and leaving for 10 minutes.

2 Mix the yeast with the sifted flours and salt and knead for 10 minutes – the dough should be sticky. Add more flour if necessary, but whatever happens do not end up with a stable dough! It should be threatening to stick to the sides of the bowl.

3 Place the dough in a bowl greased with oil and leave next to the Aga for about 1 hour or until doubled in size.

4 Meanwhile, cut the pumpkin into small chunks, place in a shallow baking tray, drizzle with olive oil and season with salt and pepper. Hang the baking tray on the second set of runners in the Roasting Oven and roast for 20–25 minutes or until the pumpkin is soft and charred around the edges. Remove from the oven and set aside.

5 Shape the dough into two rectangles.

6 Roughly divide the pumpkin and the rest of the ingredients in half. Spread each pizza with one of the halves of filling. Start with the pumpkin, spread the Parma ham on top, then layer the cheeses, tomatoes and rocket, leaving a 1–2cm border.

7 Starting at one end of the rectangle, roll up the dough as you would for a roulade and roll it on to a piece of Bake-O-Glide (you may need to flour your hands). Make sure the seam side is down and the ends are tucked and pressed in.

8 Leave to prove for about 5–10 minutes, then slide the Bake-O-Glide directly on to the floor of the Roasting Oven. Cook the calzone for about 20–25 minutes or until golden and crisp. Check after 10 minutes and slide in the Cold Plain Shelf if browning too quickly.

9 Remove from the oven and cool for a few minutes, then slice and eat.

conventional cooking:

Pre-heat the oven to 220ºC/425ºF/gas 7 and bake in the middle of the oven for 25–30 minutes.

apple and onion tart

I have an old convent recipe book which is purely devoted to apples and the basis of this recipe comes from that book. I suggest you use a mandolin to slice the onions.

serves 6

PASTRY:

175g plain flour

100g unsalted butter

50g strong Cheddar cheese, grated

1 free-range egg

salt and pepper

FILLING:

1 tbsp olive oil

knob of butter

4–6 onions depending on the size, peeled and sliced very thinly with a mandolin

2 crispy apples, peeled and grated

½ tbsp unrefined golden caster sugar

salt and pepper

1 garlic clove, peeled and crushed (optional)

1 sprig of thyme, leaves only

the merest pinch of cinnamon

3 free-range egg yolks

250ml double cream

1 Put all the pastry ingredients into a food processor and pulse until they come together to form a ball. Add a little cold water if the mixture is too crumbly. Wrap in cling film and rest in the fridge for at least 30 minutes.

2 Bring the pastry to room temperature. Roll out and line a deep, loose-bottomed 20-cm tart tin. Return to the fridge for another 20 minutes at least. Alternatively, press the dough straight into the tart tin when it has come together in the food processor, then put the tart tin in the fridge for at least 1 hour.

3 Heat the oil and butter in a frying pan, then toss in the onions, apples and sugar. Cook very gently on the Simmering Plate until the onions are deliciously caramelised and thick. Season with salt and pepper and cook for 10 minutes.

4 Add the garlic, thyme and cinnamon and cook for a further 5 minutes (alternatively, cook on the floor of the Roasting Oven). Everything should look translucent and just starting to caramelise. Pour into a bowl and cool. You can do this in advance – up to the day before.

5 When you are ready to assemble the tart, beat the egg yolks and cream into the onions. Remove the pastry from the fridge. Pour the onion mix into the tin.

6 Bake the tart on the floor of the Roasting Oven for 20 minutes or until the filling is just set. If the pastry browns too quickly, slide in the Cold Plain Shelf just above.

conventional cooking:

Pre-heat the oven to 180°C/350°F/gas 4 and blind-bake the pastry into the tin for 15–18 minutes. Pour the onion and egg mix into the baked pastry shell, then cook for 15 minutes or until the filling is just set.

ricotta torta

olive oil

2 large onions, peeled and finely chopped

zest and juice of 1½ lemons

125g breadcrumbs

1 tbsp raisins

1 tbsp fresh flat-leaf parsley, chopped

2 tbsp pine nuts, toasted and chopped, plus 1 tbsp toasted but not chopped

1 tbsp rice flour

1kg ricotta cheese

4 free-range eggs

60g Parmesan cheese, grated

handful fresh basil leaves

salt and pepper

1 To make the breadcrumbs, put some olive oil into a large frying pan and heat it in the Roasting Oven. Move to the Simmering Plate and fry a tablespoon of the chopped onion in it until soft. Add the lemon juice and zest and cook until the juice evaporates. Add the breadcrumbs and fry until golden, then add the raisins, parsley and chopped pine nuts. Transfer to a plate lined with kitchen paper and set aside.

2 In the same frying pan, pour in a little more oil and fry the rest of the onion until soft. Transfer to a bowl and cool to room temperature. (Steps 1 and 2 can be done the day before if you wish.)

3 When the onions are cool, add the rice flour, ricotta, eggs and Parmesan. Tear the basil into strips and add. Season with salt and pepper and mix well.

4 Line the base of a loose-bottomed 20.5-cm tin with Bake-O-Glide and spoon over half of the breadcrumbs. Ladle in the ricotta mixture and top with the remaining breadcrumbs.

5 Start the torta on the grid shelf on the floor of the Roasting Oven for 20–30 minutes with the Cold Plain Shelf directly above it. Remove the torta and plain shelf from the Roasting Oven and transfer the shelf to the third set of runners in the Simmering Oven. Place the torta on the plain shelf and continue cooking for 1½–2 hours or until puffed up, checking every so often.

6 For 4-oven Aga owners, start the torta on the grid shelf on the floor of the Roasting Oven for 10 minutes, then move the torta to a grid shelf on the floor of the Baking Oven and cook for a further 1–1½ hours or until puffed up. If it browns too quickly, slide the Cold Plain Shelf over the torta.

7 Remove the torta from the oven and allow to cool to room temperature. Scatter with the remaining toasted pine nuts and serve with a tomato salad dressed with olive oil and balsamic vinegar.

conventional cooking:
Cover the top of the torta with a damp piece of greaseproof paper. Pre-heat the oven to 180°C/350°F/gas 4 and bake for 1–1½ hours or until puffed up.

ricotta torta

onion seed tart filled with asparagus and lemon

serves 4–6

FOR THE PASTRY:

180g plain flour

1 tsp salt

90g cold unsalted butter, cubed

30g onion seeds

1 free-range egg, beaten

FOR THE FILLING:

4 large free-range eggs

2 tbsp double cream

1 tbsp fresh tarragon, slightly chopped

1 tbsp lemon juice

8–10 thin asparagus spears, bottoms peeled and trimmed

zest of 1 organic lemon, cut into long thin strips

salt and pepper

1 To make the pastry, sift the flour and salt into the food processor, then add the butter and half of the onion seeds and process for 30 seconds. Add the egg and process again until it forms a ball. Stop immediately, wrap in cling film and rest in the fridge for a minimum of 30 minutes.

2 Line a 23-cm square tart tin with the rest of the onion seeds so that they will provide an extra crunch and texture to the tart shell.

3 After it has rested, roll out the pastry. Line the tart tin, then rest again in the fridge for 30 minutes (you could prepare a couple of tins and pop them into the freezer).

4 To make the filling, whisk the eggs, cream, salt and pepper, tarragon and lemon juice together in a jug and pour into the pastry case. Arrange the asparagus on the filling along with the lemon zest. Place the tart on the floor of the Roasting Oven with the Cold Plain Shelf on the fourth set of runners. Bake for 20–25 minutes.

5 Remove from the oven and cool in the tin on a wire rack. Serve at room temperature.

conventional cooking:

Pre-heat the oven to 190°C/375°F/gas 5 and blind-bake the tart shell for 15 minutes. Remove and cool for about 5 minutes, then pour in the filling and proceed as above. Lower the oven temperature to 180°C/350°F/gas 4 and bake for 20 minutes.

onion seed tart filled with asparagus and lemon

apricots with honey and goats' cheese

serves 4

8 apricots

60g goats' cheese

leaves from 2 fresh thyme sprigs

1½ tbsp toasted pine nuts

2 tbsp really delicious fruity olive oil

2 coffee spoons honey

freshly ground black pepper

1 Wipe the apricots with kitchen paper to remove any fuzz and quarter them. Discard the stones.

2 Grease a shallow ovenproof dish with a little olive oil. Put the apricots in the dish and crumble the cheese over them. Sprinkle over the thyme and the pine nuts. Drizzle over the honey and pour the olive oil over everything.

3 Slide the dish on to the third set of runners in the Roasting Oven and cook for about 5–8 minutes, or until it is golden. Season with fresh pepper and serve with good sourdough bread.

conventional cooking:

Grill for 5 minutes.

broad beans with pasta and ricotta

serves 4

1kg shelled broad beans, blanched and ready to cook

500g tagliolini pasta

olive oil

1 medium onion, peeled and finely chopped

1 garlic clove, peeled and crushed

1 tsp chopped fresh oregano

1 tbsp chopped fresh flat-leaf parsley

extra virgin olive oil, for drizzling

grated zest of 1 organic lemon

60g ricotta cheese

salt and pepper

1 To prepare the broad beans, shell them, then blanch in rapidly boiling water. Drain the beans, then plunge into ice cold water. Pop each bean out of its pale green skin by pinching with thumb and forefinger.

2 Bring a large pot of salted water up to the boil on the Boiling Plate and cook the pasta until it is al dente.

3 While the pasta is cooking, heat 2–3 tablespoons of olive oil in a large frying pan, add the onion and cook on the floor of the Roasting Oven until softened. Then add the garlic, herbs and a splash of the pasta water to the pan and gently cook on the Simmering Plate.

4 Drain the pasta, reserving a little of the cooking water, and add the pasta to the onion mix. Toss in the broad beans. Season with salt and pepper.

5 Drizzle over some extra virgin olive oil and gently stir so that the pasta is thoroughly coated, adding a little of the reserved water if it is too dry. Grate the lemon zest over the pasta and crumble in the ricotta cheese. Stir, check the seasoning and serve.

conventional cooking:

Cook the pasta in rapidly boiling water over a high heat. Fry the onion in the olive oil over a medium heat and continue as above.

roasted tomato tarts

serves 6

1.5kg organic tomatoes
60ml olive oil
40ml balsamic vinegar
1 level tbsp sugar
1 garlic clove, peeled
500g good quality puff pastry
1 free-range egg yolk, beaten
18 pitted Kalamata olives
salt and pepper

1 Cut the tomatoes into small pieces and place in a single layer on a large baking tray.

2 Pour the olive oil, balsamic vinegar, sugar, salt and pepper into a bowl and whisk well. Pour this over the tomatoes and add the garlic clove to the tray. Place the baking tray on the second set of runners in the Roasting Oven and roast for 20 minutes, then move to the Simmering Oven and continue to roast for a further 40–60 minutes or until the tomatoes are browned and the juices are syrupy. Discard the garlic clove.

3 Roll out the puff pastry to a thickness of approximately 5mm. Cut it into 6 rounds, each about 12cm in diameter. Fold over 2cm of the pastry to form a border around the edge, pressing down firmly. Transfer the tart rounds to a large baking tray lined with Bake-O-Glide. Brush the pastry edges with beaten egg yolk.

4 Spoon the roasted tomatoes into the pastry and top each tart with 3 olives. Slide the baking tray onto the floor of the Roasting Oven and bake for about 10 minutes. Slide in the Cold Plain Shelf and continue baking for a further 8–10 minutes until the tarts are puffed up and golden.

5 Cool the tarts on a wire rack and serve at room temperature with a rocket and Parmesan salad.

conventional cooking:
Pre-heat the oven to 190ºC/375ºF/gas 5. Roast the tomatoes for 1 hour or until browned and with syrupy juices. Turn the temperature up to 200ºC/400ºF/gas 6 and bake the tarts for 15–18 minutes.

pumpkin tarte tatin

serves 6 for a starter or
4 for lunch

FOR THE PASTRY:

75g plain flour

50g chickpea flour

50g unsalted butter, at room
temperature and chopped into
pieces

25g Parmesan cheese, grated

1 tsp fresh rosemary, chopped

black pepper

1 large free-range egg

FOR THE FILLING:

40g unsalted butter

1 tsp brown sugar

3 whole sprigs fresh rosemary,
about 10cm long

½ tsp dried chilli flakes

1kg pumpkin, peeled and
deseeded, cut into 1cm-thick
half-moon slices

1 tbsp balsamic vinegar, plus
extra for drizzling

salt and pepper

1 First make the pastry. I usually use a food processor but you can do it by hand. Put the flours and butter into the food processor and pulse until it resembles coarse breadcrumbs. Add the cheese, chopped rosemary and pepper and pulse for a couple of seconds until the mix resembles fine breadcrumbs. Add the egg and pulse again for a few seconds or until a soft dough is formed. Flatten the dough into a disc shape, wrap in cling film and refrigerate for at least 30 minutes.

2 Put the butter and sugar into a 27-cm tarte tatin dish. Place the dish on the floor of the Roasting Oven and heat until the butter sizzles.

3 Transfer the dish to the Simmering Plate, place the rosemary sprigs on the bottom and scatter over half of the chilli flakes. Arrange the pumpkin slices carefully over the base of the dish, overlapping and filling in the gaps – what you see now will eventually be the top of the tart so make it look as good as possible. Season the pumpkin with salt, pepper and the remaining chilli flakes and spoon over the balsamic vinegar.

4 Transfer the dish back to the Roasting Oven floor and cook for 10 minutes, then cover the dish with foil and slide in a grid shelf on the fourth set of runners. Move the dish to the grid shelf and bake for another 20–25 minutes or until the pumpkin is soft, then remove the foil and transfer the dish to the Simmering or Boiling Plate for a few minutes to reduce and thicken the juices.

5 Meanwhile, remove the pastry from the fridge and roll out into a circle large enough to cover the tarte tatin dish – about 27cm round.

6 Take the dish off the heat and carefully lay the rolled out pastry over the pumpkin slices, tucking the pastry around the inside of the dish. (It is important to tuck the pastry in loosely to allow little gaps for the steam to escape, otherwise you'll end up with soggy pastry.)

7 Return the dish to the third set of runners in the Roasting Oven and bake for 20–25 minutes. If the pastry browns too quickly, slide in the Cold Plain Shelf just above. When the pastry is golden, remove the tarte tatin from the oven and allow to cool in the dish for about 10 minutes.

8 Place a flat plate over the dish and, protecting your hands, invert the plate and give it a gentle shake. Remove the tatin dish. If some of the pumpkin gets stuck, just ease it off the bottom and slot it into place. Shave over some more Parmesan, drizzle with balsamic vinegar and serve with a green salad.

conventional cooking:

Melt the butter on the hob over a medium–high heat. Add the pumpkin to the pan and cook for 10 minutes. Continue as above and cook the tart in an oven pre-heated to 200°C/400°F/gas 6 for 40–45 minutes or until the pastry is golden and cooked.

pumpkin tarte tatin

8 accompaniments

Root vegetables can be cooked very successfully in the Aga and retain most of their valuable vitamins as well as their taste. Once you learn the trick of cooking your veggies this way, you will never cook them any other way.

Cook green vegetables, such as French beans, peas, mangetout, etc., in the conventional way. Bring a pan of water to the boil and cook them in salted boiling water for however long you like, then drain and serve. However, when it comes to root vegetables, such as potatoes, carrots, etc., the Aga method is by far the best. Firstly, it eliminates lots of unwanted steam in the kitchen and, secondly, it conserves valuable heat.

Aga method of cooking root vegetables

Prepare the vegetables, say potatoes, in the usual way. Peel or scrub them and put into a saucepan of salted water. Bring the saucepan to the boil on the Boiling Plate and cook with the lid on for 4–5 minutes. Remove the pan from the heat and drain off all the water. Replace the lid and put the pan on the Simmering Oven floor. The potatoes will take approximately 25–30 minutes to cook but the timing really does depend on the size of the vegetables being cooked. I usually cook carrots for about 15 minutes as I like them with a bit of a bite.

The amazing thing about this method of cooking vegetables is that if for some reason the meal is delayed, the vegetables happily sit in the Simmering Oven for up to 3 hours without burning. It is true to say they would be well done, but they would still be edible, neither falling apart nor burnt.

Get ahead vegetables

This is a 'tricks of the trade' tip. Restaurants have been preparing vegetables like this for years.

Get ahead green vegetables

Have ready a large bowl of water with some ice in it. Put it to one side. Cook your green vegetables for 2–3 minutes in rapidly boiling water so they are tender. Using a slotted spoon, transfer them from the boiling water straight into the bowl of iced water. This is what is meant when a recipe says to 'blanch'. The iced water stops the vegetables cooking further and helps them retain their colour. Then drain well on kitchen paper towels and put into an ovenproof dish. Brush over a little melted butter or olive oil and cover with foil. Leave in a cool place or the fridge. Vegetables can be prepared in this way 24 hours in advance.

When you want to serve them, season with salt and pepper and put the dish (still covered with foil) on the floor of the Roasting Oven for 15–20 minutes. Open the door and when you hear the fat spitting they should be ready. Serve immediately. You can easily do all your vegetables this way and group them together in an ovenproof serving dish.

Get ahead roast potatoes

Prepare the potatoes in the usual way: peel, parboil on the Boiling Plate for 8 minutes, drain and fluff up by putting the lid on the pan and shaking. Put the dripping or other fat into the half- or full-size roasting tin and place on the floor of the Roasting Oven to heat up. When the fat is smoking, add the potatoes, baste with the fat and cook on the floor of the Roasting Oven for

25 minutes. Take them out of the oven, turn them over and let them cool. Cover them with foil and put aside until ready to finish off. They can be prepared up to this point 24 hours ahead of time. Do not refrigerate. Remove the foil, then put the potatoes back into the Roasting Oven 25 minutes before you want to serve them to finish off. Serve straight away. Timings may have to be adjusted to suit the size of the vegetables.

Drying fruit and vegetables in the Aga

This is where the 4-oven Aga really comes into its own. However, it is just as easy with a 2-oven Aga.

Slice the fruit or vegetables into 1–2cm slices or into halves or quarters. Lay the fruit or vegetables on a shallow Aga baking tray lined with Bake-O-Glide. Slide the tray into the Warming oven in a 4-oven Aga for 6–8 hours or overnight. The juicier the fruit, the longer it will take to dry out. It is best to scoop out the fleshy insides of fruits like tomatoes before slicing. In a 2-oven Aga slide the tray onto the third set of runners in the Simmering Oven for 3–6 hours. Leave mushrooms whole and start them in the Simmering or Warming Oven, then transfer to the lid of the Boiling Plate, protected by a tea towel or an Aga circular chef's pad until they are really dry. Store in an airtight bag or jar and rehydrate with boiling water when you want to use. Tomatoes and aubergines can also be stored in olive oil, either with or without herbs.

roast potatoes

serves 6

900g potatoes, peeled and cut into pieces roughly the same size

2 tbsp dripping

1 Line the large roasting tin with Bake-O-Glide and put about 2 heaped tablespoons of dripping into it. Slide it onto the Roasting Oven floor until it is really hot and smoking.

2 Bring the potatoes up to the boil in a saucepan of water on the Boiling Plate and cook for 5–8 minutes or until they start to give a little around the edges. Drain off all the water and, with a lid on the saucepan, shake it so that the potatoes become roughed up on the outside.

3 Remove the tin from the oven and put it on the Simmering Plate. Add the potatoes to the hot fat. Baste them and move them back to the floor of the Roasting Oven for about 50 minutes or until they are crisp.

conventional cooking:

Pre-heat the oven to 200°C/400°F/gas 6 and roast the potatoes for 1 hour.

baked potatoes

1 potato per person

Wash the potatoes and set them on a grid shelf on the third set of runners in the Roasting Oven for 45–60 minutes (the cooking time very much depends on the size of the potatoes).

mashed potatoes

Experiment with your mash by adding different flavours – sometimes I add a whole pack of garlic cream cheese to the mash. Or squeeze in some roasted garlic cloves and mash them all up together.

serves 4–6

900g potatoes, peeled and cut in half

80g butter

150ml crème fraîche

salt and pepper

1 Put the potatoes into a saucepan of water and bring to the boil on the Boiling Plate. Boil for 3 minutes. Take the pan off the heat and drain off all the water. Replace the lid and transfer the pan to the Simmering Oven for 20–30 minutes.

2 When the potatoes are tender, break them up with a knife or a potato ricer. Mash in the butter and crème fraîche. Season with lots of salt and black pepper. If the mash is too stiff, add some more crème fraîche or a little milk.

conventional cooking:

Boil the potatoes for 8–10 minutes over a high heat. Drain and continue as above.

dauphinoise potatoes

serves 4–6

2 cloves of garlic, peeled and crushed

15g butter, plus more for greasing the tin or ovenproof dish

900g potatoes, peeled and sliced very thinly

150ml crème fraîche

425ml double cream

salt and pepper

1 Put the garlic and butter into a bowl and gently melt and infuse at the back of the Aga. You can melt it in a saucepan if time is short but do not let the butter brown or the garlic burn.

2 Grease an ovenproof dish with some butter, then layer the potato slices in the dish.

3 Stir the garlic-infused butter into a bowl containing the two creams to lightly loosen them. Season the creams with salt and pepper. If the cream is too stiff, loosen it with a little milk. Pour the cream over the potatoes and season with more salt and pepper.

4 Slide a grid shelf onto the third set of runners in the Roasting Oven and cook the potatoes for 1–1½ hours. If browning too quickly, slide the Cold Plain Shelf in above it.

conventional cooking:

Pre-heat the oven to 200°C/400°F/gas 6 and bake for 1½ hours or until lightly coloured on top and the potatoes are tender.

aga oven chips

Adjust the quantities to suit the number of people you are feeding. The method is the same.

potatoes
sunflower oil
salt

1 Peel some potatoes and cut them into thick strips. Soak the potatoes in cold water for 10 minutes and drain very well on a tea towel. The drier they are, the better.

2 Put the potatoes into a large bowl and pour in some sunflower oil – about 1 tablespoon for every 2 potatoes. Toss the potatoes in the oil and make sure they are all evenly coated.

3 Spread the potatoes on a large baking tray and cook them on the Roasting Oven floor for 35–45 minutes, turning occasionally, until they are brown and crisp on all sides. Remove them from the oven, sprinkle generously with salt and serve.

conventional cooking:
Pre-heat the oven to 220°C/425°F/gas 7 and continue as above.

warm new potatoes with pancetta and pine nuts

serves 4

750g baby new potatoes
250g pancetta, cubed
3 tbsp pine nuts
1 tbsp butter
2 tbsp crème fraîche
1 bag wild rocket

FOR THE WALNUT OIL
VINAIGRETTE:
1 tbsp red wine vinegar
2 tbsp sunflower oil
1 tbsp walnut oil
1 tsp honey
1 tsp Dijon mustard
salt and pepper

1 Place the potatoes in a large pan of salted water and bring to the boil on the Boiling Plate for 3 minutes. Drain off all the water, cover and transfer them to the Simmering Oven for about 30 minutes or until they are tender.

2 While the potatoes are cooking, make the vinaigrette by whisking all the ingredients together.

3 Fry the pancetta in a frying pan on the Simmering Plate until the fat starts to run, then add the pine nuts and cook until the pancetta is crisp and the pine nuts are golden – don't let them burn. Do not wash the frying pan – just set aside.

4 When the potatoes are cooked, add the butter and crème fraîche to the potatoes and season. Spoon on all but 3 tablespoons of the vinaigrette and add the pine nuts and pancetta.

5 Divide the rocket leaves between four plates and top with the potatoes. Pour the reserved vinaigrette into the pan and scrape up all the juices and pour these over the plated potatoes and serve while still warm.

conventional cooking:
Cook the new potatoes in salted boiling water on the hob until tender, then proceed as above.

vichy carrots

serves 4

700g carrots
1 tbsp brown sugar
30g butter
salt and pepper

1 Clean the carrots and cut them into rounds, batons or, if they are small enough, leave them whole. Put them into a saucepan and cover with water. Bring to the boil on the Boiling Plate for 3 minutes.
2 Drain off all the water, then add the sugar, butter, salt and pepper to the pan. Cover with a tightly fitting lid and transfer to the Simmering Oven for 15–20 minutes.

conventional cooking:
Cook the carrots in a saucepan on the hob.

braised red cabbage

serves 4

100g duck fat
500g red cabbage, thinly sliced
2 apples, peeled and grated
100g brown sugar
250ml red wine
250ml port
salt and pepper

1 Melt the duck fat in a large casserole dish on the Simmering Plate and add the sliced cabbage. Soften the cabbage for 5–10 minutes, then add the grated apples and brown sugar. Season with salt and pepper.
2 Pour in the wine and port and bring to the boil on the Boiling Plate for about 2 minutes. Transfer the casserole to the floor of the Simmering Oven, uncovered, for 20–30 minutes. Check the cabbage, then cover with a lid and leave to braise for 1½–2 hours or until it is soft, dark and delicious.

conventional cooking:
Cook the cabbage on the hob in the usual way. Turn down the heat to simmer for 30 minutes, checking and stirring from time to time.

sautéed courgettes with basil and mint

serves 6

700g courgettes
40g butter
1 bunch basil, chopped
1 bunch mint, chopped
salt and pepper

1 Using a vegetable peeler, peel the courgettes into long thin strips.
2 Melt the butter in a large frying pan or shallow casserole on the Simmering Plate until it starts to bubble, then add the courgettes, salt and pepper. Cook for about 2–3 minutes and when they start to soften, add the basil and mint. Toss for a few minutes until tender and serve.

conventional cooking:
Cook on a hob over a medium heat as above.

spinach gratin

serves 6

150ml double cream

150ml milk

½ an onion, peeled

1 bay leaf

nutmeg

knob of butter

500g fresh spinach, washed and stalks removed

50g unsalted butter

25g flour

150g Parmesan cheese, freshly grated, plus 2 tbsp

salt and pepper

1 First infuse the cream and milk with the onion. Pour the cream and milk into a saucepan and add the onion, bay leaf, some salt and pepper and a grating of nutmeg. Bring almost to a boil on the Simmering Plate, cook for 15–20 minutes and then set aside.

2 Put a knob of butter into a non-stick frying pan and melt on the Simmering Plate, then toss in the spinach and cook for 3–5 minutes until it has wilted. Remove from the pan and drain in a fine sieve. Squeeze out the excess liquid and chop up the spinach finely.

3 Remove the bay leaf and onion from the cream. Melt the butter in a saucepan on the Simmering Plate and stir in the flour to make a roux. Cook the flour for a few minutes, then add the warmed milk/cream little by little, stirring all the time so that the sauce is smooth and silky. When all the cream has been added and the sauce is smooth, add the Parmesan. Stir in the chopped spinach and continue to cook for a minute. Taste for seasoning.

4 Pour into a gratin dish and sprinkle with the remaining Parmesan cheese. Cook on the first or second set of runners in the Roasting Oven for 10–15 minutes or until the top is golden and crispy.

conventional cooking:

Pre-heat the oven to 180°C/350°F/gas 4 and cook as above.

stir-fried mushrooms

serves 4

2 tbsp peanut oil

500g mixed mushrooms, such as oyster, button and shiitake

2 spring onions, trimmed and finely sliced

2 cloves garlic, peeled and thinly sliced

1 tbsp soy sauce

2 tbsp oyster sauce

2 tbsp dry sherry

1 tsp sugar

salt and pepper

1 Heat the oil in a deep-sided frying pan or wok until it is smoking on the Boiling Plate or on the floor of the Roasting Oven.

2 Add the mushrooms to the pan, stirring all the time. Then add the spring onions and garlic. Stir, then toss in the rest of the ingredients and cook for 2–3 minutes. Serve straight away with rice or noodles.

conventional cooking:

Cook in a wok over a high heat on the hob.

roasted garlic

I sometimes squeeze a roasted garlic clove into a baked potato, seasoned with salt, pepper and a drizzle of olive oil.

per person:

1 head of garlic
olive oil

1 Peel away the top 2–3 layers of skin from each garlic head. Place each garlic head on a piece of foil, drizzle over the olive oil and wrap each head loosely in the foil. Place the wrapped garlic on a baking tray or in an ovenproof dish.

2 Bake the garlic in the Roasting Oven, on the third set of runners, for 20–30 minutes or until the garlic is soft and tender. For 4-oven Aga owners, the Baking Oven can also be used (bake for 45–60 minutes). Remove foil from the garlic heads and serve.

conventional cooking:

Pre-heat the oven to 220°C/425°F/gas 7 and roast the garlic for 1 hour.

roasted winter vegetables with rosemary and thyme

The method for roasting vegetables is the same for all vegetables except you may have to change the timings. For example, peppers take less time than root vegetables. If you wish, add garlic to the vegetables or any other herbs.

serves 6

6 baby carrots or small carrots cut into roughly the same size

3 potatoes, washed and cut into wedges (don't peel)

3 red onions or banana shallots, outside paper removed, cut through the root into quarters

½ a swede, peeled and cut into chunks

½ tbsp freshly chopped rosemary leaves

½ tbsp fresh thyme leaves

3–4 tbsp olive oil

a pinch of sugar

salt and pepper

1 Tip all the ingredients into a large bowl or plastic bag and toss really well so that all the vegetables are well coated in the oil and herbs.

2 Line the large roasting tin with Bake-O-Glide and tip in the coated vegetables. Slide the tin onto the first set of runners of the Simmering Oven and roast for 30 minutes.

3 Transfer the tin to the floor of the Roasting Oven for another 10 minutes or until the vegetables are tender and slightly charred.

conventional cooking:

Pre-heat the oven to 220°C/425°F/gas 7 and roast the vegetables for 40–45 minutes.

roasted garlic

lentils with pine nuts, lemon and mint

serves 4

500g Puy lentils

100g pine nuts, toasted

2 tbsp good olive oil

1 bunch fresh mint, chopped

zest and juice of 1 unwaxed lemon

salt and pepper

1 Put the lentils into a saucepan of cold water. Bring to the boil on the Boiling Plate and add salt. Cover and transfer the lentils to the floor of the Simmering Oven for 20 minutes – they should be tender but not mushy.

2 While they are cooking, toast the pine nuts in a dry frying pan on the Simmering Plate and set aside.

3 Drain the lentils and put them into a warmed bowl. Pour the olive oil over and add the chopped mint, lemon juice and zest and pine nuts and toss well. Check the seasoning and serve.

conventional cooking:

Cook the lentils on a hob as above.

baked parsnips with apples

serves 4

675g parsnips, peeled and cut into large chunks

1 large cooking apple

juice of 1 lemon

30g butter

1 tsp unrefined golden caster sugar

salt and pepper

1 Bring the parsnips to the boil in a pan of water on the Boiling Plate for 3 minutes. Drain off all the water, cover and transfer to the floor of the Simmering Oven for 20–25 minutes or until very soft.

2 While the parsnips are cooking, peel and thinly slice the apple. Toss it in the lemon juice to stop it turning brown.

3 When the parsnips are tender, mash them with the butter and season with salt and pepper. Spread half of the parsnip mash over the bottom of a buttered ovenproof gratin dish, then layer the apple slices on top of the parsnips. Repeat and arrange the remaining apple slices neatly on top. Sprinkle the caster sugar over.

4 Bake on the fourth set of runners in the Roasting Oven for 25–35 minutes or until the apples are golden. If the apples brown too much, slide in the Cold Plain Shelf. For 4-oven Aga owners, cook on the third set of runners in the Baking Oven for 40–45 minutes.

conventional cooking:

Cook the parsnips as above, then bake the dish in an oven pre-heated to 200°C/400°F/gas 6 for 30–35 minutes.

baked corn-on-the-cob

Corn cooked this way retains all of its sweetness and goodness. This Aga method is so easy that you will never boil corn again. Do use freshly picked ears if possible. The quantity of corn-on-the-cob you cook depends on the number of people you are feeding.

Place the grid shelf on the floor of the Roasting Oven. With the husks still on, put the ears of corn onto the grid shelf. Cook for about 20–25 minutes. You can stack the ears but they will take a little longer and they cook more evenly in a single layer. Serve with Roasted Garlic Butter (see below) and lots of napkins!

conventional cooking:
Bring a large pan of water up to the boil, add salt, drop in the corn ears (husk removed) and cook for about 15 minutes.

roasted garlic butter

serves 8

2 whole garlic heads, tops sliced off so that the raw cloves are exposed (do not separate the cloves)

2 tbsp good-quality olive oil

250g butter, at room temperature

salt and pepper

1 Lay out a large piece of foil, put the garlic heads on top and drizzle over the olive oil. Wrap the foil tightly around the garlic and place on a baking tray. Cook in the Roasting Oven for 20–30 minutes or until the garlic cloves are soft. When cooked, set aside to cool.

2 Put the butter, salt and pepper into a bowl. When the garlic is cool enough to handle, squeeze the cloves to release the pulp onto the butter and mash it together. Transfer to a serving bowl and chill, covered, in the fridge until you are ready to serve. This will keep for up to 2 days in the fridge.

conventional cooking:
Pre-heat the oven to 220ºC/425ºF/gas 7 and cook for 1 hour.

baked pumpkin with cream and gruyère cheese

**serves 6 as a starter or
4 as a main course**

1 medium pumpkin (about 2.5kg)

200g tin sweetcorn

500g Gruyère cheese

500ml double cream

freshly grated nutmeg

25g butter

200g pancetta, cubed

salt and pepper

1 Cut off the top of the pumpkin one-quarter of the way from the top. Scoop out the seeds and remove the stringy surrounding fibres. Place the pumpkin on a deep-sided baking tray.

2 Drain the sweetcorn and tip it into the pumpkin; season with salt and pepper. Add the cheese to the sweetcorn and pour over the cream. Season with more salt and pepper and a good grating of nutmeg. Throw in the butter and top with the lid.

3 Cover the whole pumpkin with foil and bake on the fourth set of runners in the Roasting Oven for 1½–2 hours, depending on the size of the pumpkin, or until tender.

4 Meanwhile, fry the pancetta cubes in olive oil in a frying pan on the Boiling Plate until crispy. Set aside.

5 Take the foil off the pumpkin for the last 15 minutes of cooking and test for doneness by removing the lid and inserting the point of a knife. It should be tender. Remove the lid and stir gently, taste for seasoning, then scatter over the crispy pancetta and replace the lid.

6 Take the pumpkin to the table and scoop the flesh and the creamy, cheesy goo into soup bowls. Serve piping hot with lots of crusty bread.

conventional cooking:
Pre-heat the oven to 200°C/400°F/gas 6 and bake the pumpkin for 2 hours or until tender. Cook the pancetta on the hob.

lemon and thyme potato gratin

serves 4–6

30g butter, plus more for greasing gratin dish

900g potatoes, peeled and thinly sliced

1½ tsp fresh thyme

finely grated zest of an unwaxed lemon

235ml full-fat milk

salt and pepper

1 Brush a gratin dish with some melted butter. Next layer the potatoes, herbs, lemon zest, salt and pepper in the dish until all the ingredients are used up, finishing off with some of the herbs, lemon zest and seasoning on the top. Pour over the milk.

2 Cook on the third set of runners in the Roasting Oven for 35–45 minutes or until the potato is tender and the top is nicely browned.

conventional cooking:
Pre-heat the oven to 200°C/400°F/gas 6 and cook for 40–45 minutes.

baked pumpkin with cream and gruyère cheese

pistachio and apricot stuffing

This can be made ahead and put into the fridge the day before. Bring to room temperature before cooking.

serves 12

2 tbsp olive oil

2 large onions, peeled and finely chopped

60g pistachio nuts, chopped

60g butter

120g ready-to-eat dried apricots

175g fresh white breadcrumbs

4 tbsp freshly chopped flat-leaf parsley

zest of 1 unwaxed lemon

1 free-range egg, beaten

1 Heat the oil in a frying pan and sweat the onions until very soft on the Roasting Oven floor. Add the pistachio nuts and fry on the Simmering Plate until golden.

2 Next, tip in the remaining ingredients and stir to combine. Shape into 12 balls and put into a buttered baking dish. Drizzle with a little more olive oil and bake on the third set of runners in the Roasting Oven for 30 minutes or until golden.

conventional cooking:

Pre-heat the oven to 180°C/350°F/gas 4 and cook for 45 minutes.

pine nut and raisin pilaf

A wonderfully aromatic rice dish, golden with saffron threads. The sweetness of the raisins combines perfectly with the crunch of the pine nuts.

serves 4

2 tbsp olive oil

½ an onion, peeled and chopped

225g basmati rice

50g raisins

50 saffron threads (please don't count, just guess!)

½ tsp salt

360ml water

50g pine nuts

1 large tomato, chopped

1 tbsp chopped fresh mint, plus whole leaves for garnish

1 Place the oil in a saucepan with a tight-fitting lid on the Simmering Plate. Add the onion and cook until softened. Add the rice, raisins, saffron and salt and stir to coat everything thoroughly in the oil and onion. Add the water and bring to the boil. Place the lid on the pan and transfer to the Simmering Oven for 20 minutes.

2 While the rice is cooking, put the pine nuts into a frying pan and dry fry them on the Simmering Plate until they are brown and golden. Set aside.

3 When the rice is done, fluff it up with a fork and place a clean tea towel over the pan to collect excess steam. Add the pine nuts, tomato and mint and serve with a few large mint leaves on top for a garnish.

conventional cooking:

Make this on the hob.

aga rice

This is the easiest method of cooking rice I know of and once you try it you won't cook rice any other way! It is entirely up to you whether you rinse the rice. As a general rule, use just under double the amount of liquid to rice. To make knockout rice, fry an onion in a little oil and butter until soft then add the rice, stirring well to coat every grain with the oil/butter. Pour in home-made stock (see page 28) and season with salt and pepper. Cook as below. When the rice is ready, stir in a generous knob of butter.

serves 4

235g rice
1 tsp salt

1 Put the rice, 370ml water and the salt into a large saucepan and bring it up to the boil on the Boiling Plate.
2 Stir it once, then cover with a lid and put it on the floor of the Simmering Oven for 18–20 minutes.
3 Remove it from the oven, take the lid off and fluff up with a fork and cover the pan with a clean tea towel to absorb some of the steam, then serve. Brown rice will take longer: 30–40 minutes.

conventional cooking:
Cook as usual on the hob.

aga polenta

serves 4

1 tsp sea salt
3 tbsp olive oil
120g quick-cook polenta
120g Parmesan cheese, finely grated

1 Bring a pan of 500ml water to the boil on the Boiling Plate and add the salt and olive oil. Next, pour in the polenta and stir well.
2 Transfer to the Simmering Plate and cook for about 1 minute, then put a lid on the pan and place on the floor of the Simmering Oven for 15–20 minutes or until the mixture is very thick and dense. Beat in the Parmesan. Spread out on a flat surface, such as a plate lined with Bake-O-Glide, and let it cool completely. All this can be done up to a day in advance.
3 When you are ready to grill the polenta, cut it into wedges and heat a grill pan on the floor of the Roasting Oven. When the pan is really hot brush a little olive oil over the polenta wedges, take the pan out of the oven, place on the Boiling Plate and grill each side for about 2–3 minutes until they are crispy and brown. Serve with Roasted Winter Vegetables (see page 161) and shavings of Parmesan.

conventional cooking:
Follow the instructions on the packet of polenta. Use a very hot grill pan to grill the polenta.

baked polenta with garlic and parmesan

serves 6

200g polenta

90g Parmesan cheese, grated

2 garlic cloves, peeled and crushed

60g butter, cubed

30g raclette cheese, grated

1 Make up the polenta following the manufacturer's instructions.

2 When it has cooked for the required time, beat in 60g of the Parmesan cheese. Spread the polenta out on to a shallow baking tray and let it cool and set.

3 Cut it into rounds with a cookie cutter and arrange slightly overlapping in a buttered ovenproof dish. Sprinkle over the garlic, the cubed butter and the remaining cheeses.

4 Bake on the third set of runners in the Roasting Oven for 20–25 minutes or until crisp and golden. For 4-oven Aga owners, bake on the third set of runners in the Baking Oven for 30 minutes.

5 Remove from the oven and cool on a wire rack.

conventional cooking:

Pre-heat the oven to 200ºC/400ºF/gas 6 and bake for 15–20 minutes.

cous cous

You can make the cous cous with plain water, carrot juice, tomato juice or stock. Be experimental!

serves 6

1 garlic clove, peeled and crushed

½ tsp cumin

½ tsp coriander

pinch of cinnamon

about 300ml chicken stock

225g cous cous

salt and pepper

1 Put all the ingredients except the cous cous into a saucepan and bring up to the boil on the Boiling Plate. Tip the cous cous into a shallow dish.

2 Remove the pan from the heat and pour over the cous cous. If you need to add a little water, do so – the cous cous should just be covered with the liquid. Leave for 20–25 minutes until the liquid has been absorbed.

3 Fork the cous cous through (it will be a little sticky) and serve. This is a wonderful base for salads or vegetables and can be served hot or cold.

conventional cooking:

Heat on the hob.

yorkshire pudding

serves 4

3 free-range eggs

175g plain flour

175ml milk

60g dripping

salt and pepper

1 Whisk the eggs, then sift in the flour and whisk. Slowly add the milk and 110ml water, whisking continuously. Season with salt and pepper. Set aside.

2 Put the dripping into the half-size roasting tin and heat it up in the Roasting Oven until it is smoking hot. Move the tin to the Simmering Plate and pour in the batter. Hang the tin on the third set of runners in the Roasting Oven and cook for 25–30 minutes or until it has risen and is golden brown. Serve either straight away or cook it earlier in the day and re-heat for 8 minutes in the Roasting Oven before serving.

conventional cooking:

The reason Yorkshire puddings made in the Aga are so good is due to the high heat. Pre-heat the oven to its highest temperature and cook as above.

bread sauce

serves 6–8

500ml milk

6 whole cloves

1 medium onion, peeled and finely chopped

150g stale white breadcrumbs, or more if needed

30ml thick double cream or crème fraîche

40g butter

salt and pepper

1 Put the milk, cloves, chopped onion, salt and pepper into a saucepan and simmer on the Simmering Plate for 15–20 minutes or until the onion is soft. Alternatively, bring to the boil on the Boiling Plate and transfer to the Simmering Oven for 20–30 minutes. Then take it off the heat and let it infuse for an hour or longer.

2 Just before serving, remove the cloves and sprinkle in the breadcrumbs. The breadcrumbs will swell after a while, but as you don't want a sauce that is too thick, don't be too quick to add more breadcrumbs. Stir in the cream and butter and pour into a warmed serving bowl. Serve with game, turkey and chicken.

conventional cooking:

Make the sauce on the hob. Infuse the milk off the heat and continue as above.

white sauce

The sauce can be made in advance and gently re-heated. It is so useful as it is the base for many other sauces. Add cheese for a cheese sauce, or onions softened in butter for an onion sauce, and almost any herbs can be used to make the sauce of your choice. If you are making béchamel sauce, infuse the milk with a chopped onion, parsley stalks and a blade of mace for about 10 minutes. Strain the milk and follow the recipe below.

makes 425ml

40g butter
20g plain flour
425ml milk, warmed
salt and pepper

1 Melt the butter in a small saucepan on the Simmering Plate. Add the flour to the butter and stir well with a wooden spoon until the mixture turns into a glossy paste.

2 Gradually pour in the warm milk, a little at a time, stirring or whisking all the time until all of the milk has been incorporated and you have a smooth, lump-free sauce.

3 Simmer the sauce on the Simmering Plate for 3–5 minutes, whisking occasionally, so that the flour is cooked. Do not let the sauce burn or catch on the bottom. Cover the surface of the sauce with cling film so a skin doesn't form.

conventional cooking:
Cook on the hob.

hollandaise sauce

For a mousseline of hollandaise, fold some whipped cream into the sauce before serving. For a Maltaise sauce, reduce the juice of one orange together with the zest by half and add this to the basic hollandaise recipe and serve. Alternatively, add 3 tablespoons of orange juice and ½ teaspoon of zest to the finished hollandaise sauce.

makes 350ml

2 large free-range egg yolks
juice of ½ a lemon
pinch of sugar
250g unsalted butter, cut into cubes
salt and white pepper

1 Place the egg yolks, lemon juice, sugar, salt and pepper in a bowl with 1 tablespoon of water over a pan of simmering water (don't let the base of the bowl come into contact with the water) and whisk until the mix leaves a ribbon trail.

2 Whisking constantly, drop in the cubes of butter one at a time. Don't drop in the next cube until the previous one has been absorbed. This will take some time. When all the butter is used and you have a thick velvety sauce, taste for seasoning and serve.

conventional cooking:
Cook on the hob.

pomegranate glaze for roast turkey

for a 5kg turkey

4 pomegranates
4 tbsp pomegranate molasses
(see page 298)
60ml brandy
1 tbsp redcurrant jelly

1 Cut two of the pomegranates in half and hold them cut side down over a bowl. Hit the back of the fruit very hard with a wooden spoon so the pips shower into the bowl. Set them aside.

2 Use a lemon juicer to squeeze out the juice from the remaining pomegranates. Put the pomegranate juice, pomegranate molasses, brandy and redcurrant jelly into a saucepan and heat to the boil on the Boiling Plate. Reduce the liquid so that it coats the back of a spoon.

3 Use your usual method of cooking the turkey. When there is only approximately 15 minutes left of cooking time for the turkey, remove it from the oven and baste the whole bird with the pomegranate glaze. Roast for 5 minutes. Baste the bird again and roast for a final 10 minutes. Do not allow the glaze to burn. Rest the turkey for at least 20 minutes and serve.

best-ever gravy

This is my method for making gravy and I always make lots of it so that we don't run out. It doesn't matter what you are roasting, the method is still the same. I use onions as a rack for the meat to sit on while it is roasting.

1 Cut two onions in half and rest the joint on top. When the joint is ready, remove it from the tin and let it rest, covered with foil, for 15–20 minutes. Spoon off any excess fat, leaving about 1–2 tablespoons in the tin along with the onions.

2 While the meat is resting, put the tin directly onto the Simmering Plate and bring the juices to a simmer. Add 1 tablespoon of flour to the fat, onions and meat juices and whisk it in. Keep whisking until the flour absorbs all of the fat, adding a little more flour if necessary.

3 Whisking constantly so that there are no lumps, pour in about 100ml of wine and 1 tablespoon of redcurrant jelly or any other fruit jelly (such as apple jelly with pork or mint jelly with lamb). Still whisking, pour in about 500ml of home-made stock (see page 28) or less for a thicker gravy or more for a thinner consistency. This is where the quality of the stock is paramount – if you use inferior stock you will end up with inferior gravy.

4 When all of the liquid has been added, bring the gravy to a rapid simmer and cook for about 5 minutes. Check for seasoning and add salt and pepper to taste. It is very important to cook out the wine and the flour. Strain the gravy into a warmed jug and keep hot at the back of the Aga or in the Simmering or Warming Oven.

9 desserts

pancakes

These can also be served for breakfast, if you wish.

serves 4

140g plain flour

1 tbsp unrefined golden caster sugar

1 tsp baking powder

½ tsp baking soda

a pinch of salt

1 large free-range egg

237ml buttermilk

30ml sunflower oil, plus extra for greasing

1 tsp vanilla extract

honey or maple syrup and butter, to serve

1 Put all of the ingredients into a bowl and mix really well with a whisk so there are no lumps.

2 Place a round piece of Bake-O-Glide on the Simmering Plate and grease with a little oil.

3 Cooking the pancakes in batches, drop a tablespoon of the pancake mix onto the hot surface and cook until it starts to bubble. Flip the pancake over and cook for 2 minutes or until puffed up. Serve straight away with honey or maple syrup and butter.

conventional cooking:

Heat a little of the oil in a frying pan over a medium heat, drop a tablespoon of the pancake batter in and cook in batches as above.

little lemon puddings

serves 6

100g unsalted butter, plus extra for greasing

175g unrefined golden caster sugar

zest of 1 lemon

2 free-range eggs, separated

40g plain flour (or rice flour which will give a slightly grainy texture)

400ml full-fat milk

juice of 2 lemons – about 2 tbsp

1 Cream the butter, sugar and zest together until pale and fluffy. Beat the yolks in one at a time, then fold in the flour and milk. Mix in the lemon juice.

2 In a clean bowl whisk the egg whites until stiff, then fold into the lemon batter (it will look very sloppy). Divide the mix between six buttered ramekins.

3 Put the ramekins in a roasting tin and bake for 20 minutes on the fourth set of runners in the Roasting Oven with the Cold Plain Shelf on the second set of runners, until puffed up and golden. Serve straight away with double cream. (You can also make one large pudding – cook as above in the Roasting Oven for 20 minutes, then transfer to the Simmering Oven for 1 hour.)

conventional cooking:

Pre-heat the oven to 180°C/350°F/gas 4 and cook as above for 20–25 minutes.

banana and cardamom tarte tatin

This dish is traditionally made with apples (see page 174) but you can use almost any fruit. However, very soft fruit is not suitable and fruits such as plums and apricots will take longer to caramelise because of their juices. Puff pastry is usually used, but the tart works just as well with home-made shortcrust. Use a tarte tatin dish. This dessert can be made up to the cooking part and kept refrigerated until you are ready to bake it, or indeed cook it early in the day and serve at room temperature.

serves 4–6

4–6 bananas, peeled and cut into 6cm pieces (I cut them on a slant)

135g unrefined golden caster sugar

6 cardamom pods, cracked open

60g unsalted butter, diced

150g good-quality bought puff pastry

FOR THE CARAMEL:

75g unrefined golden caster sugar

30g unsalted butter

1 star anise

1 First make the caramel. Place the sugar in the bottom of the tart tin and heat it on the Simmering Plate until it turns a dark caramel colour. Take great care not to burn it. Remove it from the heat and stir in the butter and the star anise. Let it cool for a few minutes, then remove and discard the star anise.

2 Arrange the banana pieces on the caramel, packing them in very tightly. Mix the sugar with the cardamom pods and sprinkle over the bananas, then dot the butter on top.

3 Roll out the pastry large enough to cover the tatin tin. Drape the pastry over the fruit and loosely tuck it in. There needs to be room for steam to escape so that the pastry doesn't go soggy.

4 Put the tart tin on the fourth set of runners in the Roasting Oven and bake for 25–35 minutes or until the tart is golden and the fruit is tender. If the pastry is browning too quickly, slide the Cold Plain Shelf on to the second set of runners. If the juices are not sufficiently caramelised, put the tart back on the floor of the Roasting Oven to bake for a few more minutes.

5 When it is ready, remove the tart from the oven and let it stand for 5–10 minutes. To turn it out, place a plate on top of the tart mould and invert. Serve with thick Greek yoghurt.

conventional cooking:

Make the caramel on the hob over a gentle heat. Pre-heat the oven to 200°C/400°F/gas 6 and bake the tart for 40–45 minutes.

tarte tatin

serves 8

10–12 Granny Smith apples, peeled, cored and cut into quarters

150g good-quality bought puff pastry

60g unsalted butter, diced

100g unrefined golden caster sugar

½ tsp cinnamon (optional)

pinch of cloves (optional)

FOR THE CARAMEL:

75g unrefined golden caster sugar

30g unsalted butter

1 First make the caramel. Place the golden caster sugar in the bottom of the tart tin and heat it on the Simmering Plate until it turns a dark caramel colour. Take great care not to burn it. Remove it from the heat and stir in the butter and let it cool for a few minutes.

2 Arrange the apple quarters on the caramel, packing them in very tightly. Mix the sugar with the spices and sprinkle over the apples, then dot the butter around.

3 Roll out the pastry large enough to cover the tin. Drape the pastry over the fruit and loosely tuck it in. There needs to be room for steam to escape so the pastry doesn't go soggy.

4 Put the tart on the floor of the Roasting Oven for 10 minutes, then move it to the fourth set of runners and bake for 30–40 minutes. If the pastry is browning too quickly, slide the Cold Plain Shelf onto the second set of runners. The tart should be golden, the fruit tender and the juices caramelised. If you think the juices are not sufficiently caramelised, put the tart back on the floor of the Roasting Oven for a few more minutes.

5 When the tart is ready, remove it from the oven and let it stand for 5–10 minutes before turning out. Place a plate on top of the tart tin and invert. Serve with lots of double cream or vanilla ice cream.

conventional cooking:

Make the caramel on a hob over a medium-high heat. Add the apples to the pan and cook for 10 minutes. Continue as above and cook the tart in an oven pre-heated to 200°C/400°F/gas 6 for 40–45 minutes or until the pastry is golden and cooked.

apple pie

serves 8

FOR THE PASTRY:

720g plain flour

240g unrefined golden caster sugar

pinch of salt

360g cold unsalted butter, cubed

3 free-range eggs, beaten (you may need 4 if the pastry is too dry)

FOR THE FILLING:

65g flour

½ tsp ground cinnamon

½ tsp ground cardamom

half a nutmeg, grated

60g unsalted butter, cold and cubed

60g unrefined golden caster sugar

1kg cooking apples, cored, peeled and chopped

1 free-range egg yolk, beaten

1 Sift the flour, sugar and salt into the food processor, then add the butter and process for 30 seconds. Add the eggs and process again until it forms a ball (you may have to add a little cool water 1 tablespoon at a time if the mixture is dry). Stop the food processor, wrap the pastry in cling film and rest in the fridge for a minimum of 30 minutes.

2 Line a 27-cm pie dish with the pastry and chill in the refrigerator for 30 minutes. Roll out the leftover pastry to make a lid.

3 Put the flour, spices, butter and sugar into the food processor and pulse until crumbly. Transfer to a bowl and add the apples. Tip the apple mix into the lined pie dish and roll the pastry lid on top, pinching the edges of the pie together with your fingers.

4 Brush with the egg yolk and bake the pie on the floor of the Roasting Oven with the Cold Plain Shelf on the fourth set of runners for 35–40 minutes or until the crust is golden.

conventional cooking:

Pre-heat the oven to 200ºC/400ºF/gas 6. Blind-bake the pastry-lined pie dish for 10–15 minutes, then fill and bake as above.

coconut rice pudding

serves 4–6

unsalted butter, for greasing

120g pudding rice

60g unrefined golden caster sugar

600ml milk

600ml coconut milk

1 Grease a large ovenproof dish with unsalted butter. Add all the ingredients to the ovenproof dish and stir well to combine.

2 Put the dish on the third set of runners in the Roasting Oven and bake for 20–25 minutes. For 4-oven Aga owners, bake in the Baking Oven for 25–30 minutes, or until a skin has formed and the pudding is starting to turn golden on top.

3 Take the pudding out and stir, then transfer the dish to the third set of runners in the Simmering Oven for 2½ hours or until the pudding is cooked.

conventional cooking:

Pre-heat the oven to 150°C/300°F/gas 2. Cook the pudding in the centre of the oven for 30 minutes. Stir, then continue cooking for 1½ hours.

open apple and pear pies

serves 4

FOR THE PASTRY:

360g plain flour

120g unrefined golden caster sugar

pinch of salt

180g cold unsalted butter, cubed

2 free-range eggs, beaten

FOR THE FILLING:

65g flour

½ tsp ground cinnamon

60g cold unsalted butter, cubed

60g unrefined golden caster sugar

750g cooking apples, cored, peeled and chopped

750g pears, cored, peeled and chopped

150g quince cheese, chopped into tiny pieces

1 free-range egg yolk, beaten

1 To make the pastry, sift the flour, sugar and salt into a food processor, then add the butter and process for 30 seconds. Add the eggs and process again until it forms a ball (you may have to add a little cool water 1 tablespoon at a time if the mixture is dry). Stop the food processor immediately, wrap the pastry in cling film and rest in the fridge for at least 30 minutes.

2 Put the flour, cinnamon, butter and sugar into the food processor and pulse until crumbly. Transfer to a bowl, add the fruit and quince cheese and toss together.

3 Roll out the dough into 4 medium-sized rounds and transfer to a baking sheet lined with Bake-O-Glide. Pile some of the filling on to each pastry round, leaving a 5cm border. Carefully fold the border over the fruit, pleating it to make a circle. Brush with the egg yolk.

4 Bake the open pies on the floor of the Roasting Oven with the Cold Plain Shelf on the fourth set of runners for 20–25 minutes or until the pastry crust is golden.

conventional cooking:

Pre-heat the oven to 200°C/400°F/gas 6 and bake as above.

open apple and pear pies

christmas pudding

To make your Christmas pudding in advance, cook it and then put it away to mature.

serves 8–10

75g butter, softened, plus extra for greasing

75g soft dark brown sugar

75g plain flour, sifted

½ a nutmeg, grated

½ tsp mixed spice

175g raisins

100g sultanas

50g currants

50g dried sour cherries

25g flaked almonds

1 cooking apple, peeled and grated

2 free-range eggs, beaten

zest of 1 orange

zest of 1 lemon plus the juice

2 tbsp black treacle

2 tbsp brandy

1 Grease a 1-litre pudding basin. Have ready greaseproof paper, foil and string.

2 Cream the butter and sugar together. Sift in the flour, then add all the remaining ingredients and mix well.

3 Fill the basin with the pudding mixture. Cover with greaseproof paper. Make a pleat in the foil to form a lid, cover the basin and secure with string for ease of handling.

4 Stand a trivet on the bottom of a large saucepan – if you have an Aga cake baker this would be ideal; if not, use a cheap steamer from a cookshop (they are usually stainless steel and fold out). Put the pudding on the trivet and pour water into the pan so that it comes halfway up the sides of the pudding basin. Cover the pan with a lid and bring to the boil on the Boiling Plate, then move to the Simmering Plate and simmer for 30 minutes. Then transfer to the Simmering Oven for 10–12 hours – it is easiest to cook this overnight as it won't come to any harm.

5 Remove from the Simmering Oven and cool. Remove the foil and seal it with fresh new foil to store.

6 To serve, you don't need to steam it again so wrap it in foil and put it at the back of the Simmering Oven to re-heat gently – a large pudding will take about 2½ hours. Serve with atholl brose (see page 179)

conventional cooking:
Steam on top of the stove for about 3½–4 hours.

Or you can microwave the pudding. Fill the basin with the pudding mixture, make a pleat in the greaseproof paper, cover the basin, secure with the string, and pierce the top. Do not use foil! Cook on full power for 10 minutes Leave to stand for another 10 minutes, then turn out and serve flaming!

If you want to make the pudding ahead of time, after turning out, cover loosely with cling film, and cool completely. Wrap in greaseproof and foil and store in an airtight container. To reheat, stand on a serving dish, cover with cling film, pierce the top and cook on full for 5 minutes.

christmas atholl brose

This goes really well with mince pies or Christmas pudding as an alternative to brandy butter.

serves 8–10

60g toasted oatmeal – do this ahead of time in a dry pan and leave to cool

300ml double cream

85ml whisky

2–3 tbsp honey, or to taste

1 Whip the cream to firm peaks – do not over-whip. Fold in the oatmeal, honey and whisky – they will soften the cream.

2 Spoon into a glass bowl and cover with cling film and rest for at least 1 hour before serving. (You can make this and freeze up to 1 week in advance.)

apple and almond pudding

serves 6

120g self-raising flour

100g sugar

1 tsp baking powder

100g ground almonds

2 free-range eggs

1 tsp almond extract

250g sour cream

3 sharp apples, such as Granny Smith, peeled and thinly sliced

FOR THE TOPPING:

30g sliced almonds

30g unrefined golden caster sugar

1 Butter the inside of the half-sized roasting tin or a tarte tatin dish or line with Bake-O-Glide.

2 Sift the flour, sugar and baking powder into a bowl, then mix in the ground almonds.

3 Lightly beat the eggs, almond extract and sour cream together and add to the dry ingredients. Do not over-mix.

4 Spoon half the batter over the bottom of the roasting tin, then top with half the apple slices. Spread over the rest of the batter and finish with the remaining apple slices. Scatter over the sliced almonds and caster sugar.

5 Slide the tin on to the fourth set of runners in the Roasting Oven and slide in the Cold Plain Shelf above. Bake for 20–25 minutes, checking halfway through baking and turning the tin. It should be golden and springy to the touch. For 4-oven Aga owners, bake on the third set of runners in the Baking Oven for 35–40 minutes or until a cake tester comes out clean.

6 Cool on a wire rack for 10 minutes. Serve with custard.

conventional cooking:

Pre-heat the oven to 190°C/375°F/gas 5 and bake for 35–40 minutes.

panettone pudding

serves 6

255ml milk

255ml double cream

1 vanilla pod, split

25g unrefined golden caster sugar

4 free-range egg yolks

butter, for greasing dish

500g panettone loaf, cut into 1-cm thick slices and then into triangles

200ml mascarpone cheese

1 tsp vanilla extract

1 tbsp icing sugar

1 Put the milk, cream, vanilla pod and caster sugar into a saucepan and heat to just a simmer on the Simmering Plate.

2 Beat the egg yolks in a large bowl, then whisk in the warm milk vigorously so that the eggs do not curdle. Set aside.

3 Butter a baking dish and cover the bottom with half the panettone slices. Pour over half of the custard, then add the rest of the panettone and the remaining custard. Cover the dish with cling film and gently press down to soak the bread thoroughly. Set aside for 20 minutes.

4 Remove the cling film, place the baking dish in another larger roasting tin and pour in hot water to come halfway up the sides of the baking dish. Slide the tin onto the fourth set of runners in the Roasting Oven and bake for 20 minutes until just set.

5 Beat the mascarpone cheese with the vanilla extract and icing sugar. If it is too stiff, add a little milk to loosen. Remove the pudding from the oven and serve warm with the sweetened mascarpone.

conventional cooking:
Pre-heat the oven to 200°C/400°F/gas 6. Put the pudding dish in a large roasting tin and pour boiling water into the tin to come halfway up the sides of the dish and bake for 20 minutes.

panattone pudding

chocolate brioche pudding

serves 6

255ml milk

255ml double cream

1 vanilla pod, split

25g unrefined golden caster sugar

200g dark chocolate, broken into small pieces

4 free-range egg yolks

½ tsp cornflour

1 brioche loaf, cut into 1-cm thick slices, then into triangles

1 Put the milk, cream, vanilla pod and sugar into a saucepan on the Simmering Plate and heat to just a simmer. Take off the heat and add the chocolate so that it melts, stirring occasionally.

2 In a large bowl, beat the egg yolks with the cornflour. When all the chocolate has melted, whisk the chocolate custard into the egg yolks vigorously so that the eggs do not curdle. Set aside.

3 Cover the base of a ceramic baking dish with the brioche. (You may wish to grease the dish with unsalted butter, but it is not essential.) Pour over half the custard, then add the rest of the brioche and pour over the remaining custard. Cover the dish with cling film and gently press down to soak the bread thoroughly in the custard. Set aside for 20 minutes.

4 Remove the cling film, place the dish inside a larger roasting tin and pour in enough hot water to come halfway up the sides of the baking dish. Slide the tin onto the fourth set of runners in the Roasting Oven and bake for 20–25 minutes until just set. Remove from the oven and serve warm with crème fraîche.

conventional cooking:

Pre-heat the oven to 200ºC/400ºF/gas 6. Remove the cling film and place the baking dish into a larger roasting tin and pour in enough hot water to come halfway up the sides of the baking dish. Bake for about 20 minutes or until just set.

orange pudding

You will need either an electric mixer or very strong arms for this recipe!

serves 6

100g unsalted butter, at room temperature

180g unrefined golden caster sugar

4 large free-range eggs, separated

40g plain flour

400ml milk

juice of 1 lemon

juice of 2 large oranges

zest of 2 unwaxed oranges

1 Cream the butter and sugar together until they are light and fluffy. With the machine still running, add one egg yolk at a time, followed by the flour and milk, then the juices and zest. The batter should be light and cake-like.

2 In a clean bowl, whisk the egg whites to the stiff peak stage and fold in the batter. Pour the mix into a large, lightly greased pudding basin.

3 Set the basin on the trivet in the cake baker. (If you do not have a cake baker, use a deep-sided saucepan large enough to take the pudding basin.) Pour in enough boiling water to come halfway up the side of the basin and bring the whole thing to the boil on the Boiling Plate. Transfer it to the floor of the Simmering Oven for 2 hours or until it is spongy, puffed up and golden on top.

4 Serve the pudding in bowls, making sure everyone gets some of the juices at the bottom, and with lots of thick double cream.

conventional cooking:

Steam on the hob over a low heat so that the surrounding water is at a gentle simmer. Check the water from time to time and top up with boiling water if necessary.

lemon meringue pie

For a deeper filling and meringue topping, simply double the ingredients.

serves 6

1 small quantity sweet pastry (see page 195)

FOR THE MERINGUE:

3 free-range egg whites

175g unrefined golden caster sugar

FOR THE FILLING:

45g cornflour

75g unrefined golden caster sugar

237ml water

zest and juice of 3 large organic lemons

3 large free-range egg yolks

1 Roll out the pastry. Line a 20.5-cm pie tin with it and prick the bottom with a fork. Place the pie tin on the floor of the Roasting Oven and slide the Cold Plain Shelf onto the third set of runners. Bake the pie crust for 8–10 minutes or until it is cooked and golden. Remove from the oven and cool a little.

2 Slide the Plain Shelf into the Simmering Oven on the fourth set of runners.

3 Make the filling. Mix the cornflour and sugar together in a small bowl. Add 2 tablespoons of the water and mix to a smooth paste.

4 Bring the remaining water to the boil in a saucepan on the Boiling Plate. Transfer the saucepan to the Simmering Plate and, whisking all the time, pour in the cornflour paste and then add the lemon zest and juice. Whisk until the mix starts to thicken – it needs to have the consistency of thick custard. Remove it from the heat and, still whisking, add the egg yolks one at a time. Pour the filling into the pie crust and set aside.

5 Make the meringue. Whisk the egg whites in a clean bowl with an electric whisk, adding the sugar 1 tablespoon at a time, until they are at the stiff peak stage. Spread the meringue over the filling.

6 Place the pie on the Plain Shelf in the Simmering Oven and bake for 40–45 minutes, until the meringue is set and slightly coloured. Cool the pie and serve.

conventional cooking:

Pre-heat the oven to 190°C/375°F/gas 5 and blind-bake the pastry case for 20 minutes or until cooked. Lower the temperature to 150°C/300°F/gas 2 and bake the filled pastry case for 40–45 minutes.

soft fruit soufflé

People think soufflés are really difficult but in fact most of the work can be done a few days in advance, leaving only the egg whites to be whisked! Do not use this method with citrus fruits. A spicy apple and cinnamon purée also works well. Fruit chunks can be added to the bottom of the mould before filling, if you wish.

serves 4

FOR THE FRUIT BASE:

350g soft fruit, such as raspberries or strawberries

75g unrefined golden caster sugar

25g cornflour

1 free-range egg yolk

FOR THE MERINGUE:

6 free-range egg whites

40g unrefined golden caster sugar

2 tbsp unsalted butter, for greasing moulds

4 tbsp unrefined golden caster sugar, for dusting moulds

1 To make the fruit base, put the fruit and 75g caster sugar into a saucepan with 50ml water and bring to the boil on the Boiling Plate. Continue to boil for 2 minutes. Take off the heat and liquidise, strain and then put it back into a saucepan. If you use bought fruit purée, measure out 360g.

2 Mix the cornflour with 3 tablespoons of water in a bowl to make a thin paste.

3 Put the pan with the fruit base on the Simmering Plate. Start whisking the fruit purée and add the cornflour paste little by little, whisking continuously until the mixture thickens. Take off the heat, and, still whisking, add the egg yolk. The consistency should be that of clotted cream. Set aside until ready to use. (Up to this point, the whole process can be made in advance and stored in the fridge for up to 3 days. When you take it out of the fridge, gently warm the fruit mixture through so that it comes back to the clotted cream consistency.)

4 Grease 4 china ramekins very generously with unsalted butter, paying particular attention to the lip of the moulds. Sprinkle a tablespoon of caster sugar into the moulds and swirl it round to lightly dust the inside, making sure the moulds are well coated. Set on a baking sheet ready to fill.

5 In a mixer with a scrupulously clean bowl, whisk the egg whites until stiff. Add the 40g caster sugar spoonful by spoonful until it is all used up. Fold a large dollop of the meringue into the fruit purée to loosen the mix. Gently fold in the rest of the egg whites until thoroughly blended and there are no pockets of white showing.

6 Fill the prepared moulds to the top with the soufflé mixture and run a clean finger around the lip to form a neat edge. Transfer the soufflés back to the baking sheet and slide the baking tray onto the fourth set of runners in the Roasting Oven and bake for 5–7 minutes. Serve directly from the oven.

conventional cooking:
Pre-heat the oven to 180°C/350°F/gas 4 and cook for 8 minutes.

raspberry soufflés

serves 4

FOR THE FRUIT BASE:

350g raspberries

75g unrefined golden caster sugar

50ml water

FOR THE CREME PATISSIERE:

25g cornflour

3 tbsp water

1 free-range egg yolk

FOR THE MERINGUE:

6 free-range egg whites

40g unrefined golden caster sugar

2 tbsp unsalted butter, for greasing (you won't use all of it)

3 tbsp unrefined golden caster sugar, for coating (again, you won't use all of it)

1 To make the fruit base, put all the ingredients into a saucepan and bring to the boil on the Boiling Plate. Continue to boil for 2 minutes. Take off the heat, liquidise, strain and then put back into a saucepan.

2 Mix the cornflour and water together in a bowl to make a thin paste.

3 Start whisking the fruit purée on the Simmering Plate and add the cornflour paste little by little, whisking continuously until the mixture thickens.

4 Take off the heat, and, still whisking, add the egg yolk. The consistency should be that of clotted cream. Set aside until ready to use. (Up to this point, the whole process can be made in advance and stored in the fridge for up to 3 days. When you take it out of the fridge, gently warm the fruit mixture so that it comes back to clotted cream consistency.)

5 Grease 4 china ramekins generously with unsalted butter, paying particular attention to the lips of the moulds. Sprinkle a tablespoon of caster sugar into the moulds and swirl it round to dust the inside lightly, making sure the moulds are well coated. Set on a baking sheet ready to fill.

6 To make the meringue, whisk the egg whites in a mixer, with a scrupulously clean bowl, until stiff. Add the sugar spoonful by spoonful until it is all used up.

7 Fold a large dollop of the meringue into the fruit purée and fold well to loosen the mix. Gently fold in the rest of the meringue until thoroughly blended and with no pockets of 'white' showing.

8 Fill the prepared moulds with the soufflé mixture to the top, then run a clean finger round the lip to form a neat edge. Transfer the soufflés back to the baking sheet, put on the fourth set of runners in the Roasting Oven and cook for 8 minutes. Serve directly from the oven.

conventional cooking:

Pre-heat the oven to 180°C/350°F/gas 4 and cook for 8 minutes.

raspberry soufflés

poached pears with coffee

serves 6

**1 litre freshly brewed medium
strength coffee (or stronger if
you prefer)**

90g demerara sugar

**1 large cinnamon stick, broken
in half**

**6 firm pears, peeled with stems
intact**

double cream, to serve

1 Put the coffee, sugar and cinnamon stick into a large saucepan. Bring up
to the boil on the Boiling Plate and stir until all the sugar dissolves.

2 Place the pears into the boiling liquid and simmer in the Simmering Oven
for 40–45 minutes or until they are tender.

3 Remove the pan from the heat and cool the pears in the liquid, turning
them from time to time so they are evenly coloured.

4 Transfer the pears to a large dish. Sieve the coffee liquid into a clean
saucepan and bring back to the boil, then simmer to reduce until syrupy.
Pour the coffee over the pears and set aside to cool.

5 When ready to serve, place pears in individual bowls, pour over the coffee
syrup and serve with thick cream.

conventional cooking:

Poach the pears on the hob over a medium heat.

poached apricots and figs with honey
and cinnamon

serves 4–6

350g dried apricots

350g dried figs

1 cinnamon stick

2 tbsp honey

1 Place the apricots and figs in an ovenproof saucepan; add the cinnamon
stick and honey. Add just enough water to cover the fruit and cover with a
lid.

2 Place on the Boiling Plate and bring to the boil. Transfer to the Simmering
Oven for 2–3 hours or until soft and plump. Serve hot or cold with yoghurt.

conventional cooking:

Pre-heat the oven to 150°C/300°F/gas 2. Bring the fruit to the boil, then
transfer to the oven and cook for 1–2 hours or until soft and plump.

poached pears with coffee

banana, peach and rum crumble

I make no apologies for the tinned peaches! This recipe makes a lot of crumble mix. If you do not use all of the topping, freeze it for another time.

serves 6–8

FOR THE FILLING:
6–8 ripe bananas, peeled
450g tin peaches in syrup
35ml rum

FOR THE CRUMBLE TOPPING:
350g plain flour
235g butter
118g brown sugar, plus a little more for the final topping

1 Butter an ovenproof dish. Slice the bananas and arrange at the bottom of the dish. Drain the peaches, reserving about 2 tablespoons of the syrup, and put them in with the bananas. Pour over the rum and the reserved syrup and set aside.

2 In a roomy bowl, sift in the flour and rub in the butter. When the mix resembles coarse breadcrumbs, mix in the sugar. Spoon the crumble topping over the fruit and sprinkle over some more brown sugar.

3 Put the dish into an Aga roasting tin and hang the tin on the fourth set of runners in the Roasting Oven and cook for 20–25 minutes, then transfer to the second set of runners in the Simmering Oven and cook for a further 20–25 minutes or until the fruit is tender and the topping is cooked. For 4-oven Aga owners, use the third set of runners in the Baking Oven and cook for 35–45 minutes. Serve the crumble with lots of thick double cream.

conventional cooking:
Pre-heat the oven to 180°C/350°F/gas 4 and bake for 30–40 minutes.

chocolate pear crumble

serves 6

100g butter, chilled, plus a little extra for greasing

6 ripe pears

1 tsp ground ginger

80g plain flour

60g ground almonds

100g unrefined golden caster sugar

3 tbsp cocoa powder

75g dark chocolate, chilled

1 Lightly grease a deep, medium-sized ovenproof dish with butter. Peel, quarter and core the pears. Cut into chunks and put into the dish. Sprinkle over the ginger.

2 In a food processor, whiz the flour, ground almonds, sugar and cocoa powder until blended. Cut the chilled butter into small pieces, add to the bowl and pulse-process until it is mixed in and crumbly.

3 Coarsely grate the chilled chocolate, add to the processor and give it another quick whiz. Spread the crumble evenly over the pears.

4 Put the dish into an Aga roasting tin and hang the tin on the fourth set of runners in the Roasting Oven. Cook for 20–25 minutes, then transfer to the Simmering Oven and cook for a further 20–25 minutes or until the fruit is tender and the topping is cooked. For 4-oven Aga owners, cook on the third set of runners in the Baking Oven for 35–45 minutes. Serve with vanilla ice cream.

conventional cooking:

Pre-heat the oven to 180°C/350°F/gas 4 and bake for 25 minutes until golden brown.

chocolate mousse

This is the easiest chocolate mousse in the world.

serves 6–8

200g good-quality dark chocolate

1 shot espresso coffee

6 large, organic, free-range eggs, separated

1 Put the chocolate and coffee into a glass bowl and melt in the Simmering Oven or over a saucepan of gently simmering water. Stir well and remove from the heat as soon as the chocolate has melted. Stir the melted chocolate into the egg yolks.

2 Using a scrupulously clean bowl and whisk, whisk the egg whites until they form soft peaks.

3 Fold a good spoonful of the whites into the chocolate, then gently fold in the rest, making sure you don't have any white pockets. Pour into a glass bowl and cover with cling film. Chill for at least 6 hours or overnight. Serve with lightly whipped sweetened double cream.

conventional cooking:

Melt the chocolate with the coffee over a pan of water on the hob.

plum crumble tart

serves 6–8

1 small quantity sweet pastry (see page 195)

4–6 plums, stoned and cut into wedges

FOR THE CRUMBLE TOPPING:

55g plain flour

30g malt flour

160g vanilla sugar

100g unsalted butter, cut into pieces

½ tsp ground cloves or cinnamon

85g chopped hazelnuts

FOR THE HAZELNUT FILLING:

58g unsalted butter, softened

58g icing sugar

58g ground hazelnuts

1 free-range egg

1 tbsp double cream

1 Line a 20.5-cm tart tin with the pastry and chill in the fridge.

2 To make the crumble topping, put the flours, sugar and butter into a large bowl and rub together so that they resemble coarse breadcrumbs. Mix in the spice and nuts.

3 To make the hazelnut filling, beat all the ingredients together in a bowl until thick. Spread over the bottom of the pastry and top with the plums. Scatter the crumble topping over the plums.

4 Place the tart on the floor of the Roasting Oven for 30–35 minutes. Check the tart after 20 minutes; you may need to slide in the Cold Plain Shelf if the top is browning too quickly. The tart should be golden brown and the pastry cooked (there is nothing more off-putting than underdone pastry!). Serve warm with clotted cream or ice cream.

conventional cooking:

Pre-heat the oven to 190ºC/375ºF/gas 5. Blind-bake the pastry for 10 minutes. Add the filling and bake in the middle of the oven for 40 minutes or until done.

plum crumble tart

pumpkin pie

serves 6–8

1 small quantity sweet pastry
(see page 195)

3 eggs, beaten

425g pumpkin purée

175g light brown sugar

½ tsp salt

½ tsp cinnamon

½ tsp ground ginger

½ tsp ground cloves

good grating of nutmeg (about ½ tsp)

275ml evaporated milk

1 Line a 27-cm tart tin with the pastry.

2 Whisk all the remaining ingredients together and pour into the prepared tart tin.

3 Place the pie on the floor of the Roasting Oven and slide the Cold Plain Shelf onto the third set of runners. Bake for 35–40 minutes, turning the pie around after 20 minutes. The pie is cooked when a skewer inserted in the middle comes out clean.

4 Cool on a wire rack and serve with whipped cream.

conventional cooking:

Pre-heat the oven to 220°C/425°F/gas 7. Blind-bake the pastry case for 10–15 minutes before filling and baking for a further 40–45 minutes.

coconut cream pie

serves 6

1 small quantity sweet pastry
(see page 195)

FOR THE FILLING:

3 free-range eggs

135g unrefined golden caster sugar

60ml double cream

200g desiccated coconut

1 Line a 27-cm pie dish with pastry and chill in the fridge.

2 To make the filling, beat the eggs with the sugar and add the cream, then the coconut. Spoon it into the lined pie dish.

3 Place the pie on the floor of the Roasting Oven and slide in the Cold Plain Shelf on the fourth set of runners. Bake the pie for 25–30 minutes. Cool on a wire rack. This is good served with a warm chocolate sauce.

conventional cooking:

Pre-heat the oven to 190°C/375°F/gas 5 and blind-bake the pastry for 10–15 minutes. Fill the tart and continue to bake for 30–40 minutes.

sweet pastry

TO LINE ONE 20.5 CM TART TIN:

75g icing sugar

2 free-range egg yolks

120g unsalted butter, at room temperature

½ tsp baking powder

pinch of salt

250g plain flour

2 tbsp cold water

TO LINE TWO 20.5 CM TART TINS:

172g icing sugar

4 free-range egg yolks

256g unsalted butter, at room temperature

1 tsp baking powder

pinch of salt

520g plain flour

4 tbsp cold water

1 Mix together the sugar, egg yolks, butter, baking powder and salt in a large bowl. Sift the flour on to the buttery mix and rub it together until it is sandy in texture.

2 Add the water and quickly press it into a soft dough. I usually tip it on to a clean surface to mix together. Wrap the dough in cling film and refrigerate overnight or freeze.

christmas pudding snow drift

serves 4–6

400g Christmas pudding, crumbled

50ml brandy

1 litre vanilla ice cream, softened

1 lemon

4 free-range egg whites

225g unrefined golden caster sugar

1 Put the Christmas pudding in a bowl and pour over the brandy. Let it stand for 30–60 minutes.

2 Beat the Christmas pudding into the softened ice cream so that it is evenly distributed. Mould the mixture into a dome shape on a metal baking tray and re-freeze so that it is extremely hard.

3 Make sure your bowl and whisk are scrupulously clean by rubbing a lemon half over the whisk and the inside of the bowl. Put the egg whites into the bowl and start to whisk the egg whites on a medium speed, increasing the speed to high as you go. First the whites will bubble and turn frothy, then they will form into soft floppy peaks and finally they will firm up to the stiff peak stage. Add the sugar one spoonful at a time.

4 Take the ice cream out of the freezer and spread the meringue mix over it. Slide the tray onto the fourth set of runners in the Roasting Oven. Bake for 8–10 minutes or until the meringue is golden. Serve immediately.

conventional cooking:

Pre-heat the oven to 200°C/400°F/gas 6 and cook for 8–10 minutes. Serve directly from the oven.

bitter orange marmalade tart

serves 6

1 quantity sweet pastry (see page 195)

58g unsalted butter, softened

58g icing sugar

58g ground almonds

1 free-range egg

1 tbsp double cream

300–350g jar bitter orange marmalade

60g sliced almonds

1 Line a 20.5-cm tart tin with the pastry.

2 Combine the butter, sugar, ground almonds, egg and cream in a bowl to make a thick paste.

3 Spread the marmalade over the bottom of the pastry (you may not need all of it, depending on the size of the tart case). Pour the cream mixture over the marmalade case and scatter over the sliced almonds.

4 Bake the tart on the floor of the Roasting Oven for 20 minutes until puffed up and golden. Check after 10 minutes and slide in the Cold Plain Shelf on the last set of runners if the top of the tart is browning too quickly.

conventional cooking:

Pre-heat the oven to 190ºC/375ºF/gas 5 and blind-bake the lined pastry in the tart tin for 15 minutes. Cool a little and proceed as above, baking the filled tart at the same temperature for 20 minutes.

rhubarb and orange blossom water clafoutis

serves 8

600g rhubarb, cut into 2–3cm pieces

250g unrefined golden caster sugar

zest of 1 unwaxed lemon

1 tbsp orange blossom water

5 free-range eggs, whisked

1 free-range egg yolk

200ml milk

200ml double cream

1 tsp rosewater

75g plain flour

1 Place the rhubarb, 150g of the sugar, the zest and orange blossom water in a saucepan and gently heat on the Simmering Plate to dissolve the sugar. Simmer for 2–3 minutes or until the rhubarb is tender. Strain the fruit and reserve the cooking liquor.

2 Whisk the eggs, the extra yolk, the remaining sugar, the milk, cream and rosewater together until smooth, then sift in the flour and whisk again until lump-free.

3 Place the rhubarb in a large, shallow, buttered oven-proof dish or individual buttered ramekins and pour over the batter. Place the dish or ramekins on a baking tray on the third set of runners in the Roasting Oven for 15–20 minutes or until puffed up and golden on top.

4 Meanwhile, bring the reserved juices to the boil on the Boiling Plate and reduce until they are syrupy. Serve the clafoutis with clotted cream and the reduced juices.

conventional cooking:

Pre-heat the oven to 190ºC/375ºF/gas 5 and bake for 20 minutes as above.

rhubarb and orange blossom water clafoutis

rhubarb tart

serves 6

1 small quantity sweet pastry (see page 195)

500ml water

30g unrefined golden caster sugar

1 vanilla pod, split and seeds scraped out

4–6 sticks of rhubarb, cut into 4cm chunks

60g unsalted butter, softened

60g icing sugar

60g ground almonds

1 free-range egg

15ml double cream

1 Line a deep 20.5-cm tart tin with the pastry and chill in the fridge.

2 Put the water, caster sugar and the vanilla seeds scraped from the pod into a saucepan and bring to the boil on the Simmering Plate. Add the rhubarb pieces and poach for about 1–2 minutes, or until tender but not too soft. When cooked, remove from the pan with a slotted spoon and set aside. Do not discard the poaching liquor.

3 Combine the butter, icing sugar, almonds, egg and cream in a bowl and whisk with an electric hand whisk to form a thick paste. Pour the mixture into the pastry case and top with the rhubarb.

4 Place the tart on the floor of the Roasting Oven and cook for 20 minutes until puffed up and golden. Check after 10 minutes and use the Cold Plain Shelf on the last set of runners if the tart is browning too quickly.

5 While the tart is baking, bring the poaching liquor to the boil and simmer until it has reduced by half. Pour the juices into a jug and reserve.

6 Remove the tart from the oven and cool on a wire rack. Serve at room temperature with crème fraîche and the reduced poaching juices.

conventional cooking:

Pre-heat the oven to 190°C/250°F/gas 4 and blind-bake the pastry cake for 10–15 minutes, then add the filling and bake for 30 minutes. Reduce the juices on the hob.

roasted plums with nutty flapjack topping

serves 6

750g ripe plums, halved and stoned

75g unsalted butter, plus extra for greasing dish

75g runny honey

60g rolled oats

50g hazelnuts, roasted and chopped

25g brown sugar

1 Place the plum halves in a shallow, buttered ovenproof dish.

2 Melt the butter and honey in a pan on the Simmering Plate, then mix in the oats and nuts. Scatter the flapjack mix over the plums and sprinkle over the sugar.

3 Bake on the third set of runners in the Roasting Oven for 15–20 minutes, then transfer to the third set of runners in the Simmering Oven for another 25–30 minutes. For 4-oven aga owners, bake in the Baking Oven for 35–40 minutes. Serve with lots of whipped double cream and more brown sugar.

conventional cooking:

Pre-heat the oven to 180°C/350°F/gas 4 and cook for 35–40 minutes.

oven-roasted fruit

serves 6

12 ripe nectarines, plums, peaches and/or apricots, cut in half and stone removed

60g unsalted butter, cut into cubes

brown sugar or honey

1 vanilla pod, split in half

Amaretto liqueur or brandy

12–15 soft amaretti biscuits

275ml double cream

½ tbsp icing sugar

dark chocolate

1 Arrange the fruit in an ovenproof dish, cut side up, and drop a cube of butter in each indentation. Sprinkle brown sugar or drizzle honey over and spoon over some Amaretto. Add the vanilla pod to the dish.

2 Bake the fruit in the Roasting Oven for 25–30 minutes or until they are soft and tender. Remove from the oven and leave to cool.

3 Crush the amaretti biscuits and divide them between six bowls and spoon over a little more Amaretto. Whip the cream with the icing sugar – you can add more sugar if you prefer it sweeter.

4 Arrange the baked fruit on the biscuits and top with the sweetened cream. Shave over some dark chocolate and serve.

conventional cooking:

Pre-heat the oven to 200ºC/400ºF/gas 6 and cook as above.

damsons in distress

This needs to be made 2 months before serving!

serves 4

500g ripe organic damsons

220g unrefined golden caster sugar

125ml port, plus more for topping up

100ml water

1 Wash and dry the damsons and discard any bruised or mouldy ones.

2 Put the sugar, port and water into a saucepan and bring to the boil on the Boiling Plate for 2–3 minutes. Add the fruit to the syrup, return to the boil and cook for 5–7 minutes.

3 Pack the fruit into sterilised wide-mouthed jars using a slotted spoon and pour in the hot stock syrup so that the jar is half-full. Top up with more port to fill the jars within 3cm of the top. Seal and store in a dark place for a minimum of 2 months – don't be tempted to eat them earlier!

conventional cooking:

Cook on the hob.

stuffed peaches

serves 6

120g good quality dark chocolate, broken into small pieces

12 very ripe small peaches or 6 large ones, halved and stoned

118g mascarpone cheese

40ml honey

60g slivered almonds (as fresh as possible)

30ml Amaretto liqueur

1 To melt the chocolate, place in a heatproof bowl on the grid shelf on the floor of the Simmering Oven.

2 Arrange the peaches on a baking tray (slice a little off the bottom to make them sit better if they are very wobbly).

3 Mix together the mascarpone, honey, nuts and Amaretto in a bowl. Spoon some of the mix into each peach cavity.

4 Bake on the third set of runners in the Roasting Oven for 10–12 minutes.

5 Remove the bowl of chocolate from the oven and leave at the back of the Aga until needed. Stir it well, making sure all the chocolate has melted.

6 Serve each person with two peach halves, or four if you used small peaches, and drizzle over the melted chocolate.

conventional cooking:

Pre-heat the oven to 200ºC/400ºF/gas 6 and continue as above.

baked bananas

serves 4–6

8 bananas, peeled and sliced lengthways in half

3 tbsp brown sugar

juice and zest of ½ an unwaxed lemon

30ml Malibu

double cream, to serve

1 Lay the bananas in a shallow ovenproof dish and sprinkle over the sugar, zest, juice and 3 tablespoons of water.

2 Bake in the Roasting oven for 15 minutes, then pour over the Malibu and transfer to the Simmering Oven for 25–30 minutes or until the bananas are brown and the juice is syrupy. For 4-oven Aga owners, bake the entire recipe in the Baking Oven, timings as above. Serve with lots of double cream.

conventional cooking:

Pre-heat the oven to 200ºC/400ºF/gas 6 and bake the bananas for 15 minutes, then pour in the Malibu, lower the temperature to 180ºC/350ºF/ gas 4 and bake for a further 20 minutes.

stuffed peaches

glazed passionfruit tart

serves 6

225g unrefined golden caster sugar

5 free-range eggs

2 free-range egg yolks

170ml passionfruit juice (sieve fresh passionfruits to give the required amount), plus more for garnishing

160ml whipping cream

deep 23-cm tart tin lined with sweet pastry (see page 195) and blind-baked until golden

icing sugar, for glazing

1 Put the caster sugar, eggs, egg yolks, passionfruit juice and cream into a bowl, place it over a pan of simmering water on the Simmering Plate and cook until the mixture reaches 80°C on a thermometer (or, if you don't have a thermometer, until the mixture coats the back of a wooden spoon; the main thing to avoid is the mix boiling as it will split and be unusable).

2 Pour it into the baked pastry case. Put the tart on a baking dish so taking it in and out of the oven will be easy.

3 Cook the tart on the third set of runners in the Simmering Oven for 10–12 minutes. It should still have a little bit of a wobble so don't overcook it.

4 Leave to cool completely, then cut into required portions and dust with the icing sugar and glaze with a blowtorch. Slice open a passionfruit and dribble the juice – pips and all – around each slice of tart.

conventional cooking:

Pre-heat the oven to 120°C/250°F/gas ½ and bake for 10–15 minutes.

christmas tart

serves 6

1 small quantity sweet pastry (see page 195)

FOR THE FILLING:

120g unsalted butter

120g icing sugar

2 large free-range eggs

2 tbsp double cream

120g ground almonds

1 tsp pure almond extract

230g mincemeat (see page 298)

60g flaked almonds

1 Line a 23-cm loose-bottomed tart tin with sweet pastry and chill in the fridge for 30 minutes.

2 Cream the butter and sugar together in a bowl, then add the eggs and cream and mix well. Fold in the ground almonds and almond extract.

3 Spread a thin layer of mincemeat over the base of the pastry and spoon the almond mix on top. Scatter over the flaked almonds.

4 Bake the tart on the floor of the Roasting Oven for 25 minutes or until firm in the centre and golden on top. Slide the Cold Plain Shelf onto the third set of runners after 10 minutes if browning too quickly.

conventional cooking:

Pre-heat the oven to 190°C/275°F/gas 5 and blind-bake the pastry case for 10–15 minutes. Leave to cool, then add the filling and bake at 190°C/275°F/gas 5 for 25 minutes.

glazed passionfruit tart

cheesecake

serves 6–8

FOR THE BASE:

200g digestive biscuits, smashed into crumbs

50g chopped hazelnuts

60g butter, melted

FOR THE TOPPING:

175g unrefined golden caster sugar

400g cream cheese

285ml sour cream

3 large free-range eggs

1 vanilla pod, seeds scraped out

fresh strawberries

1 Mix the digestive crumbs, hazelnuts and butter in a bowl and press into a 20-cm springform tin. Cover with cling film and refrigerate until set – about 45 minutes.

2 Using a mixer, blend the sugar, cream cheese, sour cream, eggs and vanilla seeds together and pour onto the prepared biscuit base. Set a grid shelf on the floor of the Roasting Oven.

3 For 4-oven Aga owners, start the cake on the grid shelf on the floor of the Roasting Oven for 10 minutes. Move the cheesecake to a grid shelf on the floor of the Baking Oven and cook for a further 1–1½ hours. If it browns too quickly, slide the Cold Plain Shelf over the cake.

4 For 2-oven Aga owners, start the cake on the grid shelf on the floor of the Roasting Oven for 20 minutes with the Cold Plain Shelf directly above it. Remove the cake and plain shelf from the Roasting Oven and transfer the plain shelf to the third set of runners in the Simmering Oven. Place the cake on the plain shelf and continue cooking for 1½–2 hours, checking every so often.

5 Remove the cheesecake from the oven and allow to cool. Refrigerate for a few hours before serving, then serve with a topping of fresh strawberries.

conventional cooking:

Pre-heat the oven to 150°C/300°F/gas 2. Bake in the centre of the oven for 30 minutes, then turn off the oven and leave the cheesecake to cool completely in the oven.

lemon verbena baked custard

serves 6

700ml milk

3 vanilla pods

170g unrefined golden caster
sugar

4 lemon verbena teabags

6 large free-range eggs

1 Pour the milk into a saucepan. Cut the vanilla pods down the centre and scrape out the seeds from the middle using the back of a knife or a spoon. Add the seeds to the milk with the sugar and lemon verbena teabags.

2 Bring the milk to the boil on the Boiling Plate, then take it off the heat and leave the milk to infuse for 15 minutes.

3 Whisk the eggs in a large bowl. Remove the teabags from the milk, then slowly whisk the milk into the eggs. Strain the custard into six ramekins.

4 Fold a tea towel in half and place it on the bottom of the large roasting tin. Put the ramekins on the tea towel and pour boiling water into the tin to come halfway up the sides of the ramekins.

5 Bake the custards on the third set of runners in the Roasting Oven for about 15 minutes or until they are just set, or on the third set of runners in the Baking Oven for 20 minutes. Remove the ramekins from the water bath and leave to cool. Cover with cling film and refrigerate. Bring to room temperature before serving.

conventional cooking:

Pre-heat the oven to 180°C/350°F/gas 4 and bake for 20 minutes or until just set.

meringues

As a variation, try adding chocolate chips to the meringue mix once all the sugar has been added.

makes 8 large meringues

½ a lemon

4 free-range egg whites

225g unrefined golden caster
sugar

1 Before you start, make sure your bowl and whisk are scrupulously clean. Rub a lemon half over the whisk and around the inside of the bowl. Line a baking tray or the cold plain shelf with Bake-O-Glide.

2 Put the egg whites into the bowl and start to whisk the egg whites on a medium speed, increasing the speed steadily to high as you go. First the whites will bubble and turn frothy, then they will form into soft floppy peaks, and finally they will stiffen up to the stiff peak stage.

3 Add the sugar one spoonful at a time until all the sugar is used up. Spoon dollops of the meringue onto the lined plain shelf or baking tray. Slide the shelf onto the fourth set of runners in the Simmering Oven for 1½–2 hours. If you like meringues very dry, when you remove them from the oven, turn each meringue on its side and place the shelf on the Simmering Plate lid, protecting it with a tea towel. Leave to dry out for another 45–60 minutes.

conventional cooking:

Cook in a low oven, 120°C/250°F/gas ½ for 1 hour or until dry.

pavlova

serves 8

6 large free-range egg whites
(without a trace of egg yolk)

350g unrefined golden caster
sugar

2 tsp white wine vinegar

1½ tsp cornflour

300ml double or whipping cream

fruit, such as cherries,
nectarines, strawberries and/or
raspberries

1 Line a flat baking tray or a tarte tatin dish with Bake-O-Glide.

2 Put the egg whites into the bowl of an electric mixer (the bowl must be scrupulously clean). Whisk the egg whites together until they reach the soft peak stage – shiny and thick – then add the sugar 2 tablespoons at a time until it is really thick and glossy. Gently fold the vinegar and cornflour into the egg whites.

3 Spread the mixture onto the baking tray, shaping it into a circle and spreading it out from the middle so that it is about 25cm in circumference.

4 Slide the tray onto the fourth set of runners in the Roasting Oven and bake for 10 minutes, then transfer to the middle runners of the Simmering Oven and continue to cook for another 30–40 minutes. Remove it and cool on a wire rack. (The pavlova can be made to this stage the day before and stored in an airtight container.)

5 To serve, transfer the pavlova to a serving dish – it will be uncooperative and may even start to break up, but don't worry as that's all part of its deliciousness.

6 Whip the cream to soft peaks and fill the pavlova with it. Scatter over the fruit and serve.

conventional cooking:

Pre-heat the oven to 170ºC/340ºF/gas 3½. Bake in the oven for 60 minutes, then turn off the oven completely and leave the pavlova to cool in the oven.

treacle tart

serves 10–12

FOR THE PASTRY:

300g plain flour

125g cold unsalted butter, chopped

pinch of salt

1 large free-range egg

FOR THE FILLING:

540g golden syrup

zest and juice of ½ a lemon

pinch of ground ginger

125g soft white breadcrumbs

70g ground almonds

4 free-range egg yolks

225ml double cream

1 To make the pastry, put the flour, butter and salt into a food processor and process until the mix resembles fine breadcrumbs. Add the egg and 1–2 tablespoons of ice-cold water. Using the pulse button, process until the mixture just comes together. Flatten to a round, wrap in cling film and refrigerate for a minimum of 1 hour.

2 Roll out the pastry and line a 24-cm round tart tin. Set aside while you make the filling.

3 To make the filling, stir the golden syrup, lemon zest and juice together in a saucepan on the Simmering Plate for 1–2 minutes. Whisk in the remaining ingredients and mix well. Pour into the pastry case.

4 Place the tart tin on the floor of the Roasting Oven, sliding the Cold Plain Shelf on to the third set of runners, and bake for 20–30 minutes or until the tart is slightly puffed up and starting to firm up.

5 Cool in the tin for 20 minutes, then serve with double cream or crème fraîche. This tart will keep for up to 5 days in an airtight container.

conventional cooking:

Pre-heat the oven to 190°C/375°F/gas 5 and blind-bake the pastry case for 10 minutes. Fill and bake in the middle of the oven for about 40 minutes, as above.

chocolate pecan pie

serves 8

80g dark chocolate

45g unsalted butter

160g granulated sugar

235ml corn syrup or light golden syrup

3 free-range eggs

1 tsp vanilla extract

235g pecans, chopped

25cm tart tin lined with uncooked pastry (see page 195), chilled

1 Melt the chocolate and the butter together either in a bowl over simmering water or in a microwave or at the back of the Aga and set aside.

2 In a medium-sized saucepan, combine the sugar and syrup and bring to the boil on the Boiling Plate. Move to the Simmering Plate for 2 minutes, stirring constantly, then set aside to cool.

3 Beat the eggs in a large bowl, then stir in the melted chocolate-butter mixture and whisk in the sugar syrup mixture so that it is all thoroughly combined. Add the vanilla extract and stir in the pecans. Set aside until completely cool.

4 Pour the filling into the chilled pastry. Place the pie on the Roasting Oven floor and bake for 20 minutes. Then slide in the Cold Plain shelf on the second set of runners and move the pie to the grid shelf on the fourth set of runners. Continue to bake for a further 20–25 minutes. Cool and serve at room temperature.

conventional cooking:

Pre-heat the oven to 200°C/400°F/gas 6. Bake the pie for 20 minutes, then lower the temperature to 180°C/ 350°F/gas 4 and continue to cook for about 20 minutes until the pastry is golden and the filling is set.

blueberry and frangipane tart

This can also be cooked in individual tart tins, but the total cooking time may be only 15 minutes.

serves 6

1 small quantity sweet pastry (see page 195)

58g unsalted butter, softened

58g icing sugar, plus extra for dusting

58g ground almonds

1 free-range egg

1 tbsp double cream

470g blueberries

1 Line a 20.5-cm tart tin with the pastry.

2 Combine the butter, sugar, almonds, egg and cream to form a thick paste. Pour the mixture into the pastry case and top with the blueberries.

3 Place on the floor of the Roasting Oven and cook for 20 minutes until puffed up and golden. Check after 10 minutes, and slide the Cold Plain Shelf on to the last set of runners if the tart is browning too quickly.

4 Allow the tart to cook on a wire rack, then sift over icing sugar and serve with vanilla ice cream

conventional cooking:

Pre-heat the oven to 190ºC/375ºF/gas 5 and blind-bake the pastry for 15 minutes. Cool the pastry for 10 minutes, then add the filling. Lower the temperature to 180ºC/350ºF/gas 4 and bake the tart for 20 minutes.

kashmir plums

serves 6

150ml water

45ml organic honey

1 whole star anise

1 cinnamon stick

6 bruised cardamom pods

small pinch of saffron strands

12 ripe plums, halved and stoned

1 Place the water, honey and spices in a saucepan, bring up to the boil and simmer on the Simmering Plate for 5 minutes.

2 Spread 2 large pieces of foil over a deep baking tray, forming a cross. The foil must be large enough to hold all the plums and the liquid and be gathered at the top to form a completely enclosed parcel.

3 Spread the plums on to the foil and pour over the spiced liquor. Wrap up the parcel and bake the plums on the third set of runners in the Roasting Oven for 25–30 minutes or until they are soft and tender.

4 Remove the plums from the oven when they are tender. Pour the liquor back into a saucepan and reduce for 3–5 minutes on the Simmering Plate until it is thick and syrupy (sometimes this is not necessary as the cooking liqueur thickens within the foil). Serve 4 plum halves per person with a large dollop of crème fraîche.

conventional cooking:

Cook step 1 on the hob. Pre-heat the oven to 200ºC/400ºF/gas 6 and cook as above.

blueberry and frangipane tart

10 cakes

the aga way of baking

Many people think that baking in an Aga is impossible but all you need to do is know your ovens, buy good quality bakeware and keep on checking! My party trick when I do a cookery demonstration is usually to bake an all-in-one sponge cake with the Roasting Oven door off. As I do the baking part of my demonstration in the afternoon, it ties in very nicely with the 'Cleaning your Aga' part. So, whilst I am showing the basic Aga cleaning methods, the cake is slowly baking. It is quite funny to see the audience's reaction when I remove the door – something you could never contemplate with a conventional cooker.

One of the many things I learned while testing recipes for this book is that many factors determine baking times, and some cakes take an inordinate amount of time to bake in an Aga. We used three different Aga cookers – one 4-oven and two 2-oven models – and I can tell you that sometimes a cake's timing can vary from as much as 1½ hours to 6 hours depending on the Aga. So much depends on how hot the ovens are when you start your cake. On average I found oil-fuelled Agas slightly slower than gas. In all honesty, you must only use the timings as guidelines and check your food regularly when it is in the oven.

One golden Aga rule is, if it works for you carry on! Once you have recognised your cooker's hot spots and mastered its quirks, you will be the best judge of what works for you.

before the cake baker

A really good baking tip for 2-oven Aga owners is to use the Cold Plain Shelf as a hot shelf. If you have a recipe that requires a longer cooking time, over 40 minutes or so, you will want to move the cake from the Roasting Oven to the Simmering Oven. The best way to continue the baking is to slide the Cold Plain Shelf (even if you don't need it) into the Roasting Oven to heat up so

when you need to move your cake to the Simmering Oven, you move the shelf as well. Slide the now 'hot' Plain Shelf onto the desired runner, and continue baking the cake on it. The hot plain shelf gives an extra boost of heat to the cake and oven.

cake testing

To test whether a cake is done, the sides of the cake should be just coming away from the sides of the tin. Press the top of the cake lightly in the centre, if it is done it will spring back; if a dent is left you need to give it a few more minutes in the oven.

planning your baking

As it is better if the oven is a little cooler when you bake, try to plan your baking for the afternoon or after a major cooking session. Over the years I have picked up many useful tips from other Aga owners when it comes to baking. Some Aga owners swear by sliding a large roasting tray full of cold water into the Roasting Oven to cool the cooker down and then keep on changing it. Another tip is to boil the kettle and leave it on the Simmering Plate so that with the lid up the cooker will not be so hot. I prefer to plan my baking to follow a cooking session and I have lots of Cold Plain Shelves to keep me going.

a word about cakes

For me, the discovery of what makes a great cake is purely a matter of science. As with all baking, exact measurements are necessary and a good consistent set of scales is a must.

The main ingredients for making cakes are flour, fat, sugar, eggs and a raising agent (baking powder). Fruit is also a staple in many recipes. In basic terms, when flour, which contains starch and a sticky substance called gluten, is combined with the other ingredients and heat is applied, the starch grains in the flour burst. The starch can then absorb and hold the moisture obtained from the sugar, butter and eggs or fruit. When moist, the gluten becomes firm. Moisture, when heated, turns into steam and the steam created blows out the gluten. More heat sets the gluten and holds it in an expanded condition – the 'risen' cake.

Cakes are classified according to the proportions of fat, sugar and flour. Plain cakes have less fat to flour, while rich cakes have a high fat to flour ratio (the richness of the cake depends not so much on the proportion of fruit but of fat). Sponge cakes have a high proportion of air.

baking tins

Cake tins must be strong, thick and solid. Thin tins are unsuitable for the Aga because the heat passes through more quickly than in a conventional oven and can therefore burn the outside of the cake while the middle is still uncooked.

I find that I don't need to grease my own range of tins and only line the loose bottom with a pre-cut piece of Bake-O-Glide. If you are not sure how your tins will stand up, you may wish to line the sides with strips of Bake-O-Glide as well.

cooking time and oven position

As with all Aga cooking and baking, recipes are cooked according to time and position, and there is no exception to this when baking cakes. The general rule to remember regarding heat is the plainer the cake, the hotter the oven.

If a cake has a large surface a hot oven is necessary; the heat can penetrate through to the inside and cook the ingredients more quickly without burning. This speed in cooking is an aid to successful baking. When a high instant heat is applied to a raising agent, it will give off a greater force of gas and the cake will rise much better. In rich cakes, the percentage of fat and sugar is higher than that of flour and there is a smaller proportion of gluten to hold the air and the gas from the raising agent should develop slowly.

If an oven is too hot, it will burn the outside of the cake before the inside is cooked, therefore the richer the cake, the slower the oven. This is why the Simmering Oven is the perfect oven for baking fruit cakes (see below).

aga fruit cakes

Prepare your fruit cake recipe as usual, then place the tin on the third set of runners in the Simmering Oven. A 20.5cm round fruit cake will take anywhere between 4 and 10 hours. The reason for the timing variation is that no two Aga cookers are the same. My own fruit cake recipe (see pages 252–253) takes about 6 hours in the Simmering Oven.

Owners of 4-oven Agas may find that their Simmering Oven is slightly slower than a 2-oven Aga Simmering Oven. Start the cake off in the Baking Oven for 45–60 minutes, then transfer it to the Simmering Oven in as high a position as possible and cook for 4–10 hours, or longer in some cases. Another trick is to use the large grill rack from inside the large roasting tin. Put the grill rack directly on to the Simmering Oven floor and put the fruit cake directly on to it. If you feel you don't need the extra boost of the Baking Oven, bake the cake in the Simmering Oven only as above.

There is no need to line cake tins with brown paper or to cover them with newspaper. Use Bake-O-Glide for ease of cake removal.

For 2-oven Aga owners, if you have an Aga Cake Baker you can use it for baking fruit cakes. It will reduce the baking time and still give a good result but you really can't beat the Simmering Oven method.

classic chocolate cake

serves 8

150g dark chocolate
125g unsalted butter
250ml golden syrup
250ml boiling water
350g self-raising flour
50g cocoa powder
pinch of salt
1½ tsp baking powder
125g brown sugar
1 large free-range egg

1 Line a 20.5-cm square cake tin with Bake-O-Glide.

2 Melt the chocolate, butter and syrup in a jug with the boiling water.

3 Combine the flour, cocoa powder, salt, baking powder and sugar in an electric mixer, add the egg and, using the paddle attachment, start mixing. Slowly pour in the liquids and mix until the cake batter is smooth.

4 Pour the cake mix into the tin and bake on the fourth set of runners in the Roasting Oven for 30 minutes with the Cold Plain Shelf above. Transfer the now hot plain shelf and set the cake tin on it in the Simmering Oven for about 20 minutes or until a skewer inserted in the centre comes out clean.

5 Remove the cake from the oven and cool in the tin on a wire rack for 5 minutes. Run a knife around the edge of the tin, remove the cake and cool on a wire rack.

conventional cooking:

Pre-heat the oven to 180ºC/350ºF/gas 4 and bake for 30–35 minutes or until the cake springs back when pressed in the centre and comes away from the sides of the tin.

chocolate fruit cake

serves at least 12

175g candied mixed lemon and orange peel, preferably organic, roughly chopped

70g griottine cherries

30g dried sour cherries

60g raisins

170ml rum

15g cherry jam

454g jar runny honey

zest of 1 unwaxed lemon

120g whole hazelnuts

80g blanched whole almonds

80g unblanched whole almonds

80g flaked almonds

120g unsalted butter, softened

60g unrefined golden caster sugar

120g plain flour

3 large free-range eggs

200g ground almonds

300g very best dark chocolate, roughly chopped

1 Line a 20-cm diameter cake tin with Bake-O-Glide. If you are using the Cake Baker, heat it in the Roasting Oven whilst mixing the cake.

2 Put the candied peel, cherries, raisins, rum, cherry jam, honey and lemon zest in a bowl and marinate for 3 hours – the longer you marinate, the better.

3 Roast the hazelnuts and blanched almonds on the second set of runners in the Roasting Oven for 3–5 minutes or until brown. Peel and roughly chop all the whole nuts.

4 Cream the butter and sugar, sift in the flour, then add the eggs one at a time. Add 120g of the ground almonds and mix well.

5 Add the fruit and nuts to the butter and sugar mixture, along with the remaining ground almonds and the chocolate. Pour the mixture into the cake tin.

6 Put the cake tin into the Cake Baker and cook for about 1¾–2 hours on the floor of the Roasting Oven. If you are using the Simmering Oven, put a grid shelf into the Simmering Oven – the runners you use will depend how high the cake tin is. In general, aim for the fourth set of runners or on the floor. Put the tin on the grid shelf and cook for 4–8 hours or until the cake is cooked. Check the cake is cooked by inserting a skewer into the middle of the cake. If it comes out clean, the cake is done.

7 Cool the cake in the tin. The cake can be frozen for 2 months or kept well wrapped in cling film and foil for up to a month.

conventional cooking:

Pre-heat the oven to 140°C/275°F/gas 1 and bake the cake for 4–4½ hours or until a skewer inserted in the centre comes out clean.

chocolate espresso fudge cake

makes about 12 squares

85g dark chocolate

60ml espresso

240g plain flour

1 tsp baking soda

½ tsp salt

280g muscovado sugar

250ml sour cream

85g unsalted butter, softened

2 free-range eggs

FOR THE CHOCOLATE FUDGE ICING:

125ml evaporated milk

150g dark chocolate, in pieces

45g unsalted butter, cut into pieces

140g muscovado sugar

1 shot (32ml) espresso

1 Line a 34.5 x 24-cm tin with Bake-O-Glide and set aside.

2 Put the chocolate and espresso into a bowl and melt at the back of the Aga while you assemble the ingredients.

3 Sift the flour, baking soda and salt into a bowl, add the sugar, then add the sour cream and butter and beat with an electric mixer for about 2 minutes.

4 Add the eggs to the batter one at a time, then add the chocolate mix and beat again until just combined.

5 Pour the mix into the tin and slide the tin onto the fourth set of runners in the Roasting Oven with the Cold Plain Shelf on the second set of runners and bake for about 20–25 minutes. You may need to turn the cake around halfway through baking. For 4-oven Aga owners, bake the cake in the Baking Oven on the third set of runners for about 25 minutes. To test for doneness, the top of the cake should spring back when lightly pressed.

6 Cool the cake in the tin on a cooling rack for 10 minutes, then remove from the tin and finish cooling on the rack. Ice the cake with Chocolate Fudge Icing.

7 To make the icing, bring the evaporated milk up to a boil on the Simmering Plate. Remove from the heat, add the chocolate pieces and let them melt into the milk. Tip the mixture into a food processor and add the butter, sugar and espresso and process until smooth. Set the icing aside to thicken until it is the desired consistency for spreading. This is a runny icing.

conventional cooking:

Pre-heat the oven to 180ºC/350ºF/gas 4 and bake the cake as above for 20–25 minutes. Make the icing on the hob.

chocolate hazelnut cake

serves 8

8 free-range eggs

225g unrefined golden caster sugar

230g dark chocolate, finely grated

200g ground hazelnuts

100g unsalted butter, melted and at room temperature

1 tsp baking powder

zest of 1 organic orange

cocoa powder, for dusting

1 Line a 20.5-cm cake tin with Bake-O-Glide and set aside.

2 Whisk the eggs and the sugar on a high speed for 8–10 minutes until they look very light and fluffy and leave a thick ribbon trail.

3 Put the grated chocolate and hazelnuts into a bowl and add the melted butter, baking powder and orange zest. Combine thoroughly. Gently fold the whisked eggs and sugar into the chocolate mix so they are just incorporated. Carefully spoon the mixture into the prepared tin.

4 To bake, I strongly recommend that 2-oven Aga owners use a Cake Baker. Bake the cake in the Cake Baker in the Roasting Oven for 40–45 minutes or until it is pulling away from the sides and the top springs back when lightly pressed. If you don't have a Cake Baker, start the cake off on the fourth set of runners in the Roasting Oven for the first 20–25 minutes, then transfer to the Simmering Oven for 40–60 minutes or until done. For 4-oven Aga owners, bake in the Baking Oven for 40–45 minutes, sliding in the Cold Plain Shelf if required (check the cake after 25 minutes or so of baking).

5 When the cake is done, stand the cake tin on a wire cooling rack and cool in the tin for 15–20 minutes. Turn the cake out and finish cooling on the wire rack. Dust the cake with cocoa powder and serve.

conventional cooking:

Pre-heat the oven to 180°C/350°F/gas 4 and bake for 40–45 minutes. Cover the top of the cake after the first 20 minutes with damp parchment paper (scrunch up the parchment paper and run it under a tap, squeeze it out and place on the cake).

chocolate roulade

6 free-range eggs, separated
100g unrefined golden caster sugar
35g self-raising flour
35g cocoa powder
300ml whipping cream

1 Line a shallow baking tray with Bake-O-Glide.

2 Whisk the egg yolks with 40g of the sugar for about 5 minutes until they are pale. Set aside.

3 Whisk the egg whites together in a separate bowl until they reach the soft peak stage, then add the remaining sugar one tablespoon at a time until the stiff peak stage is reached.

4 Gently fold the egg yolks into the egg whites and then fold the sifted flour and cocoa into the egg mix. Spread the cake mix onto the baking tray.

5 Bake on the third set of runners in the Roasting Oven for 8–10 minutes or until the cake springs back when gently pressed in the centre.

6 While the cake is baking, lay a clean tea towel over a wire rack and then lay a piece of greaseproof paper on top of the tea towel.

7 When the cake is done, remove it from the oven, immediately invert it onto the greaseproof and peel off the Bake-O-Glide. Allow the cake to cool completely.

8 When the cake is ready, whip the cream to soft peaks and spread over the cake. With the short end of the cake facing you, roll it carefully into a roulade. Wrap the tea towel around and secure the top with clothes pegs or a bulldog clip to hold its shape. Place in the fridge.

9 When you are ready to serve, dust with icing sugar or spread with more whipped cream.

conventional cooking:
Pre-heat the oven to 200°C/400°F/gas 6 and proceed as above.

gooey chocolate cake

serves 4–6

250g good-quality dark chocolate, broken into little pieces

5 free-range eggs, separated

175g soft brown sugar

1 tbsp Dutch processed cocoa powder

25g plain flour

1 shot (32ml) espresso

FOR THE ICING:

150g cream cheese

60g unsalted butter, softened

350g icing sugar

1 tsp vanilla extract

2 tbsp cocoa powder

1 Line two 20.5-cm loose bottomed cake tins with Bake-O-Glide.

2 Melt the chocolate in a bowl at the back of the Aga or over a pan of simmering water.

3 While it is melting, cream together the egg yolks and the sugar in an electric mixer until they are thick and smooth. Stir the melted chocolate into the creamed egg yolks and sugar, then sift in the cocoa and flour and add the espresso. Mix well.

4 Whisk the egg whites in a clean bowl until they are at the soft peak stage, then fold 1 tablespoon of the whites into the chocolate mix. Fold in well, then add the rest of the whites and fold in very carefully.

5 Pour the cake batter into the prepared tins and bake on the grid shelf on the floor of the Roasting Oven with the Cold Plain Shelf just above for 20 minutes. The cakes are done when they spring back when lightly pressed in the centre.

6 Remove from the oven and let the cakes cool completely in the tins on a wire rack.

7 For the icing, beat the ingredients together in an electric mixer, then ice the cakes and sandwich together.

conventional cooking:

Pre-heat the oven to 180°C/350°F/gas 4 and bake as above in the middle of the oven.

slow oven chocolate cake

serves 6

225g dark chocolate

225g unsalted butter, softened

225g unrefined golden caster sugar

7 free-range eggs, separated

45g plain flour

½ tsp baking powder

60g ground almonds

cocoa or icing sugar, for dusting

1 Line a 20.5-cm square cake tin with Bake-O-Glide.

2 Melt the chocolate in a pan at the back of the Aga.

3 Cream the butter and sugar together until light and fluffy. Whisk the egg whites in a clean bowl so they form stiff peaks. Sift the flour into a bowl and stir in the baking powder and almonds.

4 Add the melted chocolate to the egg yolks, then add them little by little to the butter and sugar mix, alternating with the flour and almond mix until it is all used up. Stir 1 tablespoon of the egg whites into the mix, then carefully fold in the rest of the egg whites. Make sure there aren't any white pockets. Pour the cake mix into the prepared tin.

5 Bake on the third set of runners in the Roasting Oven for 10 minutes, then move to the Simmering Oven for 45–60 minutes or until the cake springs back when lightly pressed in the middle and the sides are just pulling away.

6 Cool on a wire rack, then dust the cake with cocoa or icing sugar. Store in an airtight tin. The cake will last for 3 days.

conventional cooking:

Pre-heat the oven to 190°C/350°F/gas 4 and bake for 10 minutes, then reduce the temperature to 150°C/300°F/gas 2 and continue baking for 1½–2 hours.

flourless chocolate cake

This is a dessert cake rather than an afternoon tea cake. It will collapse and behave very badly, but it is very delicious and worth the effort. It's very rich so cut into small pieces. Serve with vanilla ice cream and chocolate sauce if you dare! This cake can be made ahead of time, turned out when cool and refrigerated.

serves 8–10

350g good-quality dark chocolate, broken into small pieces

175g unsalted butter

6 large organic free-range eggs

235g unrefined golden caster sugar

FOR THE CHOCOLATE SAUCE:

100g good-quality dark plain chocolate

6 tbsp double cream

1 tsp grated orange zest

1 Line or grease the half-size roasting tin.

2 Melt the chocolate and butter together in a saucepan over a bowl of simmering water on top of the Aga.

3 Using an electric mixer, whisk the eggs and the sugar for 7–8 minutes or until very pale and fluffy. Fold the melted chocolate into the whisked eggs very gently and then pour into the prepared cake tin.

4 Bake on the fourth set of runners in the Roasting Oven with the Cold Plain Shelf on the second set of runners for 20 minutes, turning halfway through. Then transfer to the Simmering Oven for another 20 minutes or until a skewer still has a bit of the cake mix stuck to it when inserted. For 4-oven Aga owners, start the cake in the Baking Oven with the Cold Plain Shelf under the cake, then transfer to the Simmering Oven as above.

5 Remove from the oven and allow the cake to cool completely in the tin.

6 To make the sauce, melt the chocolate and cream over a bowl of hot water on the Simmering Plate. Stir until smooth; do not allow to simmer or boil. Stir in the zest and cool until at room temperature. Serve with the cake.

conventional cooking:

Pre-heat the oven to 180°C/350°F/gas 4 and bake the cake in a bain marie for 45 minutes. Turn off the oven, leave the oven door ajar and leave the cake sitting in the bain marie for another 30 minutes. Make the chocolate sauce on the hob.

chocolate brownies

makes about 10 brownies

300g dark chocolate, chopped

230g butter

340g unrefined golden caster sugar

3 large free-range eggs

2 tsp vanilla extract

1 shot of espresso or 1 tsp instant espresso powder

110g plain flour

2 tsp baking powder

pinch of salt (if you use salted butter, omit this)

100g chopped pecans or nuts of your choice

1 Melt the chocolate and butter either at the back of the Aga or in the Simmering Oven. Set aside to cool for about 5 minutes. Grease a 24 x 34-cm, 3-cm deep baking tray.

2 Stir together the sugar, eggs, vanilla extract and espresso. Pour the egg mix into the chocolate and sift over the flour, baking powder and salt. Dust the chopped nuts with a teaspoon of flour (it stops them from sinking into the mix) and add. Give the mix a really good stir, then pour into the greased baking tray.

3 Bake on the third set of runners in the Roasting Oven for 15 minutes, then tap the side of the tin to release any air bubbles. Slide in the Cold Plain Shelf on the second set of runners and move the tin to the fourth set of runners. Continue baking for a further 15–20 minutes. If you have a Baking Oven, bake on the third set of runners for 20 minutes, then continue as above. Test with a skewer, it is done when it comes out clean. Don't overcook as you want the brownies to be slightly squidgy.

4 Cool thoroughly, then cut into squares and keep in an airtight tin or in the refrigerator. These brownies can be made 3 days in advance (if you can resist eating them for that long!).

conventional cooking:
Pre-heat the oven to 180°C/350°F/gas 4 and bake for 30–35 minutes.

chocolate caramel brownies

makes about 10 brownies

300g dark chocolate, chopped

228g butter

342g unrefined golden caster sugar

3 large organic eggs

2 tsp vanilla extract

110g plain flour

2 tsp baking powder

pinch of salt (if using unsalted butter)

100g chopped hazelnuts

350g caramel candies, unwrapped and in pieces

2 tbsp milk

1 Grease a baking tray. Melt the chocolate and butter in a bowl at the back of the Aga. Set aside to cool for about 5 minutes.

2 Stir together the sugar, eggs and vanilla extract. Pour the egg mix into the chocolate and sift over the flour, baking powder and salt. Dust the nuts with a teaspoon of flour (it stops them sinking into the mix) and add.

3 Stir the mix well, then pour into a greased baking tray to a depth of 3cm. Bake in the Roasting Oven on the fourth set of runners with the Cold Plain Shelf above for 20 minutes. Tap the side of the tin to release any air bubbles and continue baking for a further 15 minutes. Don't overcook as brownies should be slightly squidgy.

4 Heat the caramels with the milk in a saucepan on the Simmering Plate until just melted and spreadable, then pour over the cooling brownies.

5 Cool thoroughly, then cut into squares and keep in an airtight tin or in the refrigerator. These can be made 3 days in advance.

conventional cooking:

Pre-heat the oven to 180ºC/350ºF/gas 4 and bake as above. Make the topping on the hob.

chocolate caramel brownies

chocolate and raspberry roulade

This was inspired by Tamasin Day Lewis's recipe for white chocolate tart.

6 free-range eggs, separated

100g unrefined golden caster sugar

35g self-raising flour

35g cocoa powder

icing sugar or cocoa powder, for dusting

FOR THE FILLING:

200ml crème fraîche

200ml double cream

150g white chocolate

250g raspberries

1 First, make the filling. Heat the crème fraîche and half the double cream in a pan on the Simmering Plate. Break up the white chocolate and put into a glass bowl. Pour in the heated creams and leave for a few minutes so that the chocolate can melt. Stir until the chocolate completely melts. Cover with cling film and put into the fridge to cool for at least 4 hours or overnight.

2 Line a shallow baking tray with Bake-O-Glide.

3 Whisk the egg yolks with 40g of the sugar for about 5 minutes or until they are pale. Set aside.

4 Whisk the egg whites together until they reach the soft peak stage, then add the remaining sugar, 1 tablespoon at a time, until the stiff peak stage is reached. Gently fold the pale egg yolks into the egg whites and then fold in the sifted flour and cocoa.

5 Spread the cake mix onto the lined baking tray and bake on the third set of runners in the Roasting Oven for 8–10 minutes or until the cake springs back when gently pressed in the centre.

6 While the cake is baking, lay a clean tea towel over a wire rack and then lay a piece of greaseproof paper over the towel. When the cake is done, remove from the oven and immediately invert it onto the towel and peel off the Bake-O-Glide. Cool the cake completely.

7 When the cake is ready to assemble, whip the rest of the cream to soft peaks and fold it and the raspberries into the cooled chocolate mix. Spread over the cake base.

8 With the short end of the cake facing you, roll it carefully into a roulade. Wrap in the clean towel and secure the top using clothes pegs or a bulldog clip to hold its shape. Place in the fridge. When you are ready to serve, dust with icing sugar or cocoa.

conventional cooking:
Pre-heat the oven to 200°C/400°F/gas 6 and cook as above.

wheat-free chocolate sponge

The quality of the eggs used will affect the cake's flavour and texture. I use two-day-old organic free-range eggs which are perfect.

serves 4–6

150g rice flour

25g potato flour

1 tbsp baking powder

175g unsalted butter, softened, or baking margarine

175g unrefined golden caster sugar

1 shot (32ml) of espresso or 1 tsp espresso instant coffee dissolved in 1 tbsp boiling water

3 tbsp organic cocoa powder, mixed with the espresso

3 large organic eggs

FOR THE FILLING:

whipped cream or chocolate buttercream icing (see page 258)

cocoa powder, for dusting

1 Line two 20-cm sponge tins, preferably loose bottomed, with Bake-O-Glide.

2 Put all the cake ingredients into the bowl of an electric mixer and, using the beater attachment, beat until well combined. Divide the mix between the prepared cake tins.

3 Place the grid shelf on the floor of the Roasting Oven and place the cake tins to the right on the grid shelf. Slide the Cold Plain Shelf onto the third set of runners above and bake the cakes for 20 minutes or until they are golden on top, are gently coming away from the sides and spring back when lightly pressed on top. For 4-oven Aga owners, place the cake tins on the fourth set of runners in the Baking Oven and only insert the cold plain shelf if the cakes are browning too quickly.

4 Remove the cakes from the oven and stand on a wire rack for a minute, then remove them from the tins and cool on the rack.

5 When the cakes are cool, spread one cake with whipped cream or chocolate buttercream icing and top with the other cake. Dust with cocoa powder and serve.

conventional cooking:
Pre-heat the oven to 160ºC/325ºF/gas 3 and bake for 20–25 minutes.

all-in-one wheat-free sponge

You can use either unsalted butter or good-quality baking margarine in this recipe. The margarine makes the cake slightly lighter, but the butter gives it a richer taste. The quality of the eggs used will affect the cake's flavour and texture. I use two-day-old organic free-range eggs.

serves 4–6

150g rice flour

25g potato flour

3 rounded tsp baking powder

175g baking margarine or unsalted butter, softened

175g unrefined golden caster sugar

1 tsp vanilla extract

3 large organic eggs

1 tbsp milk

FOR THE FILLING:

whipping cream and soft fruits

icing sugar, for dusting

1 Line two 20-cm sponge tins, preferably loose bottomed, with Bake-O-Glide.

2 Put all the cake ingredients into the bowl of an electric mixer and, using the beater attachment, beat until combined.

3 Divide the cake mix between the prepared cake tins. Place the grid shelf on the floor of the Roasting Oven and place the cake tins to the right on the grid shelf. Slide the Cold Plain Shelf onto the third set of runners and bake the cakes for 20 minutes or until they are golden on top, are gently coming away from the sides and spring back when lightly pressed on top. For 4-oven Aga owners, cook the cakes on the fourth set of runners in the Baking Oven and use the Cold Plain Shelf only if the cakes are browning too quickly. Remove the cakes and stand on a wire rack for a minute, then remove from the tin and cool on the rack.

4 When the cakes are cool, whip the cream to soft peaks and spread on one cake, then top with the fruits and the second cake. Dust the top with icing sugar and serve.

conventional cooking:

Pre-heat the oven to 160°C/325°F/gas 3 and bake for 20–25 minutes.

coffee and almond sponge meringue

serves 4–6

220g unrefined golden caster sugar

100g butter

4 large free-range eggs, separated

150g ground almonds

1 shot (32ml) espresso coffee or 1 tbsp instant coffee dissolved in 1 tbsp boiling water

1 tsp cornflour

50g sliced almonds

1 Line a 27-cm round tin with Bake-O-Glide.

2 Combine 110g of the sugar with the butter using an electric mixer.

3 Beat the yolks and slowly pour into the mixer, taking care not to curdle the mix. Add the ground almonds and espresso and mix well. Spread this mix into the tin.

4 Place the tin on a grid shelf on the floor of the Roasting Oven and bake for about 10 minutes.

5 Using a very clean bowl and an electric whisk, whisk the egg whites with the cornflour until they are at the soft peak stage, then whisk in the remainder of the sugar 1 tablespoon at a time.

6 Remove the cake from the oven and carefully spread the meringue over the cake batter and sprinkle with the sliced almonds. Return the cake to the Roasting Oven and bake for 20–30 minutes. You will probably need to slide the Cold Plain Shelf onto the runners above if the meringue browns too quickly.

7 Remove from the tin and cool on a wire rack. Serve with whipped cream.

conventional cooking:
Pre-heat the oven to 200°C/400°F/gas 6 and bake as above.

lemon meringue cake

serves 6

FOR THE LEMON CUSTARD FILLING:

250ml milk

100g unrefined golden caster sugar

3 free-range egg yolks

1 tbsp cornflour

1 tbsp plain flour

60ml lemon juice

40g unsalted butter, softened

FOR THE CAKE:

110g unsalted butter, softened

110g unrefined golden caster sugar

1 tbsp lemon zest

4 free-range egg yolks

100g plain flour

1 tsp baking powder

160ml milk

FOR THE MERINGUE:

4 free-range egg whites

½ tsp cream of tartar

200g unrefined golden caster sugar

1 First, make the lemon custard. Heat the milk in a saucepan on the Simmering Plate until almost boiling, then remove from the heat. Whisk the sugar, yolks and flours in a bowl until the mixture is thick and pale. Gradually add the hot milk and stir until smooth.

2 Rinse out the saucepan and return the custard to it. Put it back on the Simmering Plate and stir constantly until it comes to a boil and thickens. Remove from the heat and beat in the lemon juice and butter. Cover and cool to room temperature, then refrigerate until needed. This can be done in advance.

3 Line the bases of two 20.5-cm loose-bottomed cake tins with Bake-O-Glide.

4 To make the cake, cream the butter, sugar and lemon zest until light and fluffy, then add the egg yolks one at a time, alternating with the flour and baking powder. Add the milk and stir until the mix is smooth. Divide the cake batter between the prepared tins. Set aside.

5 To make the meringue, whisk the egg whites with the cream of tartar to the soft peak stage, then add the sugar little by little, whisking until it is thick, stiff and glossy. Spoon the meringue evenly over the cake batters. Place the grid shelf on the floor of the Roasting Oven and put the cake tins on top of it. Slide the Cold Plain Shelf onto the second set of runners and bake the cakes for 20–25 minutes.

6 Cool the cakes in the tins on a wire rack, then when ready to serve, place one of the cakes meringue side down and spread with the lemon custard, then place the other cake, meringue side up, on top.

conventional cooking:

Make the custard on the hob. Pre-heat the oven to 200°C/400°F/gas 6 and bake as above.

lemon meringue cake

sephardic orange cake

serves 8

2 oranges, preferably organic

6 free-range eggs

175g unrefined golden caster sugar

225g ground almonds

1 tsp baking powder

1 Place the oranges in a saucepan of water and heat to boiling point on the Boiling Plate, then transfer the pan to the Simmering Oven for 1 hour. Drain and process the oranges – skin and all – until puréed in a food processor.

2 Line a 20-cm round cake tin with deep sides with Bake-O-Glide. If you are using a Cake Baker, pre-heat it in the Roasting Oven while you mix together the cake ingredients.

3 Whisk the eggs and sugar until meringue-like in an electric mixer, then fold in the rest of the ingredients and mix well. Pour into a prepared cake tin and cook for 50–60 minutes in the Cake Baker on the floor of the Roasting Oven. For 4-oven Aga owners, bake in a regular cake tin on the fourth set of runners of the Baking Oven.

4 Cool and serve with whipped cream and a citrus sorbet.

conventional cooking:

Pre-heat the oven to 190°C/375°F/gas 5 and bake as above in a cake tin.

peach cake

You will have to use tinned peaches in winter, but in the summer choose fresh ones. In the summer I also like to mix blueberries with the peaches.

serves 6–8

420g self-raising flour

2 tsp baking powder

240g butter, softened

275g unrefined golden caster sugar

3 free-range eggs

1 tsp vanilla extract

350g chopped peaches

1 Line a 34.5 x 24-cm tin with Bake-O-Glide.

2 Put the flour, baking powder, butter, sugar, eggs and vanilla extract into an electric mixer fitted with the paddle attachment and mix to a smooth dough. Take out one third of the dough and press the rest into the prepared tin. The dough will be sticky so you may want to press it in with your hand inside a freezer bag or wet your fingers with cold water. Spread the fruit on top and scatter with clumps of the reserved dough.

3 Slide the tin onto the fourth set of runners in the Roasting Oven and bake for 20–30 minutes or until done. For 4-oven Aga owners, bake in the Baking Oven on the third set of runners for about 30 minutes. Cool the cake in the tin.

conventional cooking:

Pre-heat the oven to 190°C/375°F/gas 5 and bake for 30 minutes.

bottled damson cake

serves 8–10

600g jar bottled damsons

250ml sunflower oil

100ml milk

425g unrefined golden caster sugar

3 large free-range eggs

550g self-raising flour

100g ground hazelnuts

50g semolina

pinch of salt

2 tsp baking powder

1 tsp almond extract

FOR THE TOPPING:

100g golden syrup

50g unsalted butter

80g rolled oats

80g chopped hazelnuts

1 Drain the damsons from the bottle juices and set aside. Reserve the bottle juices for another recipe.

2 Tip the remaining cake ingredients into a large mixing bowl and mix together really well.

3 To make the topping, melt the syrup and butter in a small saucepan and then add the oats and hazelnuts.

4 Line the half-size roasting tin with Bake-O-Glide and pour in the cake mix. Spread the damsons over the cake mix, then scatter over the oat topping.

5 Slide the grid shelf onto the fourth set of runners in the Roasting Oven. Place the cake on the shelf, then slide the Cold Plain Shelf onto the second set of runners and bake for 30–35 minutes. Transfer the now hot plain shelf to the Simmering Oven, place the cake on top of it and bake for 1–2 hours or until a skewer comes out clean. For 4-oven Aga owners, bake in the Baking Oven for about 1 hour or until a skewer comes out clean.

6 Take the cake out of the oven and cool. Serve with thick double cream.

conventional cooking:

Pre-heat the oven to 190°C/375°F/gas 5. Bake for 1 hour or until a skewer comes out clean.

bottled damson cake

plum cake

serves 8–10

260ml sunflower oil

30ml walnut oil

450g unrefined golden caster sugar

3 large free-range eggs

6–8 plums, stoned and chopped into small cubes

700g plain flour

pinch of salt

1 tsp baking soda

2 tsp baking powder

generous grating of nutmeg

½ tsp cinnamon

½ tsp ground cardamom

1 tsp vanilla extract

1 Line a 20.5-cm square cake tin with Bake-O-Glide, or use the large round cake tin with the Cake Baker.

2 Tip all the ingredients into a large mixing bowl and mix together really well. Spoon into the tin.

3 Slide the Cold Plain Shelf onto the fourth set of runners in the Roasting Oven and place the cake tin on top of it. Bake for 20 minutes, then transfer the shelf to the fourth set of runners in the Simmering Oven. Place the cake on the shelf and continue baking for another 30–45 minutes or until done. This cake can also be baked in the Aga Cake Baker. For 4-oven Aga owners, cook in the Baking Oven for about 1 hour or until a skewer comes out clean.

4 Cool in the tin, then serve with clotted cream.

conventional cooking:

Pre-heat the oven to 190ºC/350ºF/gas 4 and bake for about 1–1½ hours.

cherry and almond cake

This is a lovely moist cake that keeps in an airtight tin for ages. It is also very good for tuck boxes and can be sent to keep hungry students going!

serves 6

230g butter

230g unrefined golden caster sugar

230g plain flour

½ tsp baking powder

3 free-range eggs

100g ground almonds

120g organic glacé cherries or griottine cherries

1 tsp almond extract

1 Line the base of a 20.5-cm loose-bottomed round tin with Bake-O-Glide.

2 Cream the butter and sugar together. Sieve the flour and baking powder together. Add the eggs one at a time to the creamed butter, alternating with the sieved flour to prevent the eggs from curdling. Add the ground almonds, cherries and almond extract and mix well.

3 Pour the mix into the tin. Place on the Cold Plain Shelf on the fourth set of runners in the Roasting Oven. Bake for 10 minutes, then transfer the shelf with the tin to the Simmering Oven and bake for 1½–2 hours. (In some Agas this cake can take up to 5½ hours!)

conventional cooking:

Pre-heat the oven to 130ºC/260ºF/gas ¾ and bake for 3 hours.

sour cream cake

This cake mixture can also be used to make muffins. Fill large muffin cases with the mixture and bake as in the pumpkin muffin recipe on page 26.

serves 6–8

FOR THE STREUSEL TOPPING:

150g chopped pecan nuts

185g granulated sugar

1 tsp ground cinnamon

FOR THE CAKE:

240g unsalted butter, softened, plus extra for greasing

250g unrefined golden caster sugar

300g self-raising flour

1 tsp baking powder

pinch of salt

2 free-range eggs

250ml sour cream

1 tsp vanilla extract

1 To make the topping, mix all the ingredients in a bowl and set aside.

2 Grease a 25-cm ring cake tin with butter.

3 Cream the butter and sugar together using an electric mixer. Sift the flour, baking powder and salt together in a separate bowl. In another bowl, lightly beat the eggs, sour cream and vanilla extract together. Slowly add a little of the wet mix to the creamed butter, alternating with the flour mix until it is all used up.

4 Pour half the cake mix into the tin. Sprinkle on half the streusel mix. Add the rest of the cake mix and top with the remaining streusel.

5 Slide the Cold Plain Shelf onto the fourth set of runners in the Roasting Oven and bake for 20 minutes, then move the now hot plain shelf to the Simmering Oven. Place the cake on top and continue baking for another 25–30 minutes or until done. For 4-oven Aga owners, bake in the Baking Oven for 35–45 minutes, sliding in the Cold Plain Shelf after about 20 minutes if the cake is browning too much on top.

6 Cool in the tin on a wire rack for 10 minutes, then serve the cake warm, when it will be deliciously crumbly.

conventional cooking:

Pre-heat the oven to 180°C/350°F/gas 4 and bake as above for 45 minutes.

cider vinegar 'cheese' cake

This is called 'cheese' cake not because it is made with cheese, but because it tastes so good accompanied by a thick chunk of mature Cheddar.

serves 6–8

225g unsalted butter, cut into small pieces

450g self-raising flour

225g soft brown sugar

225g sultanas

225g dried apple pieces

3 tbsp cider vinegar

300ml full-fat milk

1 tsp bicarbonate of soda

1 Line a 23-cm round or square, deep cake tin with Bake-O-Glide.

2 Put the butter and flour into a food processor and pulse until it is the consistency of fine breadcrumbs (you can do this by hand). Transfer to a large bowl and add the sugar and dried fruit.

3 Put the vinegar and milk into a large jug, then sprinkle on the bicarbonate of soda – be careful as it will froth up so the jug needs to be deep. Add the liquid to the dry mix and stir it all together quickly.

4 Pour it into the prepared tin. For 2-oven Aga owners, either use the Cake Baker or start the cake off on the third set of runners in the Roasting Oven for 20 minutes, then transfer to the Simmering Oven for 2–2½ hours. If the top browns too quickly, slide in the Cold Plain Shelf. For 4-oven Aga owners, start the cake off in the Roasting Oven for 20 minutes, then transfer to the Baking Oven for 1–1½ hours. Use the Cold Plain Shelf if it browns too quickly on top.

5 Cool in the tin. Serve with chunks of mature Cheddar cheese or slathered in butter. It will keep in an airtight tin for about 1 week. You can freeze this cake for up to 3 months, wrapped well in cling film and foil.

conventional cooking:

Pre-heat the oven to 180°C/350°F/gas 4 and bake for 1–1½ hours or until done.

gingerbread cake

serves 6–8

FOR THE TOPPING:

120g butter

175g brown sugar

3 pears, peeled, cored and sliced into quarters

FOR THE CAKE

250ml treacle

250ml boiling water

350g self-raising flour

1 tsp cinnamon

1 tsp ground ginger

½ tsp ground cloves

½ tsp ground cardamom

pinch of salt

1½ tsp baking soda

125g unsalted butter

125g brown sugar

1 large free-range egg

1 Make the topping first. Melt the butter in a 27-cm tarte tatin dish on the Boiling or Simmering Plate, then sprinkle over the sugar and cook undisturbed for about 3 minutes.

2 Arrange the pear quarters on the melted butter and sugar and continue cooking on the Simmering Plate for about 2 minutes, then set aside.

3 To make the cake, measure the treacle into a heatproof bowl and pour the boiling water over. Mix the flour, spices, salt and baking soda together in a large bowl. In the bowl of an electric mixer cream together the butter, sugar and egg until light and fluffy. Then slowly add the dry mix 3 tablespoons at a time, alternating with the treacle until it is all smooth and combined.

4 Pour the cake mix over the pears and bake on the fourth set of runners in the Roasting Oven with the Cold Plain Shelf above for 30 minutes. Transfer the cake to the Simmering Oven for a further 20 minutes or until a skewer come out clean.

5 Remove the cake from the oven and cool on a wire rack for 5 minutes. Run a knife around the edge of the tin. Protecting your hands and holding a large plate over the cake, invert the cake onto the plate so that the top becomes the bottom and the pears are on top. Serve with vanilla ice cream.

conventional cooking:

Pre-heat the oven to 180°C/350°F/gas 4 and bake for 40–50 minutes or until the cake springs back to the touch and is coming away from the edges.

walnut and coffee sponge cake

275g self-raising flour

225g unrefined golden caster sugar

225g unsalted butter, softened, or baking margarine

2 tsp baking powder

2 tsp coffee mixed with 1 tbsp boiling water

100g chopped walnuts, plus walnut halves for decorating

5 free-range eggs

FOR THE ICING:

75g unsalted butter, softened

200g icing sugar

1 tbsp coffee essence

1 Line two 20.5cm sponge tins with Bake-O-Glide.

2 Put all the cake ingredients into the bowl of an electric mixer and mix until well combined. Divide the cake mix between the prepared cake tins.

3 Place the grid shelf on the floor of the Roasting Oven and place the cake tins to the right on the grid shelf. Slide the Cold Plain Shelf onto the third set of runners and bake the cakes for 20 minutes or until they are golden on top, gently coming away from the sides and spring back when lightly pressed on top. The cakes are ready when gently coming away from the sides of the tin and spring back when lightly pressed on top.

4 Stand the cakes in their tins on a wire rack for a minute, then remove them from the tins and cool on the rack.

5 To make the icing, beat all the ingredients together until smooth. Spread half of the icing over one sponge cake and sandwich with the other. Spread the remaining icing on the top and decorate with walnut halves.

conventional cooking:

Pre-heat the oven to 180°C/350°F/gas 4 and bake for 30–35 minutes.

treacle tea cake

200g unsalted butter, very soft

75g unrefined golden caster sugar

125g treacle

250g self-raising flour

½ tsp bicarbonate of soda

1 tsp cinnamon

½ tsp ground ginger

4 free-range eggs, beaten

4 pieces of stem ginger in syrup, drained of the syrup and chopped into small pieces

icing sugar, to serve

1 Line a 20.5-cm cake tin with Bake-O-Glide.

2 Cream the butter and sugar together, then slowly add the treacle, beating all the time (I use an electric mixer for this).

3 Sieve the flour, bicarbonate of soda and the spices together. Pour a little of the egg into the butter mix, alternating with the flour mix and ending with the flour. Fold in the ginger pieces, then spoon the mix into the prepared cake tin.

4 Slide the tin onto the third set of runners in the Roasting Oven with the Cold Plain Shelf just above and bake for 20 minutes. Then transfer the now hot plain shelf to the third set of runners in the Simmering Oven and place the cake on top. Continue baking for another 40–60 minutes or until the cake is just pulling away from the sides and springs back when touched in the centre.

5 Let the cake cool in the tin for a few minutes, then turn out onto a wire rack. Dust with icing sugar and serve.

conventional cooking:

Pre-heat the oven to 180°C/350°F/gas 4 and bake for 35–40 minutes. If the cake browns too quickly, cover the top with a piece of foil.

apple cake

serves 8

230ml sunflower oil

30ml hazelnut oil

400g unrefined golden caster sugar

3 large free-range eggs

1 tsp vanilla extract

470g plain flour

pinch of salt

1 tsp baking soda

2 tsp baking powder

1 tsp cinnamon

4 large cooking apples, peeled, cored and chopped into small cubes

1 Grease a deep, round 20.5cm loose-bottomed cake tin.

2 Mix the oils and sugar together in a food processor. Add the eggs one at a time, still mixing, and then add the vanilla extract.

3 Sift all the dry ingredients together and fold into the eggy mix. Gently fold in the apples.

4 Pour the mixture into the prepared tin and bake for 15 minutes in the Roasting Oven, then transfer to the Simmering Oven and continue to bake for 1½–2 hours or until a skewer comes out clean.

For 2-oven Aga owners with a Cake Baker, bake for about 1 hour 25 minutes. For 4-oven Aga owners, bake in the Baking Oven for about 1 hour.

5 Cool on a wire rack, then serve with thick double cream.

conventional cooking:

Pre-heat the oven to 180°C/350°F/gas 4 and bake for 1 hour.

lemon squares

FOR THE BASE:

250g unsalted butter, softened

115g unrefined golden caster sugar

280g plain flour

pinch of salt

FOR THE FILLING:

6 extra large organic eggs

675g unrefined golden caster sugar

zest of 5–6 unwaxed lemons

250ml lemon juice

140g plain flour

icing sugar, for dusting

1 Line a 5-cm deep baking tray with Bake-O-Glide.

2 To make the base, cream the butter and sugar together in a food processor until pale and fluffy. Sift in the flour and salt. Mix with paddle attachment until just combined. Make a ball out of the dough, flatten and line the baking tray. Cover with cling film and chill in the fridge for a minimum of 30 minutes.

3 Bake on the fourth set of runners in the Roasting Oven for 10 minutes. Do not let it brown – use the Cold Plain Shelf if the oven is too hot. For 4-oven Aga owners, bake in the Baking Oven for 10 minutes. Allow the base to cool on a wire rack.

4 To make the filling, whisk all the ingredients together until combined, then pour onto the base. Bake on the fourth set of runners in the Roasting Oven for 20–25 minutes or until the filling is set. Slide in the Cold Plain Shelf if the oven is too hot. For 4-oven Aga owners, use the Baking Oven.

5 Cool the cake in the tin, then dust the top with icing sugar and cut into squares.

conventional cooking:

Pre-heat the oven to 180°C/350°F/gas 4 and bake the base for 15–20 minutes, then cool on a wire rack. Add the filling and bake at the same temperature for 30–35 minutes.

traybakes

Traybakes are the perfect recipes when you need to bake a large quantity of cakes, for example when you need to provide cakes for school events or when running a cake stall at a fair. They are made by the all-in-one method, baked and served from the tin. You can use a mixer or do it by hand if you prefer. I have developed a tin especially for traybakes which comes in two sizes, small (34.5 x 24cm, depth 3cm) and large (46 x 34.5cm, depth 3cm), and the quantities given here fit those tins. The small tin makes about 12 squares of cake, the large tin about 24.

SMALL:

275g self-raising flour

225g unrefined golden caster sugar

225g unsalted butter, softened, or baking margarine

2 tsp baking powder

1 tsp vanilla extract

5 free-range eggs

LARGE:

450g self-raising flour

350g unrefined golden caster sugar

350g unsalted butter, softened, or baking margarine

3 tsp baking powder

2 tsp vanilla extract

7 free-range eggs

1 Line the tins with Bake-O-Glide.

2 Put all the ingredients into the bowl of an electric mixer and mix until well combined. Pour the batter into the tin and smooth the top with a palette knife.

3 Bake on the fourth set of runners in the Roasting Oven with the Cold Plain Shelf on the second set of runners. The small traybakes take 20–25 minutes, the large ones 30–35 minutes. The cake is done when it springs back when lightly pressed in the middle and it pulls away from the sides of the tin.

4 Remove the cake from the oven and cool in the tin on a wire rack.

conventional cooking:

Pre-heat the oven to 180°C/350°F/gas 4 and bake the small traybake for 35–40 minutes, the large one for 40–45 minutes.

Variations

The variations for this cake are endless – here are some ideas. These quantities are for the small traybakes, so double them for the large.

Marmalade and ginger

Add 1 tbsp coarse-cut marmalade, the zest of 1 orange, 1 tbsp honey and 1 tsp ground ginger.

Chocolate and pistachio

Add 4 tbsp cocoa powder mixed with 2–3 tbsp boiling water, 1 tbsp golden syrup, 50g dark chocolate chips and 75g chopped pistachio nuts.

Lemon drizzle

Add the zest of 2 lemons. Make the drizzle with the juice from the lemons and 2 tbsp of unrefined golden caster sugar brought to the boil on the Simmering Plate. When the cake is warm, pour over the syrup.

Walnut and espresso with cappuccino icing (shown right)

Add 2 shots of espresso (each about 32ml) and 100g chopped walnuts to the cake mix. To ice, beat together 75g softened unsalted butter, 225g icing sugar and 1 tbsp concentrated liquid coffee. Whisk 100ml double cream to soft peak stage, then fold in the coffee mix. Dust the iced cake with cocoa powder.

all-in-one victoria sponge cake

serves 6–8

175g self-raising flour

175g soft unsalted butter

175g unrefined golden caster sugar

1 tsp vanilla extract

3 large free-range eggs

1 rounded tsp baking powder

FOR THE FILLING:

285ml whipped cream

2 punnets soft fruits, such as blueberries, strawberries, loganberries

icing sugar, for dusting

1 Line two 20-cm round sponge tins, preferably loose bottomed, with Bake-O-Glide. Put all the cake ingredients into the bowl of an electric mixer and, using the beater attachment, beat until combined. Divide the cake mix between the prepared cake tins.

2 Place the grid shelf on the floor of the Roasting Oven and place the cake tins towards the right side of the oven, on the grid shelf. Slide the Cold Plain Shelf onto the third set of runners and bake the cakes for 20 minutes or until they are golden on top, gently coming away from the sides and spring back when lightly pressed on top. Remove the cakes and stand on a wire rack for a minute, then remove the cakes from the tins and cool on the wire rack. For 4-oven Aga owners, cook the cakes on the fourth set of runners in the Baking Oven for 20–25 minutes and use the plain shelf only if the cakes are browning too quickly.

3 When the cakes are cool, whip the cream to soft peaks and spread onto one cake then top with the fruits and the second cake. Dust with icing sugar and serve.

conventional cooking:

Pre-heat the oven to 160°C/325°F/gas 3 and bake for 30–35 minutes.

cup cakes

makes 12 large cup cakes

275g self-raising flour

200g unrefined golden caster sugar

2 tsp baking powder

225g unsalted butter or margarine

4 large free-range eggs

4 tbsp milk

FOR THE BUTTERCREAM ICING:

3 large free-range egg whites

155g unrefined golden caster sugar

375g unsalted butter, at room temperature

1 tsp vanilla extract

1 Line a muffin tin with paper cup-cake cases and set aside.

2 Tip all the ingredients into a bowl and mix well until combined. Fill the cup-cake cases to the top.

3 Bake on the fourth set of runners in the Roasting Oven for 20 minutes, checking halfway through and sliding in the Cold Plain Shelf if necessary. They are done when they spring back when gently pressed on top. Remove from the tin and cool on a wire rack. For 4-oven Aga owners, bake on the third set of runners in the Baking Oven for 20–25 minutes.

4 To make the icing, place the egg whites and sugar in a large heatproof bowl, over a pot of simmering water on the Simmering Plate, and, using an electric whisk, whisk until the sugar has dissolved. When ready, take the bowl off the heat and continue whisking until it starts to form soft peaks. Add the butter bit by bit until it is all combined. Add the vanilla extract and chill until it becomes stiff but still spreadable, then use to ice the cup cakes. Add colouring if you wish.

conventional cooking:

Pre-heat the oven to 200°C/400°F/gas 6 and bake for 20–25 minutes.

all-in-one victoria sponge cake

peanut butter cup cakes

makes 12 large cup cakes

225g unsalted butter or margarine, very soft

200g unrefined golden caster sugar

275g self-raising flour

2 tsp baking powder

4 large free-range eggs

4 tbsp milk

125g peanut butter

FOR THE PEANUT BUTTER CREAM ICING:

3 large free-range egg whites

155g unrefined golden caster sugar

375g peanut butter

1 Line a muffin tin with paper cup-cake cases and set aside.

2 Cream the butter and sugar together. Sieve the flour and baking powder into a bowl. Add the eggs to the sugar and butter one at a time, alternating with the flour until all combined. Beat in the milk and peanut butter.

3 Fill the cup-cake cases half-full and level off the tops. Bake on the fourth set of runners in the Roasting Oven for 20 minutes, checking halfway through and turning the tray if necessary. They are done when they spring back when gently pressed on top.

4 Remove from the tin and cool on a wire rack.

5 To make the icing, place the egg whites and sugar in a large heatproof bowl. Set the bowl over a pot of simmering water, creating a bain marie, and whisk the sugar and egg whites until the sugar has dissolved.

6 When ready take the bowl off the heat and use an electric whisk to whisk the mix until it starts to form soft peaks. Add the peanut butter little by little until it is all combined. Chill until it becomes stiff but still spreadable, then use to ice the cup cakes

conventional cooking:

Pre-heat the oven to 200ºC/400ºF/gas 6 and bake for 20 minutes, as above. Make the icing on the hob.

fairy cakes

To make chocolate fairy cakes, use 75g self-raising flour mixed with 25g cocoa powder.

makes about 6

100g soft unsalted butter, at room temperature

100g self-raising flour

100g unrefined golden caster sugar

1 tsp baking powder

2 free-range eggs

FOR THE ICING:

225g icing sugar

2–4 tbsp water or milk

1 packet of dolly mixture sweets

1 Line a shallow muffin tin with paper cases (you will also need a roasting tin that the muffin tin will fit into).

2 Beat all the cake ingredients together in an electric mixer. Spoon the mix into the paper cases so that they are half full.

3 Put the tin into the roasting tin and slide the tin onto the third or fourth set of runners in the Roasting Oven and bake for 15–20 minutes or until the cakes have risen and are golden on top. Remove the paper cases from the tin and cool on a wire rack.

4 To make the icing, mix the sugar and liquid and beat until smooth. Spoon onto the cooled cakes and top with the sweets.

conventional cooking:

Pre-heat the oven to 200°C/400°F/gas 6 and bake the cakes directly in the muffin tin (don't put them into another tin) for 15–18 minutes.

carrot cake cup cakes

makes 12 cup cakes

350g self-raising flour, sifted

1 tsp baking powder

½ tsp salt

1 tsp ground cinnamon

350g unrefined golden caster sugar

175ml grapeseed oil

2 large free-range eggs, lightly beaten

1 tsp vanilla extract

175g chopped walnuts

175g desiccated coconut

175g puréed cooked carrots

85g crushed pineapple

FOR THE ICING:

60g unsalted butter, softened

150g cream cheese

350g icing sugar

1 tsp vanilla extract

marzipan carrots, to decorate

1 Line a 12-hole shallow muffin tin with paper cases. (You will also need a roasting tin that the muffin tin fits into.)

2 Sift the flour, baking powder, salt and cinnamon into the bowl of an electric mixer and then add the rest of the ingredients and mix well. Spoon the mix into the paper cases so they are half full.

3 Put the muffin tin into the roasting tin and slide the tin onto the third or fourth set of runners in the Roasting Oven and bake for 15–20 minutes or until the cakes have risen and are golden on top. Remove the paper cases from the tin and cool on a wire rack.

4 To make the icing, using an electric beater beat the butter and cream cheese together until smooth. Slowly add the icing sugar and vanilla extract and mix until lump-free and very smooth. Ice the cup cakes and top with a marzipan carrot if you wish.

conventional cooking:

Pre-heat the oven to 190ºC/375F/gas 5. Cook for 12–18 minutes.

carrot cake cup cakes

celebration fruit cake

for a 15-cm round cake or a 13-cm square cake:

225g currants

75g sultanas

75g raisins

40g organic glacé cherries, rinsed, dried and chopped

40g organic candied peel

zest of ½ an organic orange

zest of ½ an organic lemon

½ tbsp treacle

2 tbsp brandy

110g soft unsalted butter

110g soft brown sugar

110g plain flour

20g rice flour

pinch salt

½ tsp mixed spice

2 free-range eggs

40g chopped almonds

for a 20.5-cm round cake:

450g currants

175g sultanas

175g raisins

50g organic glacé cherries, rinsed, dried and chopped

50g organic candied peel

zest of 1 organic orange

zest of 1 organic lemon

1 tbsp treacle

3 tbsp brandy

225g soft unsalted butter

225g soft brown sugar

225g plain flour

55g rice flour

½ tsp salt

1 tsp mixed spice

4 free-range eggs

50g chopped almonds

for a 23-cm round cake or a 20-cm square cake:

575g currants

225g sultanas

225g raisins

60g organic glacé cherries, rinsed, dried and chopped

60g organic candied peel

zest of 1 organic orange

zest of 1 organic lemon

1 tbsp treacle

4 tbsp brandy

275g soft unsalted butter

275g soft brown sugar

275g plain flour

60g rice flour

½ tsp salt

1 tsp mixed spice

5 free-range eggs

60g chopped almonds

for a 28-cm round cake or a 25.5-cm square cake:

900g currants

350g sultanas

350g raisins

100g organic glacé cherries, rinsed, dried and chopped

120g organic candied peel

zest of 2 organic oranges

zest of 2 organic lemons

1½ tbsp treacle

6 tbsp brandy

450g soft unsalted butter

450g soft brown sugar

450g plain flour

65g rice flour

½ tsp salt

1½ tsp mixed spice

8 free-range eggs

120g chopped almonds

1 Read the special advice on fruit cakes below. The day before making the cake, put the fruit, peel, zests, treacle and brandy in a bowl and mix well. Cover with cling film and leave in a cool place to marinate.

2 Line your tin with Bake-O-Glide if necessary or if the tin is new.

3 When you are ready to make the cake, cream the butter and sugar together until they are pale and fluffy. Sieve the flours, salt and mixed spice together in a bowl. Add the eggs to the butter mix one at a time, alternating with the flour mix until it is all incorporated. If you are doing this with an electric mixer, do it on a very low, gentle speed. If you do it by hand, use a folding motion to mix.

4 Fold in the fruit with all the juices and the almonds. Spoon into the prepared tin.

5 Bake in the Roasting Oven for 20 minutes, then transfer to the Simmering Oven for 5–10 hours, depending on your Aga. You can bake it just in the Simmering Oven but it will take longer. The Aga baking time will vary tremendously from Aga to Aga and will take as long as it takes! The great thing about an Aga is that you can open the door and keep on checking.

conventional cooking:

Pre-heat the oven to 140ºC/275ºF/gas 1. You will need to line the tin and wrap it with a layer of brown paper around the outside and cover the top of the cake with a double layer of greaseproof paper with a small hole cut out for the steam to escape.

The 15-cm round or 13-cm square cake will take 3–3½ hours, but check it after 3 hours.

The 20.5-cm round cake will take 4–5 hours, but check it after 4 hours.

The 23-cm round or 20-cm square cake will take 4–5 hours, but check it after 4 hours.

The 28-cm round or 25.5-cm square cake will take 5–5½ hours, but check it after 5 hours.

a note on baking fruit cakes

The reason for the huge timing variations is that no two Aga cookers are the same. Owners of 4-oven Agas may find that their Simmering Oven is slightly slower than a 2-oven Aga Simmering Oven. Start the cake off in the Baking Oven for 45–60 minutes, then transfer it to the Simmering Oven in as high a position as possible and cook for 4–10 hours, or longer in some cases. Another trick is to use the large grill rack from inside the large roasting tin. Put the grill rack directly onto the Simmering Oven floor and put the fruit cake directly onto it. If you feel you don't need the extra boost of the Baking Oven, bake the cake in the Simmering Oven only as above. For 2-oven Aga owners, if you have an Aga Cake Baker you can use it for baking fruit cakes. It will reduce the baking time and still give a good result but you can't beat the Simmering Oven method. There is no need to line cake tins with brown paper or to cover with paper. Use Bake-O-Glide for ease of cake removal.

simnel cake

serves 6–8

225g plain flour

1 tsp baking powder

pinch of salt

175g unsalted butter, softened

174g soft brown sugar

3 free-range eggs

100g raisins

175g currants

100g sultanas

50g organic mixed candied peel, chopped

50g glacé cherries, rinsed, and halved

zest of 1 organic orange

zest of 1 organic lemon

2 tbsp milk

450g organic marzipan (or see the recipe on page 259)

FOR THE GLAZE:

50g good-quality apricot jam

1 tbsp water

1 Line an 18-cm round cake tin with Bake-O-Glide. If you have a Cake Baker you may want to use it.

2 Sift the flour, baking powder and salt together in a large bowl.

3 Cream the butter and sugar together until pale and fluffy. Add the eggs one at a time to the creamed butter, alternating with the flour until it is all incorporated. Carefully fold in the fruit, candied peel and zest and stir in the milk so everything is evenly incorporated.

4 Roll out one-third of the marzipan to a circle the same size as the cake tin.

5 Spoon half of the cake batter into the tin, cover with the marzipan circle and spoon on the remaining cake mix. Level the top.

6 Slide the Cold Plain Shelf onto the fourth set of runners in the Roasting Oven. Place the cake on the shelf and bake for 15–20 minutes. Transfer the now hot plain shelf to the Simmering Oven, place the cake on top and bake for 2–5 hours, depending on your oven, until the cake is golden brown and firm in the centre.

7 Cool the cake in the tin on a wire rack. When it is cool, remove from the tin and place on a cake stand.

8 While the cake is cooling, make the apricot glaze. Bring the jam and water to the boil in a saucepan, then pass through a metal sieve. Use it warm.

9 Roll out the remaining marzipan and cut out another circle to fit over the top of the cake. Roll 11 balls from the leftover marzipan scraps (first dip your hands in a little icing sugar to prevent the marzipan sticking to them).

10 Brush a little apricot glaze onto the top of the cake and roll on the marzipan circle. Flute the edges of the marzipan and make a criss-cross pattern with a knife if you wish. Brush a little apricot glaze onto the bottom of each marzipan ball and arrange them in a circle on top of the cake.

conventional cooking:

Pre-heat the oven to 160°C/325°F/gas 3 and bake as above for 2 hours.

carrot cake

serves 10–12

700g self-raising flour

1 tbsp baking powder

1 tsp salt

1 tbsp ground cinnamon

700g unrefined golden caster sugar

350ml grapeseed oil

4 large free-range eggs, lightly beaten

1 tbsp vanilla extract

350g chopped walnuts

350g desiccated coconut

350g carrots, cooked and puréed

175g crushed pineapple

FOR THE ICING:

118g unsalted butter, softened

300g pack cream cheese

700g icing sugar

1 tsp vanilla extract

1 Grease the large roasting tin and line with Bake-O-Glide.

2 Sift the flour, baking powder, salt and cinnamon into the bowl of an electric mixer, then add the rest of the cake ingredients and mix well. Pour the mixture into the tin.

3 Bake on the fourth set of runners in the Roasting Oven with the Cold Plain Shelf on the second set of runners for 40–50 minutes or until the sides pull away from the tin and a skewer comes out clean. For 4-oven Aga owners, use the Baking Oven and bake for 45–50 minutes. Cool on a wire rack until completely cold.

4 To make the cream cheese icing, using an electric beater, beat the butter and cream cheese together until smooth. Slowly add the icing sugar and vanilla extract until it is lump-free and very smooth. Spread the icing over the top of the cake.

conventional cooking:

Pre-heat the oven to 190ºC/375ºF/gas 5 and bake for 50–60 minutes.

classic scones

makes 6–8

225g self-raising flour

1½ tbsp unrefined golden caster sugar

pinch of salt

40g butter, softened

150ml milk

1 free-range egg yolk, beaten, to glaze

1 Line a baking tray with Bake-O-Glide.

2 Combine the flour, sugar and salt in the bowl of an electric mixer with the paddle hook attached. Add the butter in pieces, then add the milk. Mix until the dough just starts to hold together. Turn out onto a floured surface.

3 Roll out the dough to a thickness of 2cm and cut out with a fluted cutter. Put the scones on the baking tray and brush the tops with egg yolk. Sprinkle over a little more caster sugar if you wish.

4 Slide the baking tray onto the third set of runners in the Roasting Oven and bake for 8–10 minutes or until they are golden. Remove from the oven and cool on a wire rack.

conventional cooking:

Pre-heat the oven to 200ºC/400ºF/gas 6 and bake as above.

cheddar and mango chutney scone traybake

This traybake (and the buttermilk scones on the facing page) is very rich and quite unlike classic scones.

makes about 12 squares

475g self-raising flour

1 level tbsp baking powder

pinch of salt

150g butter, softened

2 large free-range eggs, beaten, plus 100ml mango chutney plus enough double cream to make 300ml of liquid in total, including the eggs

250g strong Cheddar cheese, grated and tossed in 1 tbsp self-raising flour

FOR THE TOPPING:

1 free-range egg yolk, beaten with 1 tbsp milk

50g Cheddar cheese, grated

1 Line a small traybake tray with Bake-O-Glide.

2 Combine the flour, baking powder and salt in an electric mixer with the paddle hook. Add the butter in pieces. Lightly beat the eggs, chutney, and cream together so they total 300ml and add to the flour and butter. Add the cheese and mix until the dough just holds together.

3 Press into the traybake tin so that it is 2cm thick and brush with the egg glaze. Mark the dough into squares. Sprinkle over the grated cheese topping.

4 Slide the tin onto the third set of runners in the Roasting Oven and bake for 20–25 minutes or until golden. Slide in the Cold Plain Shelf after 10 minutes. Remove from the oven and cool on a wire rack. Break off what you want and serve.

conventional cooking:

Pre-heat the oven to 200ºC/400ºF/gas 6 and bake for 20–25 minutes or until golden.

buttermilk scones

makes about 10 scones

475g self-raising flour

50g unrefined golden caster sugar

1 level tbsp baking powder

pinch of salt

355g butter, softened

2 large free-range eggs

120ml buttermilk

FOR THE GLAZE:

1 free-range egg yolk beaten with 1 tbsp milk

1 Line two baking trays with Bake-O-Glide.

2 Combine the flour, sugar, baking powder and salt in the bowl of an electric mixer with the paddle hook. Add the butter in pieces.

3 Lightly beat the eggs and the buttermilk together, then add them to the flour and butter. Mix until the dough just starts to hold together. Turn out onto a floured surface and knead for no more than 1 minute.

4 Roll out the dough 2cm thick and cut out the scones with a 6-cm fluted cutter. Put them onto the prepared baking trays and brush with the egg and milk glaze. Sprinkle over a little more sugar if you wish. Slide the baking tray onto the third set of runners in the Roasting Oven and bake for 8–10 minutes or until they are golden. Remove from the oven and cool on a wire rack.

conventional cooking:

Pre-heat the oven to 220°C/425°F/gas 7 and bake for 10–12 minutes until golden and well risen.

gorgonzola scones

makes about 10 scones

475g self-raising flour

1 level tbsp baking powder

pinch of salt

355g butter, softened

2 large free-range eggs

120ml double cream

235g Gorgonzola cheese, cut into small pieces and tossed in 1 tbsp self-raising flour

FOR THE GLAZE:

1 free-range egg yolk beaten with 1 tbsp milk

1 Line two baking trays with Bake-O-Glide.

2 Combine the flour, baking powder and salt in the bowl of an electric mixer with the paddle hook. Add the butter in pieces.

3 Lightly beat the eggs and the cream together and add them to the flour and butter. Add the Gorgonzola and mix until the dough just starts to hold together. Turn out onto a floured surface and knead for no more than 1 minute.

4 Roll the dough 2cm thick and cut out scones with a 6-cm fluted cutter. Put the scones on the prepared baking trays and brush with the egg glaze. Slide the baking tray onto the third set of runners in the Roasting Oven and bake for 8–10 minutes or until they are golden. Remove from the oven and cool on a wire rack.

conventional cooking:

Pre-heat the oven to 220°C/425°F/gas 7 and bake for 10–12 minutes until golden and well risen.

icings and fillings

cream cheese icing

118g unsalted butter, softened
300g cream cheese
700g icing sugar
1 tsp vanilla extract

Using an electric beater, beat the butter and cream cheese together until smooth. Slowly add the icing sugar and vanilla extract, making sure the mixture is lump-free and very smooth.

peanut butter cream icing

3 large free-range egg whites
155g unrefined golden caster sugar
375g peanut butter

Place the egg whites and sugar in a large heatproof bowl over a pan of simmering water, creating a bain marie, and whisk until the sugar has dissolved. When ready, take the bowl off the heat and, using an electric whisk, whisk the mix until it starts to form soft peaks, then add the peanut butter little by little until it is all combined. Chill until it becomes stiff but still spreadable, and then use to ice the cake.

buttercream icing

230g icing sugar
120g unsalted butter
1–2 tsp of a suitable extract for flavouring

Sieve the icing sugar into a large bowl and cream with the butter. Add extract for flavour. Suitable flavours include coffee powder, vanilla extract, almond extract and cocoa powder.

walnut filling

3 tbsp apricot jam
30g walnuts, chopped
1 tsp vanilla extract
80g ground almonds

Warm the jam at the back of the Aga and sieve it into a bowl, then mix everything together.

chocolate cake icing

75g unsalted butter
50g cocoa powder
5–6 tbsp milk
225g icing sugar

Melt the butter in a saucepan at the back of the Aga. Stir in the cocoa powder and cook on the Simmering Plate for a minute or so, then remove from the heat. Stir the milk into the icing sugar, then mix well into the butter and cocoa. Cool until it has thickened, then ice your cake.

chocolate cream cheese icing

300g cream cheese
118g unsalted butter, softened
700g icing sugar
1 tsp vanilla extract
2 tbsp cocoa powder

Beat everything together very well in an electric mixer, then use to ice and fill the cakes.

marzipan

makes enough to cover a 20-cm round cake

170g icing sugar, plus extra for kneading
170g unrefined golden caster sugar
2 organic eggs
340g ground almonds
2 drops almond extract
1 tsp lemon juice

1 Sift the sugars together in a heatproof bowl, then lightly beat in the eggs.
2 Bring a saucepan of water to the boil on the Boiling Plate, then move to the Simmering Plate. Place the bowl over the saucepan, making sure the bowl does not touch the water, and whisk the mixture until it is light and creamy and leaves a ribbon trail. Remove the bowl from the heat and set aside to cool completely.
3 When the mixture is cold, add the almonds, almond extract and lemon juice. Dust a worksurface with icing sugar and knead the paste until it is just smooth. Do not over-work the paste. If you do, too much oil will be released. Wrap the marzipan well in cling film and store in a cool, dry place.

11 biscuits

chocolate chip cookies for the christmas tree

You can make this dough up to one month before cooking; freeze in logs wrapped in greaseproof paper. If you wish, you can also make star-shaped cookies by pressing the dough into a baking tray to a thickness of 2cm, refrigerating for 1 hour and then cutting out with a star-shaped cookie cutter.

makes 20 cookies

250g unsalted butter, softened
225g soft unrefined brown sugar
110g unrefined granulated sugar
2 large free-range eggs
2 tsp vanilla extract
280g plain flour
½ tsp salt
1 tsp baking powder
450g plain chocolate chips

1 Cream the butter and sugars together until smooth and fluffy. Add the eggs one at a time and the vanilla extract.

2 Put the flour, salt and baking powder into a sieve and sift into the butter mix. Fold to combine thoroughly, then add the chocolate chips.

3 Drop 2 tablespoons of the dough one on top of the other on a baking sheet. Repeat to use up all the dough, spacing the cookies about 5cm apart. Bake for 8 minutes on the fourth set of runners in the Roasting Oven with the Cold Plain Shelf on the second set of runners. Cook in batches and remove to a wire rack.

4 While they are still hot, make a hole one-third of the way down the cookie with a clean, round pen top. Let the cookies cool completely. String a pretty ribbon through the hole and tie in a loop so that you can hang them on the Christmas tree.

conventional cooking:
Pre-heat the oven to 190°C/375°F/gas 5 and bake the cookies as above.

shortbread biscuits

These are the biscuits we serve at my Aga demonstrations. Halve the quantities if you want to make less.

makes about 50 biscuits

900g butter, at room temperature

450g unrefined golden caster sugar

1.25kg plain flour

225g semolina

5–6 drops orange extract or other flavouring (optional)

extra caster sugar, for sprinkling

1 Cream together the butter and sugar until pale and fluffy in an electric mixer with the paddle attachment. Sift in the flour and semolina and add the orange extract if using.

2 Combine well, then scrape the mixture into the large roasting tin, cover with cling film and chill overnight.

3 The next day, cut the dough into four or five blocks and remove from tin. Cut each block into 2cm thick squares and put onto a baking tray lined with Bake-O-Glide. Slide the tray onto the third set of runners in the Baking Oven for 20–25 minutes, or the fourth set of runners in the Roasting Oven with the Cold Plain Shelf on the second set of runners for 10–15 minutes, or until lightly coloured.

4 Remove the shortbread to a wire rack to cool and sprinkle with more caster sugar – this must be done while the biscuits are still hot.

5 The dough freezes well. If you want to use only a few blocks of dough, wrap the remaining blocks very well in cling film and foil and freeze until required. When you want to bake them, slice into the biscuit shapes and bake for 15–20 minutes from frozen as above.

conventional cooking:
Pre-heat the oven to 180°C/350°F/gas 4 and bake for 10 minutes.

russian shortcake

makes 12–14 pieces

145g butter

145g soft brown sugar

1 tbsp golden syrup

1 free-range egg

1½ tsp vanilla extract

260g plain flour

1 tsp baking powder

120g sultanas

FOR THE ICING:

4 tbsp icing sugar

2 tbsp butter

2 tsp golden sugar

1 tsp ground ginger

1 Line a deep Swiss roll tin with Bake-O-Glide.

2 Melt the butter, sugar and golden syrup together in a saucepan on the Simmering Plate and cool a little.

3 Beat the egg and vanilla together in a large bowl. Stir the butter mix into the egg, add the flour, baking powder and sultanas and mix well. Pour the mixture into the tin.

4 Slide the tin on to the fourth set of runners in the Roasting Oven and bake for 3–5 minutes, then slide in the Cold Plain Shelf directly above and continue baking for a further 10 minutes. Do not over-bake. For 4-oven Aga owners, bake in the Baking Oven without the cold plain shelf for 10 minutes.

5 Meanwhile, make the icing. Melt all the icing ingredients in a saucepan on the Simmering Plate. Ice the cake immediately it comes out of the oven and let the cake cool completely in the tin before removing.

conventional cooking:
Pre-heat the oven to 190ºC/375ºF/gas 5 and bake for 15–20 minutes.

pecan shortbread squares

makes about 20 bars,
enough for 1 large baking
tray or 2 small ones

FOR THE SHORTBREAD:

500g butter, at room temperature

250g unrefined golden caster sugar

515g plain flour

125g semolina

1 tbsp vanilla extract (optional)

FOR THE TOPPING:

500g unsalted butter

250ml honey

750g brown demerara sugar

zest of 1 lemon

zest of 1 orange

60ml double cream

1kg pecan nuts, chopped

500g dark organic chocolate

1 To make the shortbread, cream together the butter and sugar until pale and fluffy in an electric mixer with the paddle attachment. Sift in the flour and semolina and add the vanilla extract if using.

2 Combine well, then press the mix into one large or two small 5cm deep baking trays, cover with cling film and refrigerate overnight.

3 Remove the cling film and bake on the fourth set of runners in the Roasting Oven with the Cold Plain Shelf on the second set of runners for 10 minutes – do not let it colour. Remove to a wire rack and allow to cool.

4 To make the topping, combine the butter, honey, sugar and zests in a saucepan and cook over a low heat until the butter has melted, stirring with a wooden spoon. Bring to a boil and boil for 2–3 minutes.

5 Remove from the heat and add the cream and nuts. Stir well, then pour over the baked shortbread. Bake on the fourth set of runners in the Roasting Oven for 20–25 minutes with the Cold Plain Shelf above. For 4-oven Aga owners, bake the filled shortbread in the Baking Oven, as above. Cool in the tin on a wire rack.

6 Melt the chocolate in a bowl at the back of the Aga. Cut the pecan shortbread into squares, dip one half in the melted chocolate and leave to harden. Store in a cool place, wrapped in greaseproof paper.

conventional cooking:

Pre-heat the oven to 190°C/375°F/gas 5 and bake the shortbread for 10 minutes. Turn the temperature down to 180°C/350°F/gas 4 and bake the filled shortbread for 20–25 minutes.

chocolate almond caramel bars

makes about 12 bars

150g plain flour

1 tsp baking powder

60g ground almonds

60g unrefined golden caster sugar

125g unsalted butter, melted

125g dark chocolate, finely chopped or in chips

60ml double cream

FOR THE CARAMEL:

220g unrefined golden caster sugar

80ml double cream

50g unsalted butter, chopped

50g slightly salted butter, chopped

1 Sieve the flour and baking powder into a large bowl. Add the almonds and sugar and mix well. Pour in the melted butter and stir to combine, then press the dough into the small shallow baking tray.

2 Slide the baking tray on to the third set of runners in the Roasting Oven and bake for 10–12 minutes or until golden. Remove from the oven and leave to cool in the tin. For 4-oven Aga owners, bake in the Baking Oven on the third set of runners for 12–15 minutes.

3 Make the caramel while the base is cooling. Put the caster sugar and 80ml water into a saucepan and stir on the Simmering Plate until the sugar has dissolved. Then move to the Boiling Plate and boil without stirring until it turns amber in colour. Remove from the heat and slowly add the 80ml cream (watch out because it will spit) and both types of butter and stir to combine. Put it back on to the Simmering Plate and simmer for 3–5 minutes. Remove from the heat and leave to stand for about 20 minutes or until it starts to thicken, then pour over the cooked pastry base. Set aside until completely cool.

4 Put the chocolate into a bowl. Pour the 60ml of double cream into a saucepan and bring to a strong simmer on the Simmering Plate, then pour over the chocolate and stir until it is well combined and all the chocolate has melted. Pour the chocolate over the cool caramel and then put the baking tray into the refrigerator for about 3 hours until set. Cut into wedges or bars.

5 Store in an airtight container in the fridge. They can be made 3 days in advance.

conventional cooking:

Pre-heat the oven to 190°C/375°F/gas 5 and bake the dough for 12–15 minutes or until golden. Cook the topping on the hob.

chocolate chip biscotti

makes approximately 14

270g self-raising flour

1 tsp baking powder

145g unrefined golden caster sugar

200g dark chocolate chips

pinch of salt

3 large free-range eggs

2 tsp vanilla extract

beaten free-range egg or milk, to glaze

1 Sieve the flour and baking powder together into a large bowl, then add the sugar, chocolate chips and salt and mix well.

2 Beat the eggs with the vanilla extract and then pour them into the dry ingredients and mix well – you can do this in an electric mixer using the paddle attachment. The dough will be very soft and slightly wet.

3 Turn out the dough and make into flattish shape on a baking sheet lined with Bake-O-Glide. Brush lightly with a little beaten egg or milk. Slide the baking tray into the Roasting Oven on the fourth set of runners with the Cold Plain Shelf above for 20–30 minutes or until golden. For 4-oven Aga owners, bake in the Baking Oven for 25–35 minutes.

4 Remove the loaf from the oven and cool on a wire rack. Set the lined baking tray aside.

5 When it is cool, slice the loaf diagonally into slices 2.5cm thick. Lay the slices on the lined baking tray and bake in the Simmering Oven for about 20 minutes or until the biscotti are crisp.

6 Cool on a wire rack and store in an airtight tin.

conventional cooking:

Pre-heat the oven to 200°C/400°F/gas 6, bake the loaf for 20–30 minutes and then bake the biscotti slices for another 20 minutes.

chocolate peanut butter cookies

makes about 15 large cookies

150g organic dark chocolate

170g brown sugar

120g chunky peanut butter

60g very soft unsalted butter, at room temperature

2 large free-range eggs

1 tsp vanilla extract

170g plain flour

½ tsp baking powder

120g dark chocolate chips

1 Melt the chocolate in a large bowl at the back of the Aga.

2 Combine all the ingredients together well in the bowl and drop tablespoons of the dough on to an ungreased baking sheet, spacing them well apart.

3 Bake on the fourth set of runners in the Roasting Oven with the Cold Plain Shelf on the second set of runners for 8–10 minutes or until puffed up and set to the touch. Don't over-cook. Cool on a wire rack.

conventional cooking:

Pre-heat the oven to 190°C/375°F/gas 5 and bake for 12–14 minutes or until they are puffed up and set to the touch.

oatmeal and coconut bars

200g desiccated coconut

150g plain flour

170g brown sugar

60g granulated sugar

½ tsp salt

270g unsalted butter, cut into pieces

75g oatmeal

340ml raspberry jam

1 Lightly toast 170g of the coconut on a baking tray on the first set of runners in either the Roasting or Baking Oven for 2–3 minutes, checking frequently to make sure it doesn't burn, or in a dry frying pan on the Simmering Plate.

2 Using a food processor, make the dough. Blend together the flour, sugars, salt and butter. Using the pulse button, or folding in by hand, add the toasted coconut and the oatmeal.

3 Reserve 170g of the dough and press the rest into a greased shallow baking tray. Spread the jam over, then crumble over the remaining dough. Sprinkle over the untoasted coconut and bake on the third runners in the Roasting Oven for 20–25 minutes. Slide in the Cold Plain Shelf if the mixture browns too quickly.

4 Cool in the tray on a wire rack until it is completely cold. Lift it out and cut into bars. Can be made 3 days in advance.

conventional cooking:

Pre-heat the oven to 190ºC/375ºF/gas 5 and bake for 20–25 minutes.

yo yo biscuits

makes about 18 medium-sized biscuits

60g icing sugar
170g butter
175g self-raising flour
60g custard powder
candy-coated chocolate buttons,
to decorate

1 Line a shallow baking tray with Bake-O-Glide.

2 Cream the icing sugar and butter together. Stir in the flour and custard powder. Roll the mixture into balls and place on the baking tray. Flatten each ball with a fork and push in a chocolate button.

3 Bake the biscuits on the fourth set of runners in the Roasting Oven with the Cold Plain Shelf above for 8–10 minutes or until done. Do not over-bake – the biscuits should be yellow, not brown. Cool them on a wire rack.

conventional cooking:

Pre-heat the oven to 150°C/300°F/gas 2 and bake for 15–18 minutes or until done.

magic bars

So delicious they disappear like magic!

makes 18

120g unsalted butter
300g digestive biscuit crumbs
375ml can condensed milk
100g dark chocolate chips
250g desiccated coconut
200g chopped pecans

1 Melt the butter in a shallow baking tin in the Roasting Oven for 1–2 minutes. Sprinkle the biscuit crumbs over the butter, pour the condensed milk evenly over the crumbs, then top with the remaining ingredients and press down.

2 Bake on the third set of runners in the Roasting Oven for 25–30 minutes or until golden in colour. If it is browning too quickly, slide in the Cold Plain Shelf. Cool on a wire rack, cut into squares and store at room temperature.

conventional cooking:
Pre-heat the oven to 180°C/350°F/gas 4 and bake as above.

cheese biscuits

You can freeze this dough at the 'just combined' stage. I suggest shaping it into a log and wrapping it first in greaseproof paper, then in foil to keep in the freezer. When you want to use it, simply unwrap and, using a very sharp knife, slice it into rounds and continue as in step 3.

makes about 20–25 biscuits

145g plain flour

145g wholewheat four

60g Parmesan cheese, grated

2 tsp salt

30g unsalted butter, cut into pieces

1 tbsp thyme leaves

1 tbsp honey

175ml milk

1 free-range egg white, lightly whisked

1 tbsp nigella seeds, for sprinkling

1 Put the flours, cheese and salt into the bowl of the food processor. Pulse a couple of times to mix. Add the butter and thyme, then pulse until the mix resembles coarse breadcrumbs.

2 Mix the honey and milk in a jug, then, with the machine on slow speed, pour it through the top until the dough just comes together. Stop as soon as it does as you do not want to over-work the dough. Wrap it in cling film and refrigerate for 30 minutes.

3 Turn out the dough on to a lightly floured surface and divide into four pieces, then roll each piece very thinly. Transfer the pastry to a baking sheet lined with Bake-O-Glide and, using the cutter of your choice, cut the dough into shapes. Remove the excess dough and brush the shapes with the beaten egg white and sprinkle with some more salt and the nigella seeds.

4 Slide the baking tray onto the fourth set of runners in the Roasting Oven with the Cold Plain Shelf directly above and bake for about 10 minutes. Turn the tray and continue baking for about another 5 minutes or until the biscuits are firm to the touch and lightly coloured. For 4-oven Aga owners, slide the baking tray on to the third set of runners in the Baking Oven and bake for about 20 minutes, turning the tray halfway through the baking time.

5 Remove the biscuits from the oven and carefully transfer them on to a wire rack to cool.

conventional cooking:
Pre-heat the oven to 190°C/375°F/gas 5 and bake in the middle of the oven for 20–25 minutes, turning the baking tray halfway through baking.

olive, orange and rosemary biscotti

Biscotti are the perfect party food because you can make them ahead of time, and the dough also freezes well. Once the dough is formed into logs, freeze it like cookie dough. When you are ready to use it, defrost thoroughly and continue with the recipe. Once baked, the biscotti will keep in an airtight tin for up to a week.

makes about 18, depending how thick you slice them

270g self-raising flour
2 tsp baking powder
black pepper
200g stoned black Kalamata olives in olive oil, halved
zest of 1 organic orange (make the zests long and thin)
1 tbsp freshly chopped rosemary
3 free-range eggs
olive oil from the olives

FOR THE GLAZE:
beaten egg or milk
sea salt

1 Sieve the flour and baking powder into a large bowl. Add the pepper, olives, zest and rosemary and mix well. Beat the eggs with 2 tablespoons of the olive oil and then pour them into the dry ingredients and mix well – you can do this in an electric mixer using the paddle attachment. The dough will be very soft and slightly wet.

2 Turn out the soft dough on to a floured surface and shape into a flattish loaf. Place on a baking sheet lined with Bake-O-Glide and brush lightly with a little beaten egg or milk and sprinkle with sea salt.

3 Slide the baking tray onto the fourth set of runners in the Roasting Oven with the Cold Plain Shelf above and bake for 20–30 minutes or until golden. For 4-oven Aga owners, bake in the Baking Oven for 25–35 minutes. Remove the loaf from the oven and cool on a wire rack. Set the lined baking tray aside.

4 When cool, slice the loaf on the diagonal 2.5cm thick. Lay the slices on the lined baking tray and bake in the Simmering Oven for about 20 minutes or until the biscotti are crisp. Cool the biscotti on a wire rack and store in an airtight tin.

conventional cooking:
Pre-heat the oven to 200ºC/400ºF/gas 6 and bake for 20–30 minutes, then bake the biscotti slices for another 20 minutes.

cheese sticks

makes about 18–20, depending how you cut them

60g plain flour

½ tsp baking powder

½ tsp powdered mustard

55g butter

30g fine breadcrumbs

25g ground almonds

100g strong Cheddar cheese, grated

salt and pepper

1 free-range egg yolk

1 tbsp water

1 Line a shallow baking tray with Bake-O-Glide.

2 Sift the flour, baking powder and mustard together in a large bowl and rub in the butter.

3 Rub in the breadcrumbs, almonds and cheese and mix well. Season. Beat the yolk with the water and stir into the dry mixture to form a dough, but take care not to over-work it.

4 Roll out the dough on a floured surface to a thickness of 5mm and cut into sticks. The size depends on personal preference – the smaller and thinner, the shorter the baking time.

5 Transfer the sticks to the baking tray and bake on the second set of runners in the Roasting Oven for 5–8 minutes. Turn the baking tray around halfway through the baking time and turn the sticks over when they are golden on top – you will have to watch them carefully.

6 Cool on a wire rack and serve with drinks.

conventional cooking:
Pre-heat the oven to 200ºC/400ºF/gas 6 and bake for 8–10 minutes.

bread sticks

To ring the changes, you can sprinkle the bread sticks with different seeds such as poppy, nigella or fennel, or add spices to the basic dough mix. I like to add a good pinch of saffron to the liquid mix to give a superb flavour and colour to the sticks, or add cayenne and paprika for a real kick. Add the dry spices to the dry mix.

makes about 32 sticks, depending on length

30ml olive oil, plus extra for greasing

11ml honey

220ml warm water

20g dry yeast

380g strong flour

2 tsp sea salt

10g Parmesan cheese, finely grated

1 Combine all the liquid ingredients together in a bowl and mix well.

2 Mix all the dry ingredients together in a large bowl, then slowly add the wet to the dry and combine well until it is all incorporated into a dough. I usually do this in my Kitchen Aid using the dough hook attachment, but you can do it by hand if you wish.

3 Knead the dough for about 8 minutes or until you have a smooth and elastic dough.

4 Grease the inside of a large bowl with olive oil and pop the dough in it to prove. Cover with a tea towel and leave next to the Aga for 45–60 minutes until doubled in size.

5 When the dough has risen, divide it into four, then divide each four into eight long thin sticks. Do this in batches and lay the sticks on a baking sheet about 3cm apart. Cover the first batch with the tea towel and proceed with the second batch. When you have finished with the second batch, brush the first batch with olive oil and sprinkle over some salt.

6 Slide the tray on to the floor of the Roasting Oven and bake for 10–12 minutes. Repeat until all the dough is used up.

conventional cooking:
Pre-heat the oven to 200°C/400°F/gas 6 and bake for 10–12 minutes.

12 breads

bread-making tip

Buy a small cup-sized stainless steel beaker or mould. Fill it with cold water and put it in the Roasting Oven when baking bread. It will create the steam that is an essential ingredient in achieving a great bread crust. You can even splash water directly on to the Roasting Oven floor to create an instant burst of steam. This is good to do halfway through baking and just before the final 8 minutes of baking.

focaccia bread

makes 1 loaf

30g yeast
1kg strong flour
120ml olive oil
30g salt

FOR THE TOPPING:
1 tbsp fresh rosemary, chopped
1 tbsp fresh thyme leaves
1 tbsp fennel top, chopped
2 garlic cloves, peeled and sliced
sea salt
olive oil

1 Crumble the yeast into 200ml warm water and mix until it is smooth.

2 Put the flour, olive oil and salt into the bowl of an electric mixer with the dough hook in place. Start the motor and slowly pour in the yeast and up to 350ml warm water. You may or may not need all of the water so pour it in a little at a time. Knead until it becomes smooth and elastic. Don't be alarmed if it looks sloppy to begin with as it will pull together.

3 Lightly grease a large bowl and turn out the dough into it. Cover with a damp tea towel and place it next to the Aga for about an hour or until the dough has doubled in size.

4 While the dough is proving, mix together the herbs, garlic, salt and enough olive oil to slacken the mixture.

5 When the bread has had its first proving, knock it back by punching the air out. Line the large roasting tin with a large piece of Bake-O-Glide and shape the dough into the tin, stretching it to fit. Pour over the herb oil and, using your fingers, press the oil and herbs into the dough, giving it a dimpled effect. Leave the tin next to the Aga again for its second proving.

6 When the dough has doubled in size, place the tin on the floor of the Roasting Oven for 20–25 minutes. If it browns too quickly, insert the Cold Plain Shelf on the third set of runners. Cool in the tin for a few minutes, then remove the bread from the tin and peel off the Bake-O-Glide. Transfer to a wire rack to finish cooling.

conventional cooking:
Pre-heat the oven to 220°C/425°F/gas 7 and bake for 30–40 minutes in the centre of the oven.

rye bread

makes 2 large loaves –
eat one and freeze one!

40g fresh yeast
700ml hand-hot water
1kg strong white flour
250g rye flour
30g salt

1 Mix the yeast into 200ml hand-hot water. Put a dough hook into an electric mixer (you can do this by hand but it will be hard work) and add the flours and salt to the mixer bowl. Turn the mixer to medium speed, then pour in the yeast and water. Add a further 500ml hand-hot water a little at a time – you may not need all the water – until the dough pulls away from the sides of the bowl.

2 Knead for about 10 minutes on high. The dough has been kneaded enough when it is smooth and pliable. Place the dough into a lightly oiled large bowl and cover with a clean damp tea towel and put near the side of the Aga. Leave it to prove for 45–60 minutes or until it has doubled in size.

3 Knock back the dough by punching the air out and shape into loaf tins or into a round ball or long loaf on a piece of Bake-O-Glide on a baking sheet. Leave it to prove in a warm place for a second time, for 30–45 minutes.

4 Slide the tins or the Bake-O-Glide directly onto the floor of the Roasting Oven (discard the baking sheet) and bake for about 20–25 minutes. It is ready when the underside sounds hollow when tapped. Cool on a wire rack.

conventional cooking:

Pre-heat the oven to 220°C/425°F/gas 7 and bake for 30–40 minutes in the centre of the oven.

refrigerator white bread

makes one loaf

1kg strong white bread flour
600ml hand-hot water
25g butter, softened
30ml sunflower oil, plus more for greasing
25g salt
35g fresh yeast

1 Mix the flour, butter, oil and salt in an electric mixer with a dough hook.

2 Crumble the yeast into 425ml warm water and stir. When the yeast has melted, pour it into the flour. Add more warm water (to a maximum of 175ml) if the dough is too stiff. Hold back a little water and add only if necessary.

3 Knead for 8 minutes on a medium speed or until soft and elastic. Put the dough into a lightly oiled bowl. Cover with cling film and refrigerate overnight.

4 When you are ready to bake the bread, remove the dough from the fridge and mould into shape on a piece of Bake-O-Glide or in a tin. Let it rise near the Aga for 45–60 minutes or until it has risen.

5 Bake on the Roasting Oven floor for 20–25 minutes or until it sounds hollow when tapped underneath. (If using Bake-O-Glide, put it on a shallow baking tray and slide the paper off the tray and onto the floor of the oven.) Cool on a wire rack. The great thing about this dough is that you can pull off small amounts to bake and leave the rest in the fridge for up to 2 days.

conventional cooking:

Pre-heat the oven to 220°C/425°F/gas 7 and bake for 30–40 minutes in the centre of the oven.

apricot and hazelnut bread

makes 2 large loaves

40g fresh yeast
700ml hand-hot water
1kg strong white flour
250g rye flour
30g salt
100g no-soak apricots, chopped
100g hazelnuts, halved

1 Mix the yeast into 200ml of the water. Put a dough hook into an electric mixer (you can do this by hand but it will be hard work) and put the flours and salt into the bowl of the mixer. Turn the mixer onto a medium speed, then pour in the yeast and remaining water little by little. You may not need all of the water. When the dough starts to come together, add the apricots and hazelnuts.

2 Knead for about 10 minutes on high, until it is smooth and pliable. Place the dough in a lightly oiled large bowl and cover with a clean, damp tea towel and put near the side of the Aga. Leave it to prove for 45–60 minutes or until it has doubled in size.

3 Knock back the dough by punching the air out and shape into loaf tins or into a round ball or long loaf on a piece of Bake-O-Glide on a baking sheet. Leave it for 35–40 minutes to prove a second time, then slide the tins or the Bake-O-Glide directly onto the floor of the Roasting Oven (discard the baking sheet) and bake for about 20–25 minutes. It is ready when the underside sounds hollow when tapped. Cool on a wire rack.

conventional cooking:
Pre-heat the oven to 220°C/425°F/gas 7 and bake for 30–40 minutes in the centre of the oven.

standard white bread

makes 1 loaf

1kg strong bread flour
27g butter, softened
27g salt
34g fresh yeast
600ml warm water

1 Fit the dough hook on to an electric mixer and add the flour, butter and salt to the bowl. Mix to combine.

2 Crumble the yeast into 425ml of the warm water and stir. When the yeast has melted, pour it into the flour. Add the rest of the water if the dough is too stiff. It is best to hold back a little water and add it if necessary rather than pour it all in and have to add more flour. Knead for 8 minutes on medium speed or until the dough is soft and elastic.

3 Lightly oil a bowl and place the dough in it. Cover with cling film and stand next to the Aga to double in size.

4 Punch the dough back, then mould into shape on a piece of Bake-O-Glide or place in a tin. Stand it near the Aga for 45–60 minutes or until it has risen.

5 Put the risen dough on the floor of the Roasting Oven and place a stainless steel cup half-full of cold water next to it (the water will create steam). For extra steam, splash about 1 tablespoon of water directly on the floor of the oven towards the end of the baking time. Bake for 20–25 minutes or until the loaf sounds hollow when tapped on the underside. (If you are using Bake-O-Glide, put it on a shallow baking tray and slide the paper off the tray and on to the floor of the oven.) Remove from the tin and cool on a wire rack.

conventional cooking:

Pre-heat the oven to 220ºC/425ºF/gas 7 and bake for 30–40 minutes in the centre of the oven. If you have a fan-assisted oven or electric oven, do not put the cup of water in the oven.

brioche

makes 1 loaf

40g fresh yeast

50ml warm milk

1kg plain flour

100g unrefined golden caster sugar

12–15 free-range eggs

700ml water

20g salt

700g unsalted butter, softened

FOR THE GLAZE:

1 egg yolk, beaten with 1 tbsp milk

1 Crumble the yeast into the warm milk and mix until smooth. Put the flour and sugar into the bowl of an electric mixer with the dough hook attached and start the mixer on a slow speed. Pour in the yeast and milk and the water, then add the eggs one at a time. Next add the salt and butter and knead really well. It will appear very sloppy but persevere. When the dough comes away from the sides of the bowl it is ready.

2 Put the dough into a lightly greased large bowl and stand it to the side of the Aga for 1–2 hours or until it has doubled in size.

3 Knock back the dough and return it to the bowl. Chill in the fridge for a few hours.

4 Turn the dough out and shape it into a ball or plait or transfer to a tin. Leave to rise next to the Aga again until it has doubled in size, then glaze the top with the egg yolk mix.

5 Place the brioche on a grid shelf on the third set of runners in the Roasting Oven and bake for 40–45 minutes or until the brioche is golden and sounds hollow when tapped on the underside. If you are using a tin, unmould immediately and cool on a wire rack.

conventional cooking:

Pre-heat the oven to 200°C/400°F/gas 6 and bake for 40–45 minutes as above.

chocolate bread

This recipe is best made using an electric mixer.

makes 1 large loaf

30g unsalted butter, softened, plus extra for buttering the tins

85g unrefined golden caster sugar, plus 2 tbsp for coating the tins

30g fresh yeast

275ml warm water

365g strong bread flour

40g good-quality cocoa powder

1 tsp salt

oil, for greasing the bowl

50g good-quality dark chocolate, chopped into chunks

FOR THE GLAZE:

1 free-range egg yolk

1 tbsp double cream

2 tbsp unrefined golden caster sugar

1 Butter the insides of a large loaf tin and coat with 2 tablespoons of golden caster sugar.

2 Put the yeast into a bowl, add half the water and stir.

3 Fit the dough hook on to the mixer and combine the flour, cocoa powder, sugar and yeast mix. Add the remaining water slowly – you made not need all of it or you may need a little more depending on the flour. Mix on a low speed for about 5 minutes. Turn off the machine and let the dough rest for 10–15 minutes.

4 Add the salt and butter to the dough and continue to knead with the machine on medium speed for about 10 minutes or until the dough develops a shine.

5 Oil the inside of a large bowl. Turn out the dough, form into a ball and place inside the bowl. Cover with cling film and leave at the side of the Aga to rise.

6 When it has doubled in size, fold the chopped chocolate pieces into the dough, then lightly fold the dough into thirds (like an envelope), cover with cling film again and leave for 30 minutes.

7 Divide the dough into four equal pieces. Roll each piece into a ball and place all the balls in the prepared loaf tin. Cover with cling film and set near the Aga to double in size.

8 To prepare the glaze, mix the egg yolk and cream together. When the loaf is ready to be baked, brush very lightly with the glaze and sprinkle over the sugar.

9 Place the loaf tin on the floor of the Roasting Oven and bake for 20–25 minutes or until the bread sounds hollow when tapped on the underside (protect your hands when doing this).

10 Transfer the tin to a wire rack and cool the bread in the tin for a few minutes, then remove from the tin and cool completely on the wire rack.

conventional cooking:
Pre-heat the oven to 220ºC/425ºF/gas 7 and bake the bread as above.

walnut and raisin bread

makes 2 loaves – eat one, freeze one!

40g fresh yeast
700ml hand-hot water
1kg strong white flour
250g rye flour
30g salt
100g walnuts, roughly chopped
100g plump raisins

1 Mix the yeast into the water.

2 Fit the dough hook on to an electric mixer (you can do this by hand but it will be hard work) and put the flours and salt into the bowl of the mixer. Turn the mixer to a medium speed, then pour in the yeast and water. When the dough starts to come together, add the walnuts and raisins. Knead for about 10 minutes on a medium speed. The dough has been kneaded enough when it is smooth and pliable.

3 Place the dough into a lightly oiled large bowl, cover with a clean damp tea towel and put next to the Aga. Leave it to prove for 45–60 minutes or until it has doubled in size.

4 Knock back the dough by punching the air out and shape into loaf tins or into a round ball or long loaf on a piece of Bake-O-Glide on a baking sheet. Leave it to prove again for 30–45 minutes.

5 Slide the tins or Bake-O-Glide directly onto the floor of the Roasting Oven and bake for 20–25 minutes. It is ready when you tap the underside and it sounds hollow. Cool on a wire rack.

conventional cooking:
Pre-heat the oven to 220°C/425°F/gas 7 and bake in the centre of the oven for 30–40 minutes or until the bread sounds hollow when tapped on the underside.

onion and parma ham bread

makes 1 large loaf

1 large onion, peeled and chopped into small pieces

30g yeast

550ml warm water, plus more if needed

1kg strong flour

30g sea salt

118ml olive oil

175g Parma ham, torn into strips

FOR THE TOPPING:

1 tbsp fresh rosemary, chopped

1 tbsp fresh thyme leaves

1 tbsp fennel top, chopped

2 garlic cloves, peeled and sliced

sea salt

olive oil

1 Spread out the onion on a shallow baking tray lined with Bake-O-Glide. Put the tray on the third set of runners in the Roasting Oven and cook for 8–10 minutes until the onion is soft and slightly charred around the edges. Set aside.

2 Crumble the yeast into the warm water and mix until smooth. Put the flour and salt into the bowl of an electric mixer with the dough hook in place. Start the motor and slowly pour in the yeast mixture, then the olive oil. Add the onion and Parma ham and knead until it becomes smooth and elastic. Don't be alarmed if it looks sloppy to begin with as it will pull together.

3 Lightly grease a large bowl. Turn out the dough into it, cover with a damp tea towel and place the bowl next to the Aga for about an hour or until the dough has doubled in size.

4 While the dough is proving, mix together the herbs, garlic, salt and enough olive oil to slacken the mixture.

5 When the bread has had its first proving, knock it back by punching the air out. Line the large roasting tin with a large piece of Bake-O-Glide and shape the dough into the tin, stretching it to fit. Pour over the herb oil and, using your fingers, press the oil and herbs into the dough, giving it a dimpled effect. Leave the tin next to the Aga again for its second proving.

6 When the dough has doubled in size, place the tin on the floor of the Roasting Oven for 20–25 minutes. Place a stainless steal cup filled with cold water next to the bread to create steam in the oven. If it browns too quickly, insert the Cold Plain Shelf on the second set of runners. Cool the bread in the tin for a few minutes, then remove the Bake-O-Glide and move to a wire rack to finish cooling.

conventional cooking:

Pre-heat the oven to 200°C/400°F/gas 6 and proceed as above. If you have a fan-assisted oven or electric oven, do not put the cup of water in the oven.

onion and parma ham bread

stuffed olive focaccia bread

Read the whole recipe before starting as you have to assemble or roast the vegetables, make the tomato sauce and make the dough. If you wish, you can save time by buying fresh tomato sauce from the chilled section of a good deli or supermarket and buy a jar of roasted vegetables in olive oil. The tomato sauce can also be used on pizzas or with pasta. It can be made ahead and kept in the fridge for three days or frozen.

serves 6 as a starter or 4 for lunch

FOR THE BREAD DOUGH:

30g yeast

550ml warm water, plus more if needed

1kg strong flour

30g sea salt

125g good-quality stoned black olives, chopped

118ml olive oil

FOR THE FILLING:

approximately 600g of a selection of grilled peppers, courgettes, red onions, sun-dried tomatoes in oil, or anything else that takes your fancy

3 x 150g balls mozzarella cheese, grated or thinly sliced

FOR THE TOMATO SAUCE:

3 tbsp olive oil

1 garlic clove, peeled

50g tin anchovies in olive oil plus the oil

500g good-quality peeled tinned plum tomatoes

1 tbsp balsamic vinegar

1 bunch fresh basil

1 tsp sugar

salt and pepper

1 Crumble the yeast into the warm water and mix until smooth. Put the flour and salt into the bowl of an electric mixer with the dough hook in place. Start the motor and slowly pour in the yeast mixture, then the olives and olive oil. Knead until it becomes smooth and elastic. Don't be alarmed if it looks sloppy to begin with as it will pull together.

2 Lightly grease a large bowl and turn the dough out into it. Cover with a damp tea towel and place the bowl next to the Aga for about an hour or until the dough has doubled in size.

3 When the bread has had its first proving, knock it back by punching the air out. Line a large inverted baking tray with two pieces of Bake-O-Glide. Divide the dough in half and shape both halves into rounds on the Bake-O-Glide, stretching it to fit if necessary. Leave the tin next to the Aga for 15 minutes to allow it to rise a little.

4 Place one round of the partially risen dough on the tin on the edge of the floor of the Roasting Oven and pull the Bake-O-Glide towards the back of the oven and the tray away so that you are left with one dough round on the Bake-O-Glide on the oven floor. Bake for 8–10 minutes. Set the other dough round aside.

5 Meanwhile, make the sauce. Put the olive oil, garlic and anchovy oil in a heavy-bottomed saucepan and heat gently on the Simmering Plate. Watch it carefully and remove the garlic clove just as it starts to turn golden. (If it burns or goes brown the sauce will taste terrible.) Next add the anchovies, tomatoes, balsamic vinegar, half the basil leaves and the sugar. Season with pepper (the anchovies are salty so don't add any salt at this stage). Stir well and bring up to a simmer. Move the pan to the third set of runners in the Roasting Oven for 20–25 minutes or until the sauce is well cooked, very soft and reduced to a thick consistency. Add the remaining basil leaves and check the seasoning.

6 When the bread base is cooked, remove from the oven and build up the layers of 'stuffing' on the baked dough in this order: grilled vegetables, cheese, tomato sauce.

7 Take the raw dough and put it on top of the filling. Wrap the dough over the top of the stuffing and around to the bottom of the baked crust and pinch on the bottom so there is no visible seam. The filling should be sandwiched between the baked dough and the raw dough. Transfer the bread to the floor of the Simmering Oven (still on the Bake-O-Glide) and

stuffed olive focaccia bread

bake for 1–1½ hours. If the top browns too quickly, slide in the Cold Plain Shelf.

8 Cool in the tin for a few minutes, then remove the Bake-O-Glide and move to a wire rack to finish cooling. Cut into wedges and serve. This is ideal for picnics and lunch boxes.

conventional cooking:

Pre-heat the oven to 220ºC/425ºF/gas 7 and bake the base for 8–10 minutes, then lower the temperature to 150ºC/300ºF/gas 2 and bake the stuffed bread for 1–1½ hours. Make the sauce on the hob.

banana teabread

serves 6

2 tbsp milk

2 free-range eggs, beaten

80ml sunflower oil

3 bananas, peeled and mashed

250g self-raising flour

1 tsp baking powder

150g unrefined golden caster sugar

80g chopped walnuts
or 100g chocolate chips
or 60g desiccated coconut

1 Line a 900g loaf tin with Bake-O-Glide.

2 Whisk the milk, eggs, oil and mashed bananas together in a bowl, then add the dry ingredients and mix well. Spoon the batter into the loaf tin.

3 Slide the grid shelf on the floor of the Roasting Oven and the Cold Plain Shelf above. Place the tin on the grid shelf and bake for 25–30 minutes. Transfer the now hot plain shelf to the Simmering Oven, place the loaf tin on top of it and bake for a further 20 minutes or until the tea bread is done. For 4-oven Aga owners, bake in the Baking Oven for 50–60 minutes using the Cold Plain Shelf if it browns too quickly.

conventional cooking:

Pre-heat the oven to 190ºC/375ºF/gas 5 and bake for 50–60 minutes.

courgette teabread

serves 6

435g self-raising flour

1 tsp salt

1 tsp baking powder

generous grating of nutmeg

3 tsp cinnamon

150g chopped walnuts

200ml sunflower oil

300g unrefined golden caster sugar

300g grated courgettes

3 free-range eggs

3 tsp vanilla extract

1 Line a 900g loaf tin with Bake-O-Glide.

2 Mix all the ingredients together in a large bowl and spoon into the loaf tin.

3 Bake the teabread on the fourth set of runners in the Roasting Oven for 10 minutes, then transfer to the Simmering Oven for 1–1½ hours or until done. You can also cook this teabread in the Cake Baker in the Roasting Oven for 1 hour, or in the Baking Oven for 1 hour using the Cold Plain Shelf above if necessary.

conventional cooking:

Pre-heat the oven to 180ºC/350ºF/gas 5 and bake for 1–1½ hours.

banana teabread

chocolate chip tea cake

serves 6

90g butter

110g unrefined golden caster sugar

1 tsp vanilla extract

220ml cold sour cream

1 free-range egg, lightly beaten

220g self-raising flour

½ tsp baking powder

100g dark chocolate chips

1 Line a 450g loaf tin with Bake-O-Glide and set aside.

2 Start to melt the butter in a saucepan on the Simmering Plate. When it is half melted, remove from the heat and stir until fully melted. Stir in the sugar, vanilla extract, sour cream and egg.

3 Sieve the flour and baking powder together, then add to the wet mix and stir until just blended. Fold in the chocolate chips, then pour the batter into the lined loaf tin.

4 You can either use the Cake Baker to bake the cake in the Roasting Oven, or you can bake the loaf tin on a grid shelf on the floor of the Roasting Oven for 15–20 minutes, then slide in the Cold Plain Shelf and continue to bake for another 15–20 minutes or until it springs back when lightly pressed in the centre and is pulling away from the sides. For 4-oven Aga owners, bake on the grid shelf on the floor of the Baking Oven for 45–50 minutes, sliding in the Cold Plain Shelf halfway through baking.

conventional cooking:

Pre-heat the oven to 190ºC/375ºF/gas 5 and bake for 45–50 minutes as above.

banana and walnut muffins

makes 12

3 large bananas, mashed

3 large free-range eggs, slightly beaten

580g plain flour

120ml vegetable oil

270g unrefined golden caster sugar

2 tsp baking powder

1 tsp baking soda

pinch of salt

200g chopped walnuts

200g muesli

1 Line a 12-hole muffin tin with muffin papers and set aside. In a large bowl, mix together all of the ingredients thoroughly. Spoon the mix into the muffin tin, filling the papers to the top.

2 Put the grid shelf on the floor of the Roasting Oven and put in the muffin tin. Slide the Cold Plain Shelf onto the third set of runners and bake for 20–25 minutes or until golden. To test if they are cooked in the middle, insert the point of a knife or a skewer; if it comes out clean, they are ready. If the mix is still loose, put them back in the oven for a few minutes. For a 4-oven Aga owners, place the muffin tin on the fourth set of runners in the Baking Oven and cook for 25 minutes. Remove the muffins from the tin and cool on a wire rack.

conventional cooking:

Pre-heat the oven to 200°C/400°F/gas 6 and bake for 20–25 minutes.

healthy heavy muffins

This is more of a healthy eating muffin with a heavier texture.

makes 12

145g wholewheat flour

75g bran

3 tbsp oatmeal

2 tsp baking powder

pinch of salt

good grating of nutmeg

4 large free-range eggs, slightly beaten

100ml milk

2 tsp vanilla extract

160ml honey

1 apple, grated

2 small carrots, peeled and grated

160ml apple purée

75g dried figs, chopped

75g chopped almonds

zest of 1 organic orange

1 Line a muffin tin with muffin papers and set aside.

2 Mix together all the dry ingredients in a large bowl and all the wet in another bowl.

3 Make a well in the dry ingredients, add the fruit and nuts and pour in the wet ingredients. Using a large rubber spatula, fold the mix together using as few strokes as possible. Spoon the mix into the papers.

4 Put the grid shelf on the floor of the Roasting Oven and slide in the muffin tin. Slide the Cold Plain Shelf onto the third set of runners and bake for 20–25 minutes or until the muffins are golden. Remove from the tin and cool on a wire rack.

conventional cooking:

Pre-heat the oven to 200ºC/400ºF/gas 6 and bake for 20–25 minutes.

banana and chocolate chip muffins

makes 12

360g plain flour

240g unrefined golden caster sugar

2 tsp baking powder

1 tsp baking soda

pinch of salt

200g chocolate chips

3 large free-range eggs, slightly beaten

118ml vegetable oil

3 large bananas, peeled and mashed

1 Line a muffin tin with muffin papers and set aside.

2 Mix together all the dry ingredients in a large bowl and all the wet in another bowl.

3 Make a well in the dry ingredients, add the bananas and pour in the wet ingredients. Using a large rubber spatula, fold the mix together using as few strokes as possible. Spoon the mix into the papers.

4 Put the grid shelf on the floor of the Roasting Oven and slide in the muffin tin. Slide the Cold Plain Shelf onto the third set of runners. Bake for 20–25 minutes or until golden. Remove from the tin and cool on a wire rack.

conventional cooking:

Pre-heat the oven to 200ºC/400ºF/gas 6 and bake for 20–25 minutes.

pumpkin apple streusel muffins

This streusel topping can also be used on most other muffins.

makes 12–18

300g plain flour

400g unrefined golden caster sugar

1 tsp ground cinnamon

½ tsp ground ginger

½ tsp ground cloves

1 tsp baking powder

pinch of salt

2 free-range eggs, lightly beaten

110ml sunflower oil

235g pumpkin purée (you can use tinned pumpkin purée)

100ml milk

2 apples, peeled, cored and finely chopped

FOR THE STREUSEL TOPPING:

2 tbsp plain flour

60g unrefined golden caster sugar

½ tsp ground cinnamon

20g unsalted butter

1 Line a muffin tin with muffin papers and set aside.

2 In a large mixing bowl, combine the dry ingredients, and then add the wet and finally the apples. Stir well so that everything is thoroughly combined. Spoon the mix into the muffin papers until they are about half-full.

3 Mix the topping ingredients together and sprinkle over each muffin.

4 Bake on the fourth set of runners in the Roasting Oven for 20 minutes. Slide the Cold Plain Shelf onto the second set of runners after about 10 minutes or sooner if the muffins are browning too quickly. For 4-oven Aga owners, bake the muffins on the third set of runners in the Baking Oven for 20 minutes. The muffins are done when a skewer comes out clean.

conventional cooking:

Pre-heat the oven to 180°C/350°F/gas 4 and bake for 35–40 minutes.

cranberry, orange and pecan muffins

makes 12

220g plain flour

180g unrefined golden caster sugar

1 tsp baking powder

pinch of salt

½ tsp cinnamon

75g chopped pecans

zest of 1 organic orange

1 large free-range egg, slightly beaten

118ml vegetable oil or melted butter

160ml milk

75g fresh cranberries

1 Line a muffin tin with muffin papers and set aside.

2 Mix together all of the dry ingredients in a large bowl and all the wet in another bowl.

3 Make a well in the dry ingredients, add the cranberries and pour in the wet ingredients. Using a large rubber spatula, fold the mix together using as few strokes as possible. Spoon the mix into the muffin papers.

4 Put the grid shelf on the floor of the Roasting Oven and put in the muffin tin. Slide the Cold Plain Shelf onto the third set of runners and bake for 20–25 minutes or until they are golden. Remove from the tin and cool on a wire rack.

conventional cooking:

Pre-heat the oven to 200°C/400°F/gas 6 and bake for 20–25 minutes.

cranberry, orange and pecan muffins

13 preserves

aga preserving

There are a few golden rules when making jams, jellies and marmalades. Make them when your Aga is at its hottest, such as first thing in the morning. Always use dry, unblemished fruit. All equipment must be scrupulously clean. Jars and lids must be sterilised. If you have a dishwasher, put them through a high heat cycle, then place on a baking tray and put in the Simmering Oven for 10-15 minutes. Keep them warm when you pour in the jam. Seal jars when hot.

Warm sugar and fruits in the Simmering or Warming Oven before using. If a recipe calls for a fruit that needs to be cooked before adding the sugar, do it in the Simmering Oven. Use as little water as possible and cover the fruit with a tightly fitting lid. Bring to the boil on the Boiling Plate, then transfer to the Simmering Oven until it is ready.

Skim the scum off frequently when the jam is boiling or add a small knob of butter to disperse it.

To test for a good set, put a few saucers into the freezer before you start to cook the jam. After the first 20 minutes or so of rapid boiling, take a saucer out of the freezer and drop a small spoonful of the jam onto the cold saucer. Allow it to cool for a minute, then push your finger through the jam. If it wrinkles, it is ready; if not, boil the jam for a few minutes more. Carry on testing until a set has been reached. Always remove the jam from the heat when you are testing so that if it is ready you will not overcook it.

cranberry and walnut sauce

This sauce will keep for two weeks. Serve with turkey.

makes about 600ml

340g fresh cranberries

300g unrefined golden caster sugar

235g redcurrant jelly

235g walnuts, coarsely chopped

2 tbsp orange zest

1 Combine cranberries, sugar, redcurrant jelly and 235ml water in a large saucepan and bring to a rapid boil on the Boiling Plate.
2 Move to the Simmering Plate and simmer for 2 minutes. Skim off the foam and remove from the heat.
3 Stir in walnuts and orange zest. Pour into sterilised jars and cool.

conventional cooking:
Make this on the hob over a medium heat.

tomato and chilli chutney

To make different-flavoured chutneys, simply adjust the fruit and/or veg and spices to suit the garden glut.

makes 1½–2kg

2kg tomatoes, red and green, skinned and chopped

500g onions, peeled and chopped

1kg cooking apples, peeled (optional), cored and chopped

500g sultanas

3 hot small chillies, finely chopped

500g sugar

750ml cider vinegar, made up to 1 litre with water

1 tsp sea salt

FOR THE SPICE BAG:

12 black peppercorns

1 tsp coriander seeds

3 cloves of garlic, peeled and cracked

1 To make the spice bag, tie up the black peppercorns, coriander seeds and garlic cloves in a clean piece of muslin.

2 Skin the tomatoes by cutting a cross at the base of each one and standing them in a bowl of boiling water for 3–5 minutes. Peel off and discard the skin and chop the flesh roughly.

3 Put all the ingredients, including the spice bag, into a large preserving pan which will fit into the Simmering Oven. Bring it up to the boil on the Simmering Plate, then move to the Boiling Plate but do not allow it to catch on the bottom. Stir to dissolve the sugar. Move to the Simmering Oven for 3–4 hours or until it is thick and reduced and when a wooden spoon is dragged through it leaves a clean trail. Discard the spice bag.

4 Ladle the chutney into sterilised jars and seal. Label and keep in a dark place for 1 month or longer before eating.

conventional cooking:

Cook on the hob, simmering very gently over a low heat for 20–30 minutes once the sugar has dissolved.

prune and apple chutney

makes about

4 x 500g jars

15g butter

1 tbsp sunflower oil

6 red onions, peeled and sliced

6 Granny Smith apples, peeled, cored and cut into small chunks

300g brown sugar

250g pitted prunes, cut into pieces

200ml cider vinegar

zest and juice of 1 orange

1 tsp allspice

pepper

1 Melt the butter and oil in a large saucepan on the Simmering Plate, add the onions and cook until they are soft.

2 Add the remaining ingredients and heat slowly on the Simmering Plate until the sugar dissolves. Transfer to the Boiling Plate and boil for 3–4 minutes, then move to the Simmering Oven for 2–3 hours or until it is very thick and a spoon leaves behind a clean trail.

3 Ladle into sterilised jars, seal and label. Keeps for up to 6 months. Chutneys should be left to age for a minimum of 1 month before using.

conventional cooking:

Cook over a medium heat, then turn down the heat and gently simmer for 20–30 minutes or until the chutney is thick, as above.

apple, sage and mint jelly

You will need a jelly bag and somewhere to hang it while it drips. The upturned legs of a stool work well or buy a special jelly bag stand.

adjust the quantities to suit

cooking apples – use as many as you have

water and/or apple juice to just cover the apples

cider vinegar – 145ml to every 1 litre cooking liquor

sugar – 450g to every 570ml liquid

1 heaped tbsp chopped fresh sage leaves to every 570ml liquid

1 heaped tbsp chopped fresh mint leaves to every 570ml liquid

1 Wash the apples and cut them into chunks; do not peel or core them. Put them into a large pan and cover with water or apple juice if using so that the apple pieces are just covered.

2 Bring to the boil on the Boiling Plate, then transfer to the Simmering Oven for 45–60 minutes or until the apples are very pulpy.

3 Remove from the oven, add the vinegar and boil rapidly on the Boiling Plate for about 5 minutes. Pour some boiling water through the jelly bag, then tip in the apple pulp. Hang the bag over a large bowl to catch all of the juice. Leave for a few hours or until all the juice has strained through. If you want a clear jelly do not squeeze the bag.

4 Measure the amount of liquid in the bowl and calculate the sugar amount required. Add 450g sugar to every 570ml of juice.

5 Put the sugar and apple juice back into the preserving pan or large pan and gently dissolve the sugar on the Simmering Plate. When the sugar has completely dissolved, move to the Boiling Plate and boil rapidly for 10–12 minutes. Test for a set. When you reach setting point, stir in the sage and mint. Ladle into sterilised jars, seal and label.

conventional cooking:
Make the jelly on the hob in the usual way.

red onion confit

makes 400g

6 red onions

2 tbsp olive oil

1 tbsp butter

1 tsp unrefined golden caster sugar

1 tsp mixed spices

salt and pepper

1 Peel and slice the onions thinly. Put the oil and butter into a saucepan, add the onions and cook very gently on the Simmering Plate until the butter has melted.

2 Add the sugar, spices, salt and pepper and stir well. Transfer the pan to the Simmering Oven and cook for about 45 minutes or until the onions are soft and golden.

3 Spoon into a sterilised jar and cool. Store in the fridge for up to a week. Serve with pâté and cold meats.

conventional cooking:
Cook the onions over a medium heat on the hob, then simmer over a low heat until the onions are thick and soft.

seville orange marmalade

makes 4 x 500g jars

1.85kg preserving sugar
900g Seville oranges
1 lemon
2.2 litres water

1 Put the sugar at the back of the Aga to warm.

2 Cut the peel away from the oranges and chop up to the desired thickness and size. Place the peel in a pan and cover with 1.1 litres of water. Bring to the boil on the Boiling Plate, then place in the Simmering Oven for about an hour or until they are soft and tender. Drain and discard the water.

3 Meanwhile, cut up the orange flesh and put it into a preserving pan with all the pips and the remaining 1.1 litres of water. Bring to the boil on the Boiling Plate. Boil for 10 minutes, then transfer to the Roasting Oven for about 1–2 hours. Alternatively, cook slowly on the Boiling Plate for 20–30 minutes, but remember that this will use up a lot of your heat.

4 Remove the pan from the Roasting Oven and strain the liquid through a large sieve with a bowl underneath to catch every drop. Push the pulp with a wooden spoon to squeeze out as much pectin-rich liquid as possible.

5 Pour the liquid back into the preserving pan and add the sugar, peel and juice of 1 lemon to the liquid. Bring to the boil on the Boiling Plate and then test for a set. To reach setting point it can take 15–20 minutes. When a set is reached, pour the marmalade into sterilised jars, seal and label.

conventional cooking:

Make in the usual way on top of the stove. Bring the orange peel to the boil and simmer over a medium heat for 30–35 minutes. Continue on the hob.

strawberry jam

makes 4 x 400g jars

1kg jam sugar
2kg strawberries

1 Put the sugar into a preserving pan or large heavy-bottomed saucepan (not cast iron), and place in the Simmering Oven.

2 Hull and pick through the strawberries, discarding any blemished fruit. Put the fruit in the preserving pan and move the pan to the Simmering Plate. Stir constantly until all the sugar has dissolved and the fruit releases its juices.

3 Move to the Boiling Plate and boil rapidly for 4–5 minutes. Skim off any scum as it appears. Test for a set then, using a jam funnel, spoon into the prepared jam jars. Seal tightly with a screw-top lid while it is boiling hot.

conventional cooking:

Cook in the usual way on the hob.

mincemeat

To sterilise jars and lids, run them through the hottest wash cycle in a dishwasher.

makes 3kg

235g organic mixed candied peel

235g sultanas

350g raisins

500g apples, peeled and grated

235g suet, shredded

400g brown sugar

½ tsp cinnamon

½ tsp allspice

2cm piece of fresh ginger, grated

¼ tsp ground cloves

150g dried cranberries

150g dried sour cherries

80g flaked almonds

zest and juice of 2 oranges, preferably organic

zest and juice of 2 lemons, preferably organic

35ml brandy

grated nutmeg (about ½ a whole nutmeg)

1 Tip everything into a large, scrupulously clean heatproof bowl or casserole. Stir well and then put it on the floor of the Simmering Oven for about 2–2½ hours or until the suet has melted.

2 Stir well so that all the fruit and nuts are well coated. Cover the bowl with a clean tea towel and stand overnight in a cool place.

3 The next day, stir the mincemeat again and spoon into the jam jars. Seal the jars with the lids and store in a cool dark place. The mincemeat will keep for about 6–8 months.

conventional cooking:

Pre-heat the oven to 120°C/250°F/gas ½ and place the bowl of mincemeat in the oven for 2–3 hours or until the fat has melted. Continue as above.

blackberry butter

250g unsalted butter, at room temperature

150g ripe blackberries

1 Whiz the butter and blackberries together in a food processor to form a smooth purée.

2 Spoon into a serving dish and refrigerate until 1 hour before serving. Serve this at breakfast-time with brioche or at teatime with scones.

pomegranate molasses

250ml fresh pomegranate juice

140ml honey

½ cinnamon stick

1 crushed star anise

½ tsp ground black pepper

2 tbsp balsamic vinegar

1 Bring all the ingredients to a simmer in a saucepan on the Simmering Plate and reduce the liquid until it is thick and syrupy.

2 Sieve into a jug, then pour into a bottle. This can be kept in the fridge for a month.

index

Page numbers in *italics* refer to photographs

author's acknowledgments

My enormous thanks go to Gillian Haslam, Christine Wood,
Melvyn Evans, Sarah Lavelle, Carey Smith, Sarah Wooldridge,
my family and everyone who buys a book!